Foundations of Banking Risk

*An Overview of Banking,
Banking Risks, and
Risk–Based Banking Regulation*

RICHARD APOSTOLIK
CHRISTOPHER DONOHUE
PETER WENT

GLOBAL ASSOCIATION OF RISK PROFESSIONALS

WILEY

John Wiley & Sons, Inc.

Published by John Wiley & Sons, Inc., Hoboken, New Jersey.
Published simultaneously in Canada.

For general information on our other products and services or for technical support, please contact our Customer Care Department within the United States at (800) 762-2974, outside the United States at (317) 572-3993 or fax (317) 572-4002.

Wiley also publishes its books in a variety of electronic formats. Some content that appears in print may not be available in electronic books. For more information about Wiley products, visit our web site at www.wiley.com.

The Global Association of Risk Professionals has made every effort to ensure that at the time of writing the contents of this study text are accurate, but neither the Global Association of Risk Professionals nor its directors or employees shall be under any liability whatsoever for any inaccurate or misleading information this work could contain.

No employee of GARP is permitted to receive royalties on books or other writings he or she has authored or co-authored that are part of any program offered by GARP or which were authored as a part of their employment activities with GARP.

Library of Congress Cataloging-in-Publication Data:

Foundations of banking risk: an overview of banking, banking risks, and risk-based banking regulation / Global Association of Risk Professionals, Inc.
    p. cm.—(Wiley finance ; 507)
    Includes index.
    Summary: "GARP's Foundations of Banking Risk introduces risk professionals to the advanced components and terminology in banking risk and regulation globally. It helps them develop an understanding of the methods for the measurement and management of credit risk and operational risk, and the regulation of minimum capital requirements. It educates them about banking regulation and disclosure of market information. The book is GARP's required text used by risk professionals looking to obtain their International Certification in Banking Risk and Regulation"—Provided by publisher.
    ISBN 978-0-470-44219-7
1. Banks and banking, International—Management. 2. Risk management. 3. Banks and banking, International—Law and legislation. I. Global Association of Risk Professionals.
    HG3881.F684 2009
    332.1068'1—dc22

                      2009021635

Printed in the United States of America
10 9 8 7 6

*This book is dedicated to GARP's Board of Trustees,
without whose support and dedication to developing the profession of
risk management this book would not have been necessary or possible,
and to the Association's volunteers, representing thousands of
organizations around the globe, who work on committees and share
practical experiences in numerous global forums and in other ways,
whose goal is to create a culture of risk awareness.*

Contents

Introduction

The role of risk management is becoming more important as both banks and supervisors around the world recognize that good risk management practices are vital, not only for the success of individual banks, but also for the safety and soundness of the banking system as a whole. As a result, the world's leading banking supervisors have developed regulations based on a number of "good practice" methodologies used in risk management. These regulations, outlined in the International Convergence of Capital Measurement and Capital Standards, also known as the Basel II Accord, codify the risk management practices of many highly regarded banks.

The importance of these risk management methodologies as a basis for regulation is hard to overstate. The fact that they were developed with the support of the international banking community means that they have gained worldwide acceptance as the standards for risk management in banks.

The implementation of risk-based regulation means that bank staff, as well as bank supervisors, will need to be educated and trained to recognize risks and how to implement risk management approaches. Consequently GARP offers this program, the *Foundations of Banking Risk*, to develop in bank staff a basic understanding of banking, banking risks, and bank regulation and supervision.

To complete the *Foundations of Banking Risk*, students will also be required to review and understand certain assigned additional readings and take and pass an assessment exam consisting of multiple-choice questions.

This study text has been designed to assist students in preparing for the *Foundations of Banking Risk* assessment exam. It is presented in a user-friendly format to enable candidates to understand the key terms and concepts of banking, banking risks, and risk-based regulation.

This study text contains many technical terms used in banking and risk management. These terms are either defined in the text or in the glossary. Since the material is at the introductory level candidates are not expected to have a reasonable understanding of risk management or experience in banking. They are not expected to know terms commonly used in the finance industry.

Each chapter contains a number of examples of actual financial events, as well as case study scenarios, diagrams, and tables aimed at explaining banking, banking risks, and risk-based regulations.

This study text has adopted the standard codes used by banks throughout the world to identify currencies for the purposes of trading, settlement and the displaying of market prices. The codes, set by the International Organization for Standardization (ISO), avoid the confusion that could result as many currencies have similar names. For example, the text uses USD for the U.S. dollar, GBP for the British pound, EUR for the euro, and JPY for the Japanese yen.

Acknowledgments

GARP's *Foundations of Banking Risk* has been developed under the auspices of the Banking Risk Committee of the GARP Risk Academy who guided and reviewed the work of the contributing authors. The Committee, chaired by **Professor Xavier Freixas**, dean of the undergraduate School of Economics and Business Administration and professor at the Universitat Pompeu Fabra in Barcelona (Spain) and Research Fellow at CEPR, oversees the strategic development of the Academy's academic program.

The committee and the authors thank **Professor George M. McCabe**, professor of Finance at the University of Nebraska–Lincoln, **Jaidev Iyer**, managing director of GARP, and **Dr. Satyajit Karnik** and **William H. May**, at the GARP Research Center, who contributed to the development of the program. Finally, the authors also thank Maryann Appel, who tirelessly and effectively designed and formatted the graphics and text in this book.

CHAPTER 1

Functions and Forms of Banking

C hapter 1 introduces banks and the banking system, the role banks play in facilitating economic activity, and the relevant risks banks face. The three core banking functions—collecting deposits, arranging payments, and making loans—and their attendant risks are described. As this chapter intends to provide a foundation for the more detailed discussions in subsequent chapters, most of the key topics are presented within a risk management framework. A glossary is provided at the end of the book.

Chapter Outline

Banks and Banking
- 1.1 Banks and Banking
- 1.2 Different Bank Types
- 1.3 Banking Risks
- 1.4 Forces Shaping the Banking Industry

Key Learning Points
- Banks provide three core banking services: deposit collection, payment arrangement, and loan underwriting. Banks may also offer financial services such as cash, asset, and risk management.
- Banks play a central role in facilitating economic activity through three interrelated processes: financial intermediation, asset transformation, and money creation.
- Retail banks serve primarily retail customers, and wholesale banks serve primarily corporate customers. A country's central bank regulates other banks, provides services to other banks and sets monetary policy on behalf of the country's government.
- The main risks that banks face are credit, market, and operational risks. Other types of risk include liquidity, business, and reputational risk.
- Multiple forces shape the banking industry, including regulation, competition, product innovation, changing technology, and the uncertainty surrounding future interest and inflation rates.

Key Terms

- Asset transformation
- Banking book
- Basel Accords
- Brokerage services
- Business risk
- Central bank
- Commodity risk
- Credit risk
- Equity risk
- Financial intermediation
- Foreign exchange risk
- Inflation rate
- Interest rate
- Interest rate risk
- International or global banks
- Investment banking services
- Liquidity risk
- Market risk
- Money creation
- Money multiplier
- Operational risk
- Regulatory reserve capital
- Reputational risk
- Reserve requirements
- Retail banks
- Risk management
- Trading book
- Underwriting
- Universal banks
- Wholesale banks

Functions and Forms of Banking

1.1 BANKS AND BANKING

Banks and banking have been around for a long time. To understand banking risk and regulation, we first must understand the range of services banks provide and the key role banks play in a modern economy.

1.1.1 Core Bank Services

Banks offer many products and services. While there is variation among banks and across regions, the core services that banks traditionally provide are:

- **Deposit collection**—the process of accepting cash or money (deposits) from individuals and businesses (depositors) for safekeeping in a bank account, available for future use.
- **Payment services**—the process of accepting and making payments on behalf of the customers using their bank accounts.
- **Loan underwriting**—the process of evaluating and deciding whether a customer (borrower) is eligible to receive a loan or credit and then extending the loan or credit to the customer.

As banking has evolved, the complexity of the three core banking functions noted above has increased. For instance, in early banking, depositors of funds with a bank received in return a certificate stating the amount of money they deposited with the bank. Later, deposit certificates could be used to make payments. Initially a cumbersome process, the concept of using deposit certificates for payments further evolved into "passbooks," checks, and other methods to conveniently withdraw deposits from the bank. Today, deposits, withdrawals, and payments are instantaneous: withdrawals and payments can now be made through debit cards, and payments are easily made via electronic fund transfers. See Figure 1.1 for examples of bank products and the services each provides.

Underwriting has many different meanings in finance and banking. This book focuses on lending or credit. Banks underwrite loans in two steps. First, the bank analyzes the borrower's financial capacity, or the borrower's ability and willingness to repay the loan or credit. This process will be discussed in detail in Chapter 5. Then, the bank pays out, or funds, the loan (money or cash) to the borrower.

Figure 1.1 Examples of bank products and core bank services

Services	Examples of Bank Products
Collecting deposits, or deposit collection	• Checking accounts • Certificates of deposit • Savings accounts
Arranging payments, or payment services	• Debit cards • Electronic banking • Foreign exchange • Checking accounts
Underwriting loans	• Commercial and industrial loans • Consumer loans • Real estate/mortgage loans • Credit cards

Providing all these core services is not enough for an institution to be called a bank in a modern economy, however. In addition to taking deposits, making loans, and arranging payments, a modern bank will also hold a banking license and be subject to regulatory supervision by a banking regulator.

1.1.2   Banks in the Economy

Through the core bank services mentioned, banks are critical facilitators of economic activity.
- Banks channel savings from depositors to borrowers, an activity known as **financial intermediation**.
- Banks create loans from deposits through **asset transformation**.
- Banks, through financial intermediation and asset transformation, engage in **money creation**.

When a bank accepts deposits, the depositor in effect lends money to the bank. In exchange, the depositor receives interest payments on the deposits. The bank then uses the deposits to finance loans to borrowers and generates income by charging the borrowers interest on the loans the bank issues. The difference between the interest that the bank receives from the borrowers and the interest it pays to the depositors is the main source of revenue and profit to the bank.

When underwriting a loan, a bank evaluates the credit quality of the borrower—the likelihood that the borrower will repay the loan. However, depositors, who lend money to the bank in the form of deposits, typically do not evaluate the credit quality of the bank or the bank's ability to repay the deposits on demand. Depositors assume that their deposits with the bank are safe and will be returned in full by the bank when so demanded by the depositors. This puts depositors at risk since, as we will see in later sections, banks occasionally do fail and are not able to repay deposits in full upon demand (Section 3.1). To protect depositors against bank failures, governments have created safety nets such as deposit insurance (Section 3.4). These safety nets vary from country to country and generally do not provide unlimited protection, thus leaving a certain percent of deposits exposed to the risk that a bank will default and the depositors will not be able to receive their deposits in full.

By collecting funds in the form of deposits and then loaning these funds out, banks engage in **financial intermediation**. Throughout the world, bank loans are the predominant source of financing for individuals and companies. Other financial intermediaries such as finance companies and the financial markets also channel savings and investments. Unlike other financial intermediaries, though, banks alone channel deposits from the depositors to the borrowers. Hence, banks are also called *depository financial intermediaries*.

Financial intermediation emphasizes the qualitative differences between bank deposits and bank loans. Bank deposits (e.g., savings accounts, checking accounts) are typically relatively small, consisting of money entrusted to the bank by individuals, companies, and other organizations for safekeeping. Deposits are also comparatively safe and can typically be withdrawn at any time or have relatively short maturities. By contrast, bank loans (e.g., home mortgage loans, car loans, corporate loans) are generally larger and riskier than deposits with repayment schedules typically extending over several years. The process of creating a new asset (loan) from liabilities (deposits) with different characteristics is called **asset transformation** (see Figure 1.2).

Figure 1.2 **Asset transformation**

1.1.3 Money Creation

Banks earn revenues from the financial intermediation/asset transformation process by converting customer deposits into loans. To be profitable, however, the interest rates that the bank earns on its loans must be greater than the rate it pays on the deposits that finance them. Since the majority of deposits can be withdrawn at any time, banks must balance the goal of higher revenues (investing more of the deposits to finance loans) with the need to have cash on hand to meet the withdrawal requests of depositors. To do this, banks "reserve" a relatively small fraction of their deposit funds to meet depositor demand. Banking regulators determine the **reserve requirements,** the proportion of deposits a bank must keep as reserves in the vault of the bank. Keeping only a small fraction of the depositor's funds available for withdrawal is called the *fractional reserve banking system.* This system allows banks to create money.

Money creation is the process of generating additional money by repeatedly lending, through the fractional reserve banking system, an original deposit to a bank.

EXAMPLE

Suppose Universal Bank has collected deposits totaling USD 100 and retains 10% of those deposits as reserves to meet withdrawals. Universal Bank uses the remaining 90%, or USD 90, for lending purposes. Suppose the USD 90 is lent to one person, who then spends all the funds at one store. This USD 90 is effectively "new" money. The store then deposits the USD 90 in Competitor Bank. At that point there are deposits in the two banks of USD 190 (the initial deposit of USD 100 plus the new deposit of USD 90). Competitor Bank now sets aside 10% of the USD 90, or USD 9, in reserves, and loans the remaining USD 81, which is then deposited by the borrower in Third Bank. There is now USD 100 + USD 90 + USD 81, or USD 271 of deposits in the three banks. As this process continues, more deposits are loaned out and spent and more money is deposited; at each turn, more and more money is made available through the lending process.

Figure 1.3 below shows the amount of money that an initial USD 100 deposit generates, assuming a 10% reserve requirement, transaction by transaction. Over the course of 21 separate transactions, USD 801 of deposits is generated, from an initial deposit of only USD 100. Allowed to continue indefinitely, this process would generate a total of USD 1,000 in deposits—the original USD 100 deposit plus USD 900 created through subsequent loans.

Figure 1.3 Money creation (USD 801 in new lending from initial USD 100 deposit)

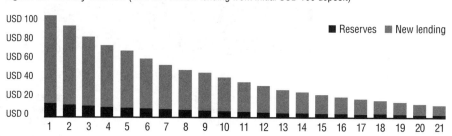

In the example on the previous page, the cycle started with an initial deposit of USD 100; no additional money was put into the system. Portions of the original USD 100 repeatedly flowed through the system, increasing both bank deposits and bank loans. The amount of money created at each deposit is 90% of the previous step (100% less the 10% held in reserve).

Reserve requirements limit how much money an initial deposit can create in the fractional reserve banking system. The **money multiplier**, the inverse of the reserve requirement, is a formula used to determine how much new money each unit of currency deposited with a bank can create. As the following example shows, the higher the reserve requirement the more the bank must keep as regulatory reserves in the vault of the bank and the less money banks can create.

EXAMPLE

With a reserve requirement of 10%, the money multiplier is 10 (1/10% = 10). Thus, the amount of money that can be created on a USD 100 deposit is USD 1,000. Out of USD 1,000, USD 900 (or 90%) is new money and USD 100 (or 10%) is the original deposit.

With a reserve requirement of 20%, the money multiplier falls to 5 (1/20% = 5). Thus, the amount of money that can be created on a USD 100 deposit would be USD 500. Out of this USD 500, USD 400 (or 80%) is new money and USD 100 (or 20%) is the original deposit.

Globally, banks represent the largest source of financing for businesses and are therefore critical to economic development. Banks provide debt financing by underwriting loans and bonds and otherwise helping companies secure financing by issuing bonds in the credit or debt markets. Banks can also help companies secure financing by issuing equity in the stock market and occasionally taking ownership stakes in companies. Debt and equity are the two types of financing and two sources of capital.

Banks also provide financing for consumers, who use bank loans to purchase and finance assets they might not otherwise be able to afford, such as a car or a house. Credit cards, another type of bank loan, provide consumers with convenient access to credit that enables purchases and can stimulate economic growth. Chapter 4 will discuss in greater detail the various loan products and how they are used. Through their core functions—financial intermediation, asset transformation, and money creation—banks play a central role in advanced economies.

EXAMPLE

The interrelationship between bank functions and economic activity has been vividly shown by the global credit and banking crisis that started in 2007. Because banks have been unable to collect on loans that were made to low credit quality borrowers called "subprime borrowers," banks became unable to recirculate deposits and lend to other parties. This in turn meant there was less credit available for the use of companies and individuals who depend on bank loans to finance their purchases. Consequently, the companies and individuals made fewer deposits, creating less money. The effects were widely felt around the world and led to a substantial reduction in credit, which first led to a reduction in the demand for goods and services and further reduced the amount of money being deposited at banks. This caused an even further tightening of credit availability.

1.1.4   Payment Services

Depositors can use their deposit accounts at banks to make and receive payments between depositors and between banks. Payments refer to the settlement of financial transactions between parties and usually involve the transfer of funds between the parties. There are various payment systems that facilitate transfer of funds for transactions and include checks, payment orders, bill payment, and electronic payments in the form of wire services and other electronic settlement systems. Payment systems can also help large corporations and government organizations handle their payment for goods and services.

Apart from settlement for payments, banks can also offer payment services by providing their customers with foreign currencies to make international payments. In arranging international payments, banks facilitate international transactions by offering facilities that allow for creating payment documents that foreign banks accept and by accepting payment documents that foreign banks have issued. Using international payment networks between banks, banks can also send payments according to their customers' requests.

1.1.5   Other Banking Services

Apart from its core services, a bank usually offers other financial services, some in competition with nonbank financial service providers that typically include finance companies, brokerage firms, risk management consultants, and insurance companies. Banks and the companies offering these services typically receive fees, or "fee income," for providing these services. Fee income is the second main source of revenue to banks after the interest the bank receives from its borrowers. Other banking services may include:

- *Cash management.* As a part of their core deposit collection and arranging payments function, banks provide cash or treasury management services to large corpora tions. In general, this service means the bank agrees to handle cash collection and payments for a company and invest any temporary cash surplus.

- *Investment- and securities-related activities.* Many bank customers demand investment products—such as mutual funds, unit trusts, and annuities—that offer higher returns, with higher associated risks, than bank deposits. Traditionally, customers have turned to non-banks for these investment products. Today, however, most banks offer them in an effort to maintain customer relationships.

Banks also offer other securities-related activities, including brokerage and investment banking services. **Brokerage services** involve the buying and selling of securities (e.g., stocks and bonds) on behalf of customers. **Investment banking services** include advising commercial customers on mergers and acquisitions, as well as offering a broad range of financing options, including direct investment in the companies themselves.

- *Derivatives trading.* Derivatives such as swaps, options, forwards, and futures are financial instruments whose value is "derived" from the intrinsic value and/or change in value of another financial or physical asset, such as bonds, stocks, or gold. Derivative transactions help institutions manage various types of risks, such as foreign exchange, interest rate, commodity price, and credit default risks. Derivatives and their use are discussed in Chapter 6.

- *Loan commitments.* Banks receive a flat fee for extending a loan commitment of a certain amount of funds for a period of time whether the full amount is drawn down by the borrower or not. When the borrower uses the whole or parts of the loan commitment, the used portion of the commitment is recorded on the balance sheet. The unused portion remains off balance sheet.

- *Letters of credit.* When a bank provides a letter of credit, it guarantees a payment (up to the amount specified in the letter of credit) on behalf of its customer and receives a fee for providing this guarantee.

- *Insurance services.* Many banks, particularly those outside the United States, offer insurance products to broaden their customer base. Insurance services are a logical progression for banks since insurance products have financial intermediation and asset transformation features similar to traditional bank products. Life insurance policies, for instance, are similar to many of the long-term deposit products that banks offer; all are savings tools, but they deliver their savings benefits differently.

- *Trust services.* Some bank customers, particularly wealthy individuals, corporate pension plans, and estates, prefer to have professionals manage their assets. Therefore, many banks offer trust services that professionally manage a customer's assets for a fee. These assets under management do not show up on the balance sheet of the bank.

- *Risk management services.* As banks have expanded into more complex businesses, they have had to confront more complicated and composite risks such as interest rate, exchange rate, and price risks. Banks have developed sophisticated skills and complicated tools to manage these complex risks. For a fee, banks now offer the same risk management skills and tools to their customers.

1.2 DIFFERENT BANK TYPES

This section illustrates different types of banks by focusing on the types of customers served and the range of services offered. Variations of the types of banks described here exist in different parts of the world.

1.2.1 Retail Banks

Retail banks' primary customers are individuals, or "consumers." Many retail banks also offer services to small and medium enterprises (SMEs). Retail banks may have different specializations:

- *Retail and consumer banks, savings and loans companies (thrifts, building societies), and credit unions.* These offer loans primarily to individuals to finance house, car, or other purchases (e.g., AIG Retail Bank in Thailand, Woodlands Bank in the United States, Országos Takarékpénztár és Kereskedelmi Bank in Hungary).

- *Private banking firms.* These provide wealth management services including tax and investment advice typically to rich individuals (e.g., Coutts & Co in the United Kingdom and Bank Julius Baer in Switzerland).

- *Postal banks.* These offer banking services to customers in post offices. This structure, where the postal service owns or collaborates with a bank, is widely used through-out the world (e.g., Postbank A.G. in Germany, Japan Post Bank in Japan), although not in the United States.

Although retail banks can come in many forms, most have a small network of local branches that enable them to focus on retail consumers in one specific geographic area such as a city or a region of a country. However, there are a number of very large retail banks that have extensive branch networks that cover entire countries or portions of countries (e.g., JPMorgan Chase, Industrial and Commercial Bank of China, Deutsche Bank) and link to retail branches in networks owned through their affiliated entities in other parts of the world (e.g., Citigroup, HSBC).

1.2.2 Wholesale Banks

Wholesale banks' customers are primarily corporate and non-corporate businesses. Although the range of business customers varies, it usually includes larger domestic and international companies. Wholesale banks also offer advisory services tailored to the specific needs of large businesses. Types of wholesale banks include:

- *Commercial banks.* They offer a wide range of highly specialized loans to large businesses, act as an intermediary in raising funds, and provide specialized financial services, such as payment and risk management services.

- *Correspondent banks.* These offer banking services to other banks, including loans and various investment alternatives.

- *Investment or merchant banks.* They offer professional advice to corporations and governments about raising funds in the capital markets such as the stock, bond, or credit markets. In the case of companies, they also provide advice on buying or selling companies whole or in part; in the case of governments, they will advise on privatizing public assets. They may also serve as underwriters and investors in these activities.

BANKING IN FOCUS

The number of investment or merchant banks has diminished since 2008 due to the effects of the global credit crisis that started in 2007.

In 2008, in the wake of the collapse of the subprime mortgage market, investment banks Bear Stearns and Lehman Brothers went out of business. Bear Stearns was sold to JPMorgan Chase and Lehman Brothers declared bankruptcy. Merrill Lynch, the third largest investment bank in the United States, merged with Bank of America. Two of the remaining major U.S. investment banks, Goldman Sachs and Morgan Stanley, legally converted their operations to those of bank holding companies. This move allowed them to accept deposits and thereby raise funds through customer deposits to support their ongoing operations.

This is a monumental change to banking because the investment banking model—which relies on accessing the credit markets for financing while being exposed to financial market risks—has been called into question.

Typically, independent investment banks are not able to accept deposits and are reliant on the credit markets to borrow the funds they need to operate. When the credit markets become difficult to operate in, as happened in 2007 and 2008, the ability to obtain credit and borrow dries up and investment banks are forced to rely on their retained earnings or the sale of assets to stay in business. This has been shown to be insufficient to sustain operations.

Although the large investment banks in the United States have either converted to banks or collapsed, there are still investment banks remaining in the United States. Many of them are smaller, highly specialized investment banks. They are not as reliant on wholesale funding and typically focus on providing advice to corporate customers about raising financing in the financial markets (e.g., Lazard Ltd.).

Many wholesale banks finance international trade and often operate in several countries through representative offices or smaller branches. These banks are known as *international*, *multinational*, or *global banks*. Banks that offer financial services, including insurance, along with the core banking functions are called universal banks. Citibank, HSBC, and Deutsche Bank are examples of large **universal banks**.

1.2.3   Central Banks

Central banks are the principal monetary authority of a country or a group of countries and are crucial to the functioning of all banks, financial markets, and the economy. Central banks manage the amount of money and credit in an economy—usually in an effort to contain inflation rates and/or to foster economic growth. They typically accomplish this through their daily activities of buying and selling government debt, determining and maintaining core interest rates, setting reserve requirement levels, and issuing currency. Some central banks are also charged with maintaining certain foreign exchange rate levels for the home currency. Central banks also arrange payments between banks and act as regulators and supervisors for banks within a country. In their regulatory capacity, central banks supervise other banks and focus on the safety and soundness of its country's financial system. Examples of central banks include the European Central Bank (European Union), the Bank of England (United Kingdom), Bank of Japan (Japan), the People's Bank of China (China), and the Federal Reserve System (United States).

An **interest rate** is the price of credit, or the rate a lender charges a borrower for using borrowed funds. The **inflation rate** is the change in the purchasing value of money.

EXAMPLE

BankCredit lends EUR 1,000,000 to Compagnie Petit, a French corporation. In exchange for using these funds, the bank charges 6% interest rate per year. At the end of the year, Compagnie Petit must pay EUR 60,000 in interest to the bank as well as repay the original EUR 1,000,000.

At the beginning of the year, Jean Molineaux paid EUR 100 for various groceries at the store. At the end of the year, the same groceries at the same store cost EUR 105. Since the price of the same groceries increased 5% during the year, the purchasing power of the money declined by approximately 5%. This decline in purchasing power is the inflation rate.

1.3   BANKING RISKS

There are multiple definitions of risk. Each of us has a definition of what risk is, and all of us recognize a wide range of risks. Some of the more widely discussed definitions of risk include the following:

- The likelihood an undesirable event will occur
- The magnitude of loss from an unexpected event
- The probability that "things won't go right"
- The effects of an adverse outcome

Banks face several types of risk. All the following are examples of the various risks banks encounter:

- Borrowers may submit payments late or fail altogether to make payments.
- Depositors may demand the return of their money at a faster rate than the bank has reserved for.
- Market interest rates may change and hurt the value of a bank's loans.
- Investments made by the bank in securities or private companies may lose value.
- Human input errors or fraud in computer systems can lead to losses.

To monitor, manage, and measure these risks, banks are actively engaged in risk management. In a bank, the **risk management** function contributes to the management of the risks a bank faces by continuously measuring the risk of its current portfolio of assets and other exposures, communicating the risk profile of the bank to other bank functions and by taking steps either directly or in collaboration with other bank functions to reduce the possibility of loss or to mitigate the size of the potential loss.

From a regulatory perspective, the size and risk of a bank's assets are the most important determinants of how much **regulatory reserve capital** the bank is required to hold. A bank with high-risk assets faces the possibility that those assets could quickly lose value. If the market—depositors—perceives that the bank is unstable and deposits are in peril, then nervous depositors may withdraw their funds from the bank. If too many depositors want to withdraw their funds at the same time, then fear that the bank will run out of money could break out. Section 3.1 discusses how bank runs occur. And when there is a widespread withdrawal of money from a bank, the bank may be forced to sell its assets under pressure. To avoid this, regulators would want a bank with high-risk assets to have more reserves available. Therefore, understanding banking regulation requires understanding financial risk management.

This section introduces the various types of risk a bank may face and provides examples that demonstrate each risk. Later chapters explore these risks and their regulatory implications in more detail. The risks discussed below are those identified by the **Basel Accords**, the cornerstone of international risk-based banking regulation. The Basel Accords, described in greater detail in Section 3.3 and throughout the book, are the result of a collaborative attempt by banking regulators from major developed countries to create a globally valid and widely applicable framework for banks and bank risk management.

The Basel II Accord, the most recent of these accords, focuses on three types of risk:
1. Credit risk
2. Market risk
3. Operational risk

The Basel Accord also recognizes that there are other types of risk that may include these different core risk types (see Figure 1.4).

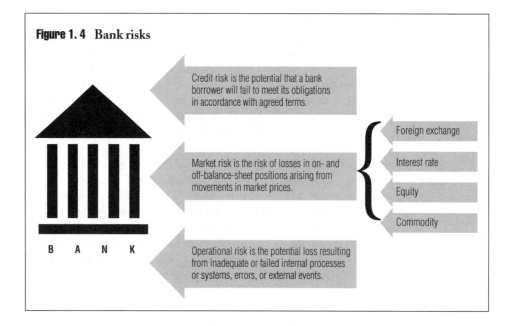

Figure 1. 4 Bank risks

Credit risk is the potential that a bank borrower will fail to meet its obligations in accordance with agreed terms.

Market risk is the risk of losses in on- and off-balance-sheet positions arising from movements in market prices.

Foreign exchange

Interest rate

Equity

Commodity

Operational risk is the potential loss resulting from inadequate or failed internal processes or systems, errors, or external events.

B   A   N   K

1.3.1   Credit Risk

Credit risk is the potential loss a bank would suffer if a bank borrower, also known as the counterparty, fails to meet its obligations—pay interest on the loan and repay the amount borrowed—in accordance with agreed terms. Credit risk is the single largest risk most banks face and arises from the possibility that loans or bonds held by a bank will not be repaid either partially or fully. Credit risk is often synonymous with default risk.

EXAMPLE

In December 2007, the large Swiss bank UBS announced a loss of USD 10 billion due to the significant loss in value of loans made to high-risk borrowers (subprime mortgage borrowers). Many high-risk borrowers could not repay their loans, and the complex models used to predict the likelihood of credit losses turned out to be incorrect. Other major banks all over the globe suffered similar losses due to incorrectly assessing the likelihood of default on mortgage payments. This inability to assess or respond correctly to this risk resulted in many billions of U.S. dollars in losses to companies and individuals around the world.

Default risk affects depositors as well. From the depositors' perspective, credit risk is the risk that the bank will not be able to repay funds when they ask for them.

The underwriting process aims to assess the credit risk associated with lending to a particular potential borrower. Chapter 5 contains a detailed description of the underwriting process. Once a loan is underwritten and the credit is received by the customer, the loan becomes a part of the bank's **banking book**. The banking book is the portfolio of assets (primarily loans) the bank holds, does not actively trade, and expects to hold until maturity when the loan is repaid fully. Section 2.2 discusses the banking book further. A bank's credit risk is the aggregate credit risk of the assets in its banking book.

1.3.2   Market Risk

Market risk is the risk of losses to the bank arising from movements in market prices as a result of changes in interest rates, foreign exchange rates, and equity and commodity prices. The various components of market risk, and the forces that give rise to them, are covered more extensively in Chapter 6. The components of market risk are as follows:

*   **Interest rate risk** is the potential loss due to movements in interest rates. This risk arises because bank assets (loans and bonds) usually have a significantly longer maturity than bank liabilities (deposits). This risk can be conceptualized in two ways. First, if interest rates rise, the value of the longer-term assets will tend to fall more than the value of the shorter-term liabilities, reducing the bank's equity. Section 2.2 discusses bank assets, liabilities, and equity further. Second, if interest rates rise, the bank will be forced to pay higher interest rates on its deposits well before its longer-term loans mature and it is able to replace those loans with loans that earn higher interest rates.

EXAMPLE

American savings and loans (S&Ls), also called thrifts, are essentially mortgage lenders. They collect deposits and underwrite mortgages. During the 1980s and early 1990s, the U.S. S&L system underwent a major crisis in which several thousand thrifts failed as a result of interest rate risk exposure.

Many failed thrifts had underwritten longer-term (up to 30-year) fixed-rate mortgages that were funded by variable-rate deposits. These deposits paid interest rates that would reset, higher or lower, based on the market level of interest rates. As market interest rates increased, the deposit rates reset higher and the interest payments the thrifts had to make began to exceed the interest payments they were receiving on their portfolios of fixed-rate mortgages. This led to increasingly large losses and eventually wiped out the equity of thousands of S&Ls and led to their failure. As shown on the next page in Figure 1.5, as interest rates rose, the payments the S&Ls had to make on variable rate deposits became larger than the payments received from the fixed rate mortgage loans leading to larger and larger losses.

Figure 1.5   Gains vs. losses for American S&Ls as interest rates rise

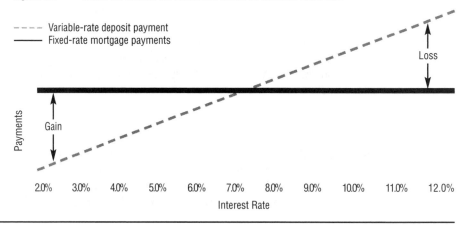

- **Equity risk** is the potential loss due to an adverse change in the price of stock. Stock, also referred to as shares or equity, represent an ownership interest in a company. Banks can purchase ownership stakes in other companies, exposing them to the risk of the changing value of these shares.

EXAMPLE

As the functionality and use of the Internet expanded in the late 1990s, stock prices in technology and Internet sector companies (known as dot-coms) increased rapidly. Interest in these companies grew and pushed stock prices higher and higher, in part driven by speculation of future increases. Unfortunately, from March 2000 to October 2002, this dot-com bubble burst, and the stock price of many of these companies including Amazon, Dell, AOL (America Online) and Yahoo! fell markedly, resulting in shareholder losses of 50% or more.

- **Foreign exchange risk** is the risk that the value of the bank's assets or liabilities changes due to currency exchange rate fluctuations. Banks buy and sell foreign exchange on behalf of their customers (who need foreign currency to pay for their international transactions or receive foreign currency and want to exchange it to their own currency) or for the banks' own accounts.

EXAMPLE

Early in 1992, Swedish companies found it increasingly difficult to obtain credit. Because interest rates were high and the banking system was strained, banks that could lend funds charged high interest rates. Many SMEs turned to the Swedish banks for foreign currency loans; at the time, foreign interest rates were lower than domestic interest rates. Both the banks and the borrowers were willing to assume the currency exchange risk in order to obtain the foreign loans and their lower interest rates. At that time, the Swedish krona (SEK) had a stable exchange rate, linked to the ECU, a basket of European currencies, and there was no expectation that it would change.

But later that year—November 19, 1992—the Swedish government, after a lengthy and expensive struggle to maintain the strength of its currency, effectively devalued the currency, and allowed the SEK to float freely against other currencies by removing the linkage between the SEK and the ECU. The value of the SEK fell significantly, approximately 10% against the major currencies.[1] On November 19, 1992, therefore, it took 10% more SEK for Swedish companies to make the interest payments on their foreign currency loans than it did the day before. While the interest rates on these loans did not change, the amount of SEK the borrower had to have to repay them increased by 10% because the value of the currency was 10% lower. (For example, a SEK 10 interest payment became a SEK 11 interest payment.) While a 10% change may not seem like much, it presented a significant hardship to some borrowers—particularly for those companies that did not generate foreign currency revenue. As a result, many small and medium-sized companies in Sweden failed, making an already weak banking system and economy even more unstable.

- **Commodity risk** is the potential loss due to an adverse change in commodity prices. There are different types of commodities, including agricultural commodities (e.g., wheat, corn, soybeans), industrial commodities (e.g., metals), and energy commodities (e.g., natural gas, crude oil). The value of commodities fluctuates a great deal due to changes in demand and supply.

EXAMPLE

During the 1970s, two American businessmen, the Hunt brothers, accumulated 280 million ounces of silver, a substantial position in the commodity. As they were accumulating this large position—approximately 1/3 of the world's supply—the price of silver rose. For a short period of time at the end of 1979, the Hunt brothers had "cornered" the silver market and effectively controlled its price. Between September 1979 and January 1980, the price of silver increased from USD 11 to USD 50 per ounce, during which time the two brothers earned an estimated USD 2 to 4 billion as a result of their silver speculation. At its peak, the position held by the brothers was worth USD14 billion. Two months later, however, the price of silver collapsed to USD 11 per ounce, and the brothers were forced to sell their substantial silver holdings at a loss.

---

1.   For example, on October 5, 1992, when the SEK was linked to the ECU, one USD cost SEK 5.30. On December 23, 1992, after the SEK was allowed to float, one USD cost SEK 7.12. The value of the SEK declined relative to the USD by 34% in the fall of 1992.

Market risk tends to focus on a bank's **trading book**. The trading book is the portfolio of financial assets such as bonds, equity, foreign exchange, and derivatives held by a bank to either facilitate trading for its customers or for its own account or to hedge against various types of risk. Assets in the trading book are generally made available for sale, as the bank does not intend to keep those assets until they mature. Assets in the bank's banking book (held until maturity) and trading book (not held until maturity) collectively contain all the various investments in loans, securities, and other financial assets the bank has made using its deposits, loans, and shareholder equity.

Distinguishing between the trading and banking books is essential for how the banks operate and how they manage their risks. The Basel Accord does not provide a definition for the term **banking book**; this is an important and easily forgotten point. In effect, what is included in the banking book is what is not included in the bank's trading book, which is defined by the Basel II Accord. The trading and banking books will be the subject of discussion in later chapters (see Section 2.2).

1.3.3   Operational Risk

Operational risk is the risk of loss resulting from inadequate or failed internal processes, people and systems or from external events. This definition includes legal risk, but excludes strategic and reputational risk.

EXAMPLE

In 1995, Baring Brothers and Co. Ltd. (Barings) collapsed after incurring losses of GBP 827 million following the failure of its internal control processes and procedures. One of Baring's traders in Singapore hid trading losses for more than two years. Because of insufficient internal control measures, the trader was able to authorize his own trades and book them into the bank's systems without any supervision. The trader's supervisors were alerted after the trades started to lose significant amounts of money and it was no longer possible for the trader to keep the trades and the losses secret.

Compared to credit and market risk, operational risk is the least understood and most challenging risk to measure, manage, and monitor. There is a wide range of loss events that can be categorized as operational risk events. Chapter 7 discusses how banks measure and manage the different types of operational risks they are exposed to as part of the banking business.

1.3.4   Other Risk Types

Beyond the three main types of risk—credit, market, and operational—there are other risks banks face and must manage appropriately. Here is a listing of some of them:

- **Liquidity risk** relates to the bank's ability to meet its continuing obligations, including financing its assets. Liquidity risk will be discussed in greater detail in Chapters 3 and 6.

EXAMPLE

In August 2007, Northern Rock, a bank focused on financing real estate in the United Kingdom, announced that it needed emergency funding from the Bank of England. Northern Rock was a relatively small bank that did not have a sufficient depositor base to fund new loans from deposits. It financed new mortgages by selling the mortgages it originated to other banks and investors and by taking out short-term loans, making it increasingly vulnerable to changes in the financial markets. How much financing Northern Rock could raise depended on two factors. The first was the demand for mortgages it originated to sell to other banks. The second was the availability of credit in the credit market to finance these mortgages. Both of these depended on how the overall banking marketplace, particularly the availability of funding to finance lending, was performing. When the credit markets came under pressure in 2007, the bank found it increasingly difficult to sell the mortgages it had originated. At the same time, Northern Rock could not secure the required short-term financing it required. Effectively Northern Rock could not finance its assets, was unable to raise new funds, ran out of money, and, notwithstanding the emergency financing from the Bank of England, was ultimately taken over by the government.

- **Business risk** is the potential loss due to a decrease in the competitive position of the bank and the prospect of the bank prospering in changing markets.

EXAMPLE

In the mid-1990s, BestBank of Boulder, Colorado (USA), attempted to build its credit card loan portfolios quickly by issuing cards to many low-quality, "subprime," borrowers. Unfortunately, too many low-quality borrowers failed to pay their BestBank credit card debts. In July 1998, BestBank was closed after incurring losses of about USD 232 million. This serves as a classic example of a bank seeking to grow its business by lending money to high-risk customers: Although the bank was apparently generating high returns for a period of time, it failed to adequately provide for and guard against bad debts in its business strategy.

- **Reputational risk** is the potential loss resulting from a decrease in a bank's standing in public opinion. Recovering from a reputation problem, real or perceived, is not easy. Organizations have lost considerable business for no other reason than loss of customer confidence over a public relations problem, even with relatively solid systems, processes, and finances in place.

EXAMPLE

In early 1991, Salomon Brothers, then the fifth largest investment bank in the United States, was caught submitting far larger purchase orders for U.S. government debt than it was allowed. When the U.S. government borrows funds, it sells the debt at an auction and invites selected banks to purchase these securities, called Treasuries. To ensure that Treasuries are correctly priced and all investors willing to lend money to the U.S. government receive a fair price and interest rate, each bank invited to bid at this auction can only purchase a limited amount of the securities. By falsifying names and records, Salomon Brothers amassed a large position in the Treasuries, ultimately controlling the price investors paid for these securities. When its illegal activities became known, the price of Salomon shares dropped significantly, and there were concerns in the financial markets about Salomon's ability to continue doing business. Salomon Brothers suffered considerable loss of reputation that was only partially restored by Warren Buffett, a well-respected U.S. investor, who injected equity in the firm and took a leadership role in the firm. The U.S. government subsequently fined Salomon Brothers USD 290 million, the largest fine ever levied on an investment bank at the time.

1.4   FORCES SHAPING THE BANKING INDUSTRY

There are numerous other aspects of banking that have not been covered in this chapter but will be briefly touched upon in later parts of the book—either directly or as part of a discussion about other topics.

- *Regulation, deregulation, and globalization.* Deregulation led to a relaxing of restrictive banking regulations in many countries around the globe. This allowed many banks to compete against each other and with other financial services providers with less direct government oversight and more freedom in how they structured their businesses. The theory behind the movement resulting in less oversight was that increased competition among banks would increase their bank efficiency. Deregulation puts market pressures on banks from organizations that offer similar banking services. Additionally, it was felt that banks would, in their own self-interest, effectively regulate themselves with little need for heavy-handed oversight from government regulators. The reasoning is that it is in the bank's self-interest to ensure they functioned properly to compete in an increasingly competitive world. However, as it became apparent in 2008, banks were unable to police themselves effectively. Their lack of discipline resulted in a virtual collapse of the global financial system. It has also become clear that many banks are now considered "too big to fail" due to their global connectivity and importance to the worldwide financial system. Now, governments are considering numerous banking regulation reforms and are, for the first time, considering adopting some type of cooperative system to allow for the rapid sharing of information among world financial regulators with the intent of more proactively addressing future financial services-related risks and issues.

- *Competition.* Competition from specialized financial service providers has taken market share from banks and forced them to increase their efficiency. Examples of non-depository financial intermediaries that now compete with banks include:

  - Retirement systems—pension plans and retirement funds
  - Collective investment pools—mutual funds, unit trusts, and hedge funds
  - Finance companies—leasing and equipment finance
  - Payment services
  - Insurance companies
  - Hedge funds
  - Private equity companies

- *Securitization.* Bundling together various debt capital assets, such as mortgages, credit cards, and loans, and selling securities representing various types of ownership in the resulting portfolio, is a relatively new financial product. The securitization process is explained in greater detail in Section 5.3. Securitization is a threat to banks since it enables nonbanks to offer loans and financing at a lower cost than that which banks historically charge. Securitization, however, can also benefit banks by offering them a way to sell some of the higher-risk assets they would prefer not to hold on their books.

- *Technological advances.* Improvements in computing power, telecommunications, and information technology have allowed banks to offer new ventures such as Internet-based banking. Technological advances continue to reduce the cost of routine banking services, such as payments and withdrawals.

- *Inflation and interest rate uncertainty.* Both bank balance sheets and profits are highly sensitive to changes in interest rates. When inflation increases, interest rates tend to increase, and many banks—as we will see in later sections—will suffer. When interest rates change considerably and frequently, banks must focus on managing these risks.

In this chapter, we laid the foundation for understanding banks, the banking industry, and the risks they face. Later chapters discuss in greater detail the relationship between bank risks and regulation.

CHAPTER 2

Managing Banks

C hapter 2 builds on the first chapter and introduces bank management topics that are particularly relevant to risk management and regulation. This chapter examines bank corporate governance, the financial statements banks use to communicate their activities, the function of asset and liability management in banking, and how banks manage loan losses.

Chapter Outline

- 2.1 Bank Corporate Governance
- 2.2 Balance Sheet and Income Statement
- 2.3 Asset and Liability Management
- 2.4 Loan Losses

Key Learning Points

- Bank corporate governance refers to the framework banks use to manage their operations and deal with the often-conflicting interests of bank stakeholders.
- Banks report their assets, liabilities, and the effects of their various business transactions in financial statements. Financial statements provide a comprehensive view of performance for shareholders, depositors, stakeholders, and regulators.
- Banks manage their assets and liabilities with the overall objective of reducing risks while maximizing returns to shareholders.
- Banks treat performing and nonperforming loans differently; banks build up reserves in their financial statements to reduce the potential negative effects of nonperforming loans.

Key Terms

- Asset and liability management
- Assets
- Balance sheet
- Banking book of the bank
- Charged-off loan
- Collateral
- Corporate governance
- Dividends
- Equity
- Fair market value
- Income statement
- Interest rate risk
- Interest rate risk in the banking book
- Leverage
- Liabilities
- Liquidity
- Liquidity risk
- Loan loss reserve
- Marked-to-market

- Net income
- Nonperforming loan
- Paid-in capital
- Past-due loan
- Performing loan
- Private offering
- Provision for loan losses
- Public offering
- Repurchase agreement, "repo"
- Retained earnings
- Savings accounts
- Scenario analysis stress testing
- Shareholders
- Solvency
- Stakeholders
- Stress Testing
- Trading book of the bank
- Transaction accounts
- Written-down loan

Managing Banks

2.1 BANK CORPORATE GOVERNANCE

A bank is required to consider the sometimes conflicting requirements of its individual customers, borrowers, depositors, investors, employees, shareholders, regulators, and the public, collectively called **stakeholders**. All stakeholders have an interest in the future success of the bank. For instance, if the bank is successful, customers benefit from continued business relationships, depositors have continued access to their money, and employees have jobs and receive salaries. Banks attempt to balance the conflicting interests of all its stakeholders, yet recognize that ultimately all decisions should increase the value of the bank and wealth of the owners of the bank, the **shareholders**. Shareholders elect the board of directors that supervises management that controls the day-to-day operations of the bank. **Corporate governance**, the set of relationships between the board of directors, shareholders, and other stakeholders of a company, is a framework banks use to enhance their success. Corporate governance creates a relationship structure that helps management to:

- Set corporate and strategic business objectives and run daily operations
- Consider the interests of all its stakeholder groups, separately as well as jointly
- Manage the bank in a safe and sound manner
- Comply with relevant laws and regulations
- Protect the interests of its depositors

The structure of a bank's corporate governance depends on its host country's legal system, business customs, and the historical development of the bank. Although there is no single structure that can be prescribed as ideal, there are generally accepted governance concepts and ideas that have been shown to support an adequately functioning governance system. Good corporate governance seeks to establish rules that help corporations, such as banks, create internal processes that benefit both the bank and its stakeholders.

Several national and international organizations, agencies, corporations, and institutions have attempted to define what creates good corporate governance. Some of the elements identified as described in this section.

2.1.1 Board of Directors

The board of directors has the ultimate responsibility for the management and performance of a company and is responsible for its governance.

The board of directors should do the following:
- Set the overall strategic direction of the bank, including the establishment of the bank's risk tolerance levels
- Hire and fire; oversee, guide, and review the performance of senior management; and set senior management compensation
- Monitor the performance of the bank, review regular financial and risk reports
- Be qualified, both personally and professionally, to act as directors with integrity and in the interest of shareholders
- Meet regularly with senior management and internal auditors to establish and approve policies
- Review reporting lines, authority, and responsibilities of the bank's senior management
- In particular, outside directors should be independent of internal and external influences and provide sound advice without participating in the daily management of the bank

Specialized committees support the overall work of the board and allow board members to oversee specific areas. These committees will cover areas such as risk management, audit, compensation, and board nominations. Particularly in smaller banks, a board-level committee can be tasked to review major loan decisions.

When the board of directors establishes the bank's strategy and risk tolerance levels, it effectively decides what types of assets the bank should primarily underwrite. Essentially, any bank can choose between pursuing a low-risk strategy and a high-risk strategy.
- A *low-risk strategy* entails underwriting high-quality bonds (in particular, government bonds) and loans with stringent underwriting standards (Chapter 4), including collateral demands. These assets are considered conservative, with little risk of default. Chapter 6 will discuss bonds.
- A *high-risk strategy* entails underwriting lower-quality bonds (in particular, lower rated corporate bonds) and loans with less stringent underwriting standards (Chapter 4). All these assets are considered risky, having a greater risk of default.

Whether a bank pursues a low-risk strategy or a high-risk strategy, the board of directors has to determine how prudently, or conservatively, the bank should be managed. A prudent bank closely monitors the loans it underwrites, has more than adequate liquidity, and generally has stringent internal controls on all aspects of its operations. From a regulatory perspective, a prudently managed bank that pursues a low-risk strategy is optimal. A bank that is not prudently managed and pursues a high-risk strategy usually causes considerable concern to regulators.

While a bank's organizational structure is a business decision reserved to the bank's CEO, the board of directors may provide advice as to the broad design of the bank's organizational structure to the CEO. However, it should be noted that there is a line drawn between the board's oversight responsibilities and the bank's daily management and day-to-day decision making, which lie in the hands of the bank's CEO and its senior management. A typical organization structure is depicted in Figure 2.1.

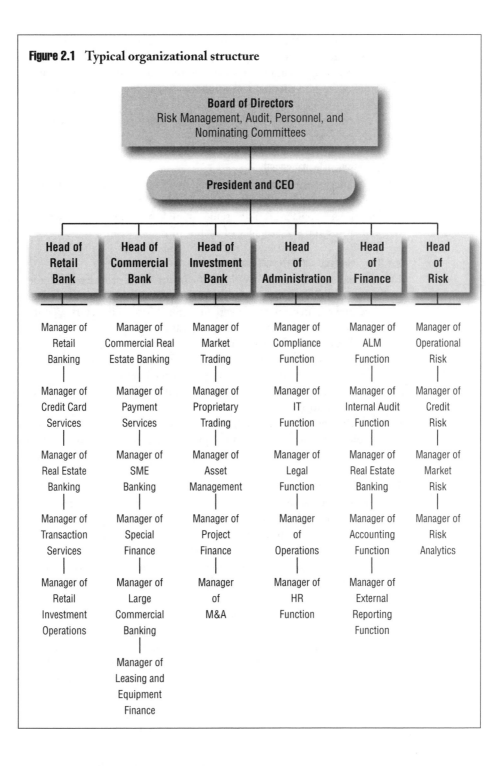

Figure 2.1 Typical organizational structure

At the head of the organization is the board of directors. Immediately below the board of directors is the company's president, who oversees the senior management. The senior managers, in turn, oversee the activities of business units, junior managers, and employees. This hierarchical structure ensures that corporate activities are coordinated across the various businesses.

A company or a bank's organizational structure should include the following features:

2.1.2   Senior Management

Senior management has comprehensive oversight of managers (managers are held directly responsible for the development of a specific line of business or operational function.) An important task for senior managers is to communicate the responsibilities and ensure the performance of each staff member.

2.1.3   Internal and External Auditors

Internal and external auditors validate the information provided by senior management to the board of directors, regulators, and the public. Both internal and external auditors play a central role in corporate governance. The board of directors supports and protects the auditor's interaction in the following ways:

*   The board supports auditor independence by engaging auditors to prepare an unbiased assessment of the company's financial position based on accepted standards and report the findings directly to the board.
*   Boards engage external auditors to judge the effectiveness of the company's internal controls.
*   Boards should review, in a timely and effective manner, the auditor's findings and recommendations and require prompt correction by senior management of problems identified by auditors.

2.1.4   Transparency

Transparency helps stakeholders, investors, the public, and regulators to evaluate the performance of the bank and how effectively senior management and the board fulfill their responsibilities. The degree of transparency relates to the degree of disclosure. At a minimum, public disclosure should include:

*   The size and qualifications of the board of directors and its subcommittees
*   The structure, qualifications, and responsibilities of the company's senior management
*   Information about the bank's basic organizational structure, including its legal structure
*   Information regarding senior employee incentive structure and compensation policy (typically restricted to a few senior and well-compensated employees)
*   The nature and extent of transactions with affiliates and related parties

2.2   BALANCE SHEET AND INCOME STATEMENT

One corporate governance responsibility that a bank's board and senior management team must fulfill is to record correctly and account for all the bank's transactions. Transactions include the bank's loans, investments, and other assets as well as deposits. These records form the underlying basis for the bank's financial statements: its balance sheet, income statement, statement of cash flows, and the notes to these statements. Through financial statements, a bank is able to communicate its financial position to its stakeholders and regulators. This section focuses on the balance sheet and the income statement.

- The **balance sheet** shows all the assets, liabilities, and equity the bank has at one particular point in time, such as at the end of a year. It is a snapshot of what the bank owns (assets) and owes (liabilities), and the difference between them, the bank's equity.
- The **income statement** records all the revenues (income) and costs (expenses) that the bank has encountered over a specific time period, such as one month, one quarter, or one year.

2.2.1   Bank Assets

A bank typically has cash, investments in securities and loans, real estate holdings, and other **assets** on its balance sheet. The majority of a bank's assets are held in either the bank's banking or trading books. A small proportion of the bank's assets are held in cash, either in the vault of the bank to meet immediate needs for payments and withdrawals, as reserves at the central bank or deposited with other banks to fulfill its regulatory reserve requirements (see Chapter 1).

Figure 2.2 below shows a simple balance sheet for a hypothetical bank, FirstBank, a typical medium-sized bank that provides credit for commercial and industrial purposes. The bank finances its assets—the bonds it owns and the loans it underwrites—using a combination of deposits and borrowings. We will use this hypothetical balance sheet as our example throughout the remainder of this chapter.

Figure 2.2   FirstBank balance sheet

Assets in million USD		Amount	Liabilities in million USD	Amount	
Cash		10	Short-term deposits	300	
Government bonds		100	Long-term deposits	250	
			Subtotal deposits		*550*
Loans to local government, net	190		Short-term financing	200	
Loans to SMEs, net	200		Long-term bonds	150	
Loans to large corporations, net	500		*Subtotal other liabilities*		*350*
Total loans		*890*	Total liabilities	900	
			Equity		100
Total		**1,000**	**Total**		**1,000**

From a management perspective, the bank's assets are divided in two "books" that contain assets of similar characteristics.

*   The **trading book of the bank** includes the investments the bank has made in securities such as bonds, equities, and commodities. The trading book is chiefly exposed to market risk. Chapter 6 will discuss in further detail the risks of the various financial assets usually found in the trading book.

*   The **banking book of the bank** refers to the loans the bank has made. The primary risk in the banking book is credit risk. Interest rate risk is also a major consideration when managing the bank's banking book (see Section 2.3.1). Chapters 4 and 5 will discuss in detail the risks of the various loan types that banks routinely underwrite.

Figure 2.3 below depicts the difference between the trading book and the banking book for our hypothetical bank, FirstBank.

Figure 2.3	**Trading and banking books**		
Assets in million USD		**Amount**	**Book**
Cash		10	
Government bonds		100	Trading
Loans to local government		190	
Loans to SMEs		200	Banking
Loans to large corporations		500	
Total		**1,000**	

FirstBank's trading book consists of the government bonds the bank owns, and the banking book consists of three distinct portfolios: local government loans, SME loans, and large corporate loans. The value of the banking book equals the value of the bank's loans.

In addition to the above, banks will usually own real estate (building and other premises) and machinery and equipment (computer and other technology networks) used to support operations.

2.2.2   Bank Liabilities

A bank's **liabilities** consist of its deposits and its borrowings. Most of a commercial bank's liabilities are the deposits made by its customers (depositors). These deposits are generally placed in either transaction accounts or savings accounts. Figure 2.2 shows the balance sheet with the various liabilities the bank holds.

*   **Transaction accounts** are accounts where the depositor can withdraw the deposits on demand using checks, debit cards, or similar payment instructions. Transaction accounts usually allow a large number of withdrawals with minimal time restrictions. For the convenience of immediate access to deposits, banks pay no, or low, interest to the depositors. Checking or debit accounts are examples of transaction accounts.

- **Savings accounts** typically limit the number of withdrawals a depositor can make over a specified period of time, and offer higher interest rates to depositors. Because access to funds in a savings account is limited and withdrawal in certain cases may be restricted by time, savings accounts are important to a bank's asset and liability management function (see Section 2.3.2 for more details). Examples of savings accounts are time deposits, passbook savings, and certificates of deposits.

A bank may also borrow money from other banks overnight or from its central bank for various time periods. Additionally, banks may issue bonds and other debt instruments that are publicly traded. Figure 2.4 shows FirstBank's debt financing.

Figure 2.4	**The bank's debt financing**		
Liabilities in million USD	**Amount**		**Liability type**
Short-term deposits	300		Transaction deposit
Long-term deposits	250		Savings deposit
Total deposits		*550*	
Short-term financing	200		Other bank liability
Long-term bonds	150		Other bank liability
Other debt financing		*350*	
Total liabilities		**900**	

2.2.3   Equity

The difference between the bank's assets and liabilities equals its **equity**.

$$\text{Assets} - \text{Liabilities} = \text{Equity}$$

EXAMPLE

FirstBank has USD 1,000 million in assets with USD 900 million in liabilities; the difference of USD 100 million is the bank's equity.

Equity represents the ownership stake of the bank's shareholders and consists of two parts:
1. **Paid-in-capital**, the capital that the owners have provided to the bank
2. **Retained earnings**, all the earnings the bank has generated since its inception, less any income it returned to the owners as dividends

A bank can raise equity in two ways. First, it can sell new stock (equity) to its existing shareholders or the public. When the bank turns to the public to sell new equity in the form of shares, the process is called a **public offering**. An alternative approach to raising equity is a **private offering**, when the bank turns to a selected group of qualified investors to raise the equity capital. Second, the bank can generate net income that is added to its existing equity capital as retained earnings. **Dividends** are discretionary payments from the bank to the shareholders. The bank returns part of the income the bank earns to its owners through dividends. The board of directors usually decides whether to pay dividends.

Typically, equity consists of preferred and common stock. One of the fundamental differences between preferred and common stock is that common stock allows its owners to make decisions that affect the bank by voting as shareholders with the other shareholders, including voting for the board of directors. Owners of preferred stock generally do not have this right, which they gave up in exchange for a set dividend payment and priority over the common shareholders in the event the bank is liquidated. Preferred stock is considered a hybrid security, as it has both debt- and equitylike features. The debtlike features include set return and the fact that preferred shareholders, in case the bank is liquidated, receive payments before the common shareholders. The equitylike features include that preferred shareholders may receive dividends that may be structured to reflect corporate profits and the fact that if the bank is liquidated, they receive payment after the bondholders but before the common shareholders.

2.2.4   Income Statement

The income statement records the effects of the financial transactions the bank carried out over a specified time period, usually quarterly or annually. The income statement specifically shows the effect costs have on the revenues generated. The difference between the revenues earned and the costs incurred over a set time period is called profit (or loss). In sum, profit, or loss, is the difference between the bank's income and its expenses.

The bank's greatest source of income is the difference between the interest rate the bank earns on the loans it makes and the interest rate it pays to the depositors for their deposits. This difference is called the interest rate margin. Banks only profit when their interest income (paid by the borrowers to the bank) is greater than interest expenses (paid by the bank to the depositors). Managing the bank's net interest income, the difference between interest income and interest expense, is an important function of bank managers.

EXAMPLE

Using the balance sheet presented in Figure 2.2 and the bank's stated rates of return, we can calculate its net interest income. Looking at the assets (left) side of the balance sheet, we see that the USD 10 million in cash FirstBank holds on hand currently earns nothing. The interest income the bank derives from the next four items and their total is shown in Figure 2.5.

Figure 2.5   The bank's interest income

Assets in million USD	Amount	Annual return	Annual interest income
Cash	10	0%	10 * 0% = 0
Government bonds	100	2%	100 * 2% = 2
Loans to local government, net[1]	190	3%	190 * 3% = 6
Loans to SMEs, net	200	5%	200 * 5% = 10
Loans to large corporations, net	500	7%	500 * 7% = 35
Total			**53**

Looking at the liabilities (right) side of the same balance sheet, the bank's interest expense comes from the first four items, and is shown in Figure 2.6.

Figure 2.6   The bank's interest expense

Liabilities in million USD	Amount	Annual cost	Annual interest expense
Short-term deposits	300	1%	300 * 1% = 3
Long-term deposits	250	2%	250 * 2% = 5
Short-term financing	200	3%	200 * 3% = 6
Long-term bonds	150	4%	150 * 4% = 6
Total			**20**

Interest income	USD 53 million
– Interest expense	USD 20 million
= Net interest income	USD 33 million

A second major source of revenues generated by the bank comes from the various fees banks charge their customers for services provided. For example, fees are charged for opening an account, applying for a loan, arranging a payment, or receiving advice for complex financial services. Fee income is a substantial source of income. Many banks try to maintain some type of balance between the revenues they earn from interest income and fee income.

The most significant cost the bank has apart from its interest expenses is for personnel (employees). Other important costs are the cost for the premises where it operates and the physical infrastructure (computer and other networks) the bank owns.

After all costs have been deducted from the bank's revenue, the bank's earnings before taxes are calculated. Banks, as most all other companies, pay tax on their earnings to local, state, and national governments. After the bank pays any taxes due, the remainder is the bank's **net income**. If the net income is negative, it is called a loss.

---

1.   For reasons of presentation simplicity, this number is rounded from USD 5.7 million to USD 6.0 million.

EXAMPLE

In building on the example above, assume FirstBank generates USD 15 million in fee income but has USD 23 million in personnel and other expenses. Thus, its earnings before taxes may be calculated as:

Net interest income	USD 33 million
+ Fee income	USD 15 million
– Personnel and other expenses	USD 23 million
= Earnings before taxes	USD 25 million

These examples present a very simplified approach to calculating profits and losses. In reality, there are numerous, and often complex, tax, legal, regulatory, and other considerations that banks, and any company, must take into account before it can calculate profit(s) or loss(es).

Banks can use their positive net income in any number of ways. As mentioned earlier, the net income can be added to the bank's already existing equity capital as retained earnings, thereby increasing the amount of the bank's equity capital, or the bank can return part of this income to its shareholders as dividends or through the repurchase of existing stock.

2.2.5   The Role of Bank's Equity

Equity plays an important role in the management of the bank. If the bank makes a loan to a borrower that defaults on its obligation, the bank will lose some of its assets, affecting the bank's equity and reducing the shareholders' stake in the banks. The depositors, who have entrusted their money for safekeeping at the bank, expect to be protected from any losses the bank suffers on its loans.

As noted in Chapter 1, the processes of financial intermediation and asset transformation are key to bank operations and are also at the core of bank risks. Underwriting, the process of evaluating a borrower's ability to repay funds to the bank, places the bank in a unique position. The bank must determine how much credit can be extended (if any) and the conditions (or terms) it must impose on the loan to decrease the possibility of loss. In addition, the bank must consider the total amount of credit risk it is willing to take across all its borrowers (see Section 2.1.1 on corporate governance). In fact, how well a bank succeeds in its underwriting process affects the bank's profits, financial health, and survival.

FirstBank has extended many loans to SMEs, including a USD 4 million loan to Mega Construction. Suppose that just after making the loan to Mega Construction the bank's balance sheet looks as in Figure 2.7.

Figure 2.7   FirstBank's balance sheet

Assets in million USD	Amount		Liabilities in million USD	Amount	
Cash		10	Short-term deposits	300	
Government bonds		100	Long-term deposits	250	
			Subtotal deposits		*550*
Loans to local government, net	190		Short-term financing	200	
Loans to SMEs, net	200		Long-term bonds	150	
Loans to large corporations, net	500		*Subtotal other liabilities*		*350*
Total loans		*890*	Total liabilities	900	
			Equity		100
Total		**1,000**	**Total**		**1,000**

Now, let us suppose that Mega Construction is unable to repay the loan and defaults. This loan default impacts the bank in several ways:

- The bank will not receive any additional interest income from the loan. Assuming the interest rates on loans to SMEs are 5%, the bank would lose USD 200,000 in annual interest income. In the meantime, FirstBank still has to pay interest to its depositors. This will reduce the net interest income of the bank.
- If FirstBank cannot recover the loan it has provided to Mega Construction, the bank loses USD 4 million, which it *charges off*, or removes, from its balance sheet. (Section 2.4 will discuss in greater detail how banks manage nonperforming loans.) The charge-off affects the bank's balance sheet by reducing two items:
  1. Assets by the loss of USD 4 million
  2. Equity by the loss of USD 4 million

Losses to the bank reduce first its equity. Deposits are usually insulated from these losses, as equity and other sources of capital—such as the bank's own borrowings—bear the primary impact of losses. Banks create various reserves to counterbalance some of the effects of loan losses; how these reserves work will be discussed in Section 2.4. Some countries provide deposit insurance as an additional guarantee for bank depositors, further reducing the potential risk to depositors (see Section 3.4 for more on deposit insurance).

After the USD 4 million loss, the bank's balance sheet looks like Figure 2.8, showing total assets and liabilities (plus equity) of the USD 996 million.

Figure 2.8   FirstBank's balance sheet after the loss

Assets (in USD millions)	Amount	Liabilities	Amount
Cash	10	Short-term deposits	300
Government bonds	100	Long-term deposits	250
Loans to local government, net	190	Short-term financing	200
❶ Loans to SMEs, net	196	Long-term bonds	150
Loans to large corporations, net	500	❷ Equity	96
Total	996	Total	996

The two effects of the loss on the balance sheet of the bank are the following:

1. *The value of loans is reduced by the amount of the loss.* The USD 4 million loan loss reduces the "Loans to SME" from USD 200 million to USD 196 million.
2. *The value of equity is reduced by the amount of the loss.* The USD 4 million loan loss reduces equity from USD 100 million to USD 96 million.

As we can see in Figure 2.8, the USD 4 million loss is small in relation to all of the bank's assets, just 0.4% of assets of USD 1,000 million. It is, however, a considerable loss in relation to the bank's equity of USD 100 million. It is 4% of the capital. The bank's equity absorbs the losses the bank suffers when loans or other investments go sour. That is why banks carefully evaluate their borrowers; should losses accumulate, the bank's equity would be in peril. Losses tend to accumulate during bad economic times, the same times when banks are most vulnerable.

If the losses are large enough, the entire capital of the bank disappears. In fact, in this particular case, the bank can only withstand an additional USD 96 million in losses before its equity becomes zero. With USD 996 million in loans outstanding, if a little less than 1/10 of the total amount the bank lent to the customers is lost, the equity of the bank becomes zero. In fact, in most countries, a bank would be closed by the regulators before it lost all of its equity. A bank with a larger equity base is better able to absorb potential losses from nonperforming and defaulted loans and is considered more stable.

In the example above, 90% of the assets are financed through debt. *Leverage* or (*gearing* in the UK) is the ratio of debt to equity.

EXAMPLE

Initially, Bank A's USD 1,000 million in assets were financed through USD 900 million in debt and USD 100 million equity. The leverage was 9-to-1; each dollar of equity supported USD 10 in assets. In relation to many other businesses, banks are highly leveraged.

Banks compared to other businesses are inherently highly leveraged. Let's revisit FirstBank's balance sheet with the loan loss example above to see how quickly bank equity can disappear when a bank has higher leverage and suffers losses.

EXAMPLE

Looking at the same loss of USD 4 million discussed earlier, the impact on FirstBank will be far greater when leverage increases. Let us assume that instead of 9-to-1 leverage, FirstBank's initial leverage was 19-to-1. In this scenario, the bank's assets of USD 1,000 million would be financed with USD 950 million in debt and only USD 50 million in equity. Here, each dollar of equity supports USD 19 in debt (USD 950/USD 50 = USD 19). Figure 2.9 shows the combined effects of losses and smaller equity base.

Figure 2.9 Simplified balance sheet—smaller equity base or higher leverage

Assets (in USD millions)	Amount	Liabilities	Amount
Cash	10	Short-term deposits	300
Government bonds, net	100	Long-term deposits	250
Loans to local government, net	190	Short-term financing	250
❶ *Loans to SMEs, net*	*196*	Long-term bonds	150
Loans to large corporations, net	500	❷ *Equity*	*46*
Total	**996**	**Total**	**996**

1. The value of loans is reduced by the amount of the loss. The USD 4 million loan loss reduces the "Loans to SME" from USD 200 million to USD 196 million.
2. The value of equity is reduced by the amount of the loss. The USD 4 million loan loss reduces equity from USD 50 million to USD 46 million.

Losing USD 4 million, or 0.4% of its assets in this case, reduces equity from USD 50 million to USD 46 million, but this erosion will reduce equity by 8% (USD 3 / USD 50 = 8%). The bank now can only withstand an additional USD 46 million in losses before its equity becomes zero. With USD 996 million in loans outstanding, if a little less than 5% of the total amount the bank lent to the customers is lost, the equity of the bank becomes zero.

The higher the leverage, the faster the equity disappears when the bank has to take losses on loans that default. The impact losses have on equity is why bank regulations and regulators have historically focused on the bank's equity. Regulators consider the bank's equity the core tool to motivate bank managers and owners to reduce risks and to provide a sufficient cushion against losses.

More equity and lower leverage represents the following:
- Bigger commitment by the owners, on the aggregate, to the future of the bank, as they have more of their wealth tied to the fortunes of the bank and potentially to lose.
- Greater cushion for the bank to absorb and withstand potential losses.

In fact, over the years, both regulators and economists have found that prudently managed banks have higher capital-to-total-assets ratios and suffer losses less frequently. They have found that the amount of capital a bank must have to support its operations reduces the risks a bank will take and increases the likelihood that the equity of the bank is sufficient to withstand loan losses as well as liquidity pressures. In fact, contemporary banking regulation, such as the Basel II Accord (described in Section 3.3), is risk based and links the riskiness of the bank's assets to its equity.

2.3   Asset and Liability Management

Banks face two additional key risks that have not yet been discussed: **interest rate risk** and **liquidity risk**.
- *Interest rate risk refers to the potential loss in value of an asset due to changes in interest rates.* For example, a bank pays one interest rate to its depositors and receives another from its debtors. If interest rates change, the profitability of the bank changes as well. Interest rate risk affects both the banking book and the trading book.
- *Liquidity risk refers to the potential inability of a bank to meet its payment obligations when they are due.* In particular, a bank must manage its ability to pay its depositors interest and to repay depositors seeking to withdraw any part of their money. Liquidity risk is also called *funding liquidity risk*.

The liquidity discussed in this section is different from another type of liquidity, the ability to trade in markets without significant price concessions, which will be discussed in Chapter 6.

The bank's **asset and liability management** (ALM) function manages both the interest rate risk in the bank's banking book and liquidity risk. In particular, the ALM function in a bank focuses on:
- Maintaining liquidity for the bank
- Analyzing the shape and structure of the bank's balance sheet
- Maintaining a stable net interest margin

2.3.1   Interest Rate Risk

Interest rate risk in the banking book refers to a possible monetary loss caused by adverse changes in interest rates affecting the underlying structure of the bank's business: its lending and deposit-taking activities. The dangers of not managing banking book interest rate risk were highlighted by the savings and loan crisis that affected the United States during 1980s and 1990s.

EXAMPLE

In the United States, savings and loan associations (S&Ls), also known as thrifts, are banks that are predominantly mortgage lenders. During the 1980s and early 1990s, many S&Ls collapsed due largely to a mismanagement of interest rate risk that allowed a severe mismatch of assets and liabilities.

During the 1980s, S&Ls underwrote fixed-rate, 30-year mortgages at around 6% and financed these loans from short-term deposits at interest rates around 2%. The mortgages were relatively profitable, until U.S. interest rates rose and the S&Ls had to pay 9 to 10% on their deposits, the same deposits that financed the funds that were loaned out for 30 years at only 6%. In the end, several hundred S&Ls collapsed.

Ultimately, the U.S. government financed the collapsed S&Ls; some reports put the bailout figure around USD 150 billion. There are, however, estimates that reach up to USD 500 billion. (See Section 1.3.2 about the S&L crisis.)

In managing the bank's assets and liabilities, the ALM function has to consider and balance several factors simultaneously:

- *The bank's balance sheet, a dynamic portfolio of loans and deposits.* As new loans are extended, as existing loans mature, and as new deposits arrive, existing deposits may be withdrawn.
- *The interest rate on liabilities and assets.* Some will be fixed, but the interest rate on other liabilities and assets will change periodically according to market rates, resulting in fluctuations in the value of floating-rate liabilities and assets.
- *Timing differences between changes in market rates and in the interest rates on retail products such as bank loans to customers.*
- *The bank's current liquidity needs.* The current market interest rates for all maturities and competition among banks determine the interest rates offered on deposit products.
- *Commercial (e.g., corporate loans) and retail (e.g., home mortgage loans) products.* both allow for the early termination of the loans, but the terms and conditions can be widely different among individual commercial or retail loans, as well as between commercial and retail loans in general.

To manage interest rate risk in the banking book, banks consider the impact of interest rate changes on both their assets and liabilities, and the particular features of their assets and liabilities, including, among other things, terms and timing. How well the bank manages its assets and liabilities, the revenues from its assets, and the costs of its liabilities has a direct impact on the net interest margin of the bank.

2.3.2   Liquidity Risk

Liquidity is defined by the Basel Committee as the ability of a bank to fund increases in assets and meet obligations as they come due, without incurring unacceptable losses. From both a bank's and its regulator's point of view, the structure of the bank's assets and its related liquidity needs may highlight potential weaknesses over time. Liquidity corresponds to the bank's ability to make payments to its customers punctually. Ultimately, its ability, or inability, to make these payments in a timely manner will directly affect the banking institution's **solvency**, or its ability to pay its debts with available cash.

Solvency is different from a bank's ability to make a profit. A bank can be solvent (have more assets than liabilities) and not make a profit if its expenses are greater than its revenues. A solvent bank may be able to generate cash to make payments by selling off assets, but if these transactions are at a loss, then the sale of its assets could erode the bank's solvency, leading to insolvency. A bank can be profitable without being solvent if its revenues are greater than its expenses but its assets are worth less than its liabilities.

Banks actively manage their liquidity risks to ensure that they have sufficient funding to pay their obligations when they become due. Liquidity obligations run to both a bank's depositors and its loan customers. Depositors demand liquidity; they expect to be able to withdraw their deposits at any time without delay. Since fractional reserve banking means that banks can keep only a fraction of their deposits available for immediate withdrawal, improperly managing the bank's liquidity risk could lead to serious consequences (see Section 3.1 on liquidity and bank runs). Customers who borrow money from the bank require that the bank provide them with access to the funds they have borrowed without delay when the funds are needed. If a highly leveraged bank needs to secure liquidity quickly to fulfill its obligations, but can only do so by selling its assets hastily and at low prices, then it can easily become insolvent.

As with interest rate risk, banks model how their liquidity requirements may change over time in a wide array of circumstances. Banks have several tools at their disposal to assess their liquidity. Among these tools, scenario analysis and stress testing play a chief role in enabling a bank to examine its liquidity in a variety of adverse situations. **Scenario analysis**, or what-if analysis, analyzes the potential outcome of various scenarios by setting up several possible situations and analyzing the potential outcomes of each situation. Scenario analysis often includes multiple steps and complex programming. **Stress testing** analyzes the potential outcome of a specific change to a risk model parameter (e.g., asset correlations and volatility), or to the business and operating environment that is fundamental, material, and adverse.

EXAMPLE

FirstBank considers a scenario in which it loses its main depositor, a large car manufacturer. When the ALM department conducts a scenario analysis, it models how the bank would meet its liquidity needs without the car manufacturer's funds. The ALM department also conducts a stress test whereby it analyzes the potential impacts on its liquidity should a large number of its loans default and a substantial number of smaller depositors withdraw their deposits at once, while the bank cannot secure funding elsewhere. This type of analysis allows the bank, and its supervisory agency, to gain a clearer picture of the risks the bank is facing and to proactively determine how to deal with those risks.

A particular concern of liquidity monitoring relates to the potential for a run on a bank. Banks need to have sufficient and readily available funds to meet regular withdrawals of deposits and to fulfill its loan obligations. (see Chapter 1). If a bank is rumored to be in financial difficulty, depositors may rush to withdraw their funds. Unanticipated demand could reduce the bank's cash on hand, very likely causing the bank to become illiquid and, ultimately, insolvent.

EXAMPLE

In September 2007, Northern Rock, a British bank, found itself in a liquidity crisis. In prior years, mortgage lending in the United States to subprime borrowers (that is, lesser-qualified borrowers who are required to make either little or no down payment on their home loans) had grown considerably. As the U.S. housing market slowed in early 2007, the rate of subprime mortgage defaults increased sharply, leading to considerable losses to the banks and financial institutions that owned these loans. Because of the U.S. subprime crisis, financial institutions globally became nervous about lending to mortgage banks.

As a large mortgage lender in mid-2007, Northern Rock suddenly found it very difficult to obtain the short-term loans from other banks or other funding sources it needed to repay its depositors. After the news was released publicly in mid-September 2007 that the bank had a liquidity problem and needed immediate assistance from the Bank of England, depositors rushed to withdraw their funds, further exacerbating the problem. At the time, UK government deposit protection only covered up to GBP 31,700 (100% of the first GBP 2,000 in deposits and 90% of the next GBP 33,000 in deposits, GBP 29,700), possibly contributing to depositor anxiety. Subsequent to these events, in October 2008, UK deposit insurance was temporarily increased to GBP 50,000. By January 2008, Northern Rock had borrowed in excess of USD 25 billion from the Bank of England. In February 2008, it was announced that the British government would nationalize the bank, taking it over to protect the depositors and assure that it would be able to fulfill its obligations.

Banks, including central banks, often provide support to each other to meet short-term liquidity needs through **repurchase agreements**. A repurchase agreement (also known as a repo) allows one party to sell an asset for cash with the understanding, supported by a legal repurchase agreement, that it will be repurchased at a later date at an agreed-on price (usually higher than the sales price).

EXAMPLE

Atlas Bank needs USD 10 million for five days. It enters into a repurchase agreement with Capital Bank, whereby it sells to Capital Bank a USD 10 million bond for USD 10 million and agrees to repurchase it for USD 10,005,000. At the end of the five days, Atlas pays Capital Bank USD 10,005,000 and receives the bond back. Atlas has increased its liquidity for five days at a cost of USD 1,000 for each day. Figure 2.10 shows the flow of money between the two banks involved in this repurchase agreement transaction.

Figure 2.10   Repurchase agreement

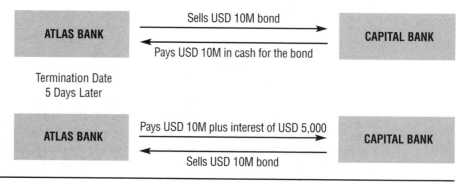

In a repo transaction, the actual ownership of the security passes to the buyer from the seller. The repo markets are a major source of funding for the liquidity needs of banks around the globe.

In addition to the liquidity needs described above, bank supervisors often require banks to maintain a minimum holding of either cash or assets that can be readily turned into cash in case the bank encounters an unexpected cash demand. Highly liquid assets generally include the bank's deposits held at the central bank and domestic government debt held by the bank.

Finally, since the collapse of Herstatt Bank (see Section 3.3.1 for further details), bank supervisors have also been concerned with banks' ability to meet their obligations to each other. A particular concern for regulators are the ripple effects of a bank owing money to other banks as a result of its position in a payments system, (e.g., a check clearing system or a government bond payment and delivery system). If a bank's customers who use these payment systems default, the bank may not have sufficient cash to be able to pay its banking counterparties on behalf of their customers (the other banks). To counter this risk, banks often rely on collateral, usually high-quality government bonds and other securities.

Collateral are assets pledged by a borrower to secure a loan or other credit and to act as a guarantee to the lender in the event of a default. If the borrower is unable or unwilling to repay the debt, the lender has the option to accept the collateral as full or partial payment of the loan's principal, accrued interest, fees, and expenses. (The role of collateral will be explained further in Section 4.4.5.)

EXAMPLE

Bank Little, a small bank, and Bank Large, a large international bank, engage in various transactions with each other. In most of these transactions, Bank Little buys securities, mostly government bonds, from Bank Large. The terms of payment for these transactions is three days. For example, for a transaction entered on Monday, payment is expected on Thursday. During this three-day period, Bank Large effectively extends credit to Bank Little and assumes the risk that Bank Little may not be able to pay for the transaction at the end of the three days.

Since Bank Little is smaller than Bank Large, there is a concern that Bank Little may be exposed to significant liquidity risks and may not be able to pay for its government bond transactions as contracted. To reduce the risk of this happening and to further support the transactions between the two banks, Bank Little posts collateral with Bank Large equal to a certain percentage of the value of the transaction. Bank Large will usually specify the amount and type of collateral it will accept from Bank Little. If Bank Little is unable to pay for its transactions with Bank Large, the collateral Bank Little posted to Bank Large can be used by Bank Large to pay for the purchase of the government bonds. This reduces the risk to Bank Large. Figure 2.11 shows this.

Figure 2.11   The use of collateral

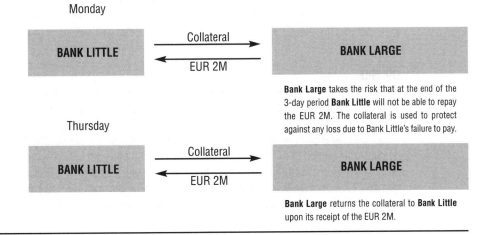

2.4 LOAN LOSSES

Banks recognize that some of the loans they underwrite may default, and they anticipate the impact this could have on both the bank's earnings and its profits. As we will see in later chapters, banks have developed sophisticated and highly structured approaches to predict, manage, and reduce potential loan losses. Since loan losses diminish the equity capital and consequently may affect the long-term survival of the bank, banks must incorporate into their planning and budgeting processes a reasonable level of loan losses as a "cost of doing business," similar to expenses they budget for employees, office space, and equipment. For good corporate governance, a bank's board of directors should set and approve the bank's loan loss policies. That is why each year banks set aside part of their income to offset the potential impact of loan losses in a way similar to salaries and other common expenses.

Complex rules govern the way banks are required to report publicly the assets they have in their trading and banking books. Regulators, shareholders, and other stakeholders have an interest in having high-quality, reliable, and up-to-date information on the financial position of the bank. One core concern is how well the recorded value of loans and other assets reflect their true value. This issue of asset valuation is one of the underlying reasons for the credit crisis that began in 2007.

This section discusses how banks record and value assets in their trading and banking book, and, in general, what rules they are required to follow to properly treat and value loans that do not perform. The section also describes methods to manage loan losses and the reserves that are held by the bank to deal with them.

2.4.1   Valuing Assets in the Trading Book

Assets in the trading book are usually held for sale, and their value on the balance sheet of the bank should reflect what these assets would fetch in the financial markets (Chapter 6). Thus, the value of these assets has to be **marked-to-market**, that is, their value on the balance sheet must reflect the fair market value. The **fair market value** is the price the asset would bring if sold immediately on the market to a willing buyer.

EXAMPLE

FirstBank, our hypothetical bank, has purchased a bond for USD 1 million. As a result of severe financial turmoil, the bond dropped in value 10%, and it can only be sold for USD 900,000. The bank's financial records must record the fair market value of the bond at USD 900,000 and not the purchase price of USD 1 million. The difference of USD 100,000 is an unrealized loss (a book loss that has not been actually incurred as the bond has not yet been sold in the market). The unrealized loss will reduce the bank's assets and equity at the time it is recorded. The effects of this loss are similar to the loss the bank suffers if one of its loans defaults and the ensuing loss reduces the bank's earnings.

Several months later, the financial turmoil subsided and the price of the bond increased to USD 1,010,000. As a result of the price of the bond increasing in the market, the previous loss of USD 100,000 is erased and both the bank's assets and equity increase in value. Although the bond can be sold for USD 1,010,000 in the market, at a gain of USD 10,000, this gain is considered an "unrealized gain" until the bond is sold. Most accounting rules are generally more restrictive in treating unrealized gains than unrealized losses. The bank must initially record the bond on its books at the purchase price of USD 1,000,000. The unrealized gain of USD 10,000 will have to wait for a period of time or until the bond is actually sold for that gain to be recognized in the financial statements.

2.4.2   Value of Assets in the Banking Book, Performing Loans

Assets held in the banking book, mostly loans, are usually not made available for sale. This is as opposed to assets held in the trading book as already noted, which are usually held for sale.

Loans whose borrowers make payments as agreed on with the bank are considered **performing loans**. Loans whose borrowers fail to make, or make delayed, payments may be considered **nonperforming loans** (see below).

In the banking book, if the loans held by the bank are not sold off to third parties, then for accounting purposes they are considered to be held until they are repaid or to maturity. Since these assets are held long-term, changes in their value do not necessarily have to reflect their fair market value. Their value, however, does have to reflect what the bank reasonably can expect to receive from the borrower. If the bank expects the loan to be repaid in full, no adjustments are necessary.

EXAMPLE

FirstBank has extended a USD 5 million, 5 year, loan to Mega Construction Inc. and records the loan on its balance sheet as USD 5 million since it expects to hold the loan until the loan is fully repaid. Regardless of how well Mega Construction performs over the next 5 years (absent bankruptcy or other materially adverse problem), FirstBank can carry the loan on its books at that face value.

2.4.3   Value of Assets in the Banking Book, Nonperforming Loans

If a bank does not expect full or partial repayment of a loan on time, it must then be classified as a **nonperforming loan** and adjustments must be made to the recorded value of the loan in the bank's financial statements. The bank has to adjust the recorded value of nonperforming loans on its balance sheet so that shareholders, management, regulators, and other stakeholders can correctly assess the strength of the bank. The loan's new recorded value must be changed to reflect the expected amount the bank can reasonably recover from the borrower. As a consequence of a borrower not repaying the loan, in full, the bank must categorize the nonperforming loan as past due, written down, or charged off.

- A **past-due loan** is where the repayment of principal and interest are in doubt because the borrower has missed several payments to the bank or the bank has a clear indication that the borrower may not repay the loan, i.e., there is clear doubt about the borrower's ability or willingness to pay. A past-due loan may be fully repaid by the borrower.

- A **written-down loan** is a loan that is past due, and the bank has made a determination that it will not be able to recover fully the amount it has lent to the borrower. As such, the bank has to adjust the value of the loan in its financial statements to the value that the bank expects to recover from the borrower. The amount by which the bank reduces the value of the loan is also called the write-down.

- A **charged-off loan** is a loan that has been removed from the bank's financial statements because the bank believes that it will collect nothing of the loan from the borrower. A charged-off loan will reduce the bank's equity. Even though a loan may be completely charged off, the bank may continue to try to collect on it.

EXAMPLE

Due to unforeseen circumstances, Mega Construction Inc., the borrower from the previous example, became unable to make principal and interest payments in a timely manner. Mega Construction, a home builder, has been materially impacted by the softening real estate market and is largely incapable of selling its already built property inventory. As a result, it has not been able to raise sufficient funds to make loan payments as scheduled.

When FirstBank first received an indication that Mega Construction would not be able to continue making its loan principal and/or interest payments on time, it flagged the loan as non-performing or doubtful. As is true with any bank, nonperforming loans receive additional attention from FirstBank's management, as well as its regulators. Initially, FirstBank exercises forbearance by working with Mega Construction and providing additional time to make the payments or, alternatively, to reduce at least temporarily the interest rate on the loan. Under this situation, FirstBank may not have to make any adjustments to the value of the loan. If Mega Construction Inc. is able to catch up with its payments, the loan will no longer be classified as non-performing.

However, if the forbearance does not help Mega Construction and it is not able to catch up with the payments, FirstBank will then typically decide it is unlikely the borrower will make all the payments it owes the bank. In that case, the bank must adjust the value of the loan recorded on its balance sheet. This can be achieved by either a write-down or through a specific provision (more about provisions in the next section).

When a loan is written down, the value of the loan is reduced to a value the bank expects to recover. For example, if FirstBank believes that it can only recover 80% of the outstanding loan, it would reduce the value of the loan by 20%, or USD 1 million. The loan will then be recorded at its net value or USD 4 million, with the USD 1 million that was written down reducing the bank's assets and consequently its equity.

If the situation worsens further and it becomes more likely that Mega Construction Inc. will be unable to repay even 80% of the USD 5 million loan, the bank will have to write down the loan even further to a value that it deems to be reasonable. If FirstBank does not expect the loan to be repaid at all—due to significantly worsening economic conditions or other factors—the bank faces no other option but to charge off and remove the entire remaining loan of USD 4 million as it is recorded on the bank's balance sheet.

In the above scenario, the bank charged off the loan in two steps. First, it wrote down the loan. Next, because Mega Construction was unable to make any payments, the bank had to remove the entire loan from its balance sheet.

How a bank deals with nonperforming loans depends on the regulatory rules under which it operates, how conservative the bank's risk management policies are, and the degree of prudence the bank's management exercises in its overall bank management.

Prudent management is a function of the bank's corporate governance and reflects the risk management culture promoted by the bank's board of directors and the operational structure of the bank. Very conservatively, or prudently, managed banks may aggressively charge off the entire loan as soon as the loan becomes nonperforming. Other banks may exercise a less conservative approach and delay writing down or even charging off loans for as long as they can. While regulators provide guidance on how to treat nonperforming loans on the bank's books, banks, particularly those that have limited financial strength, may tend to be less conservative when it comes to writing down or charging off assets and keep them on their books at face value much longer for obvious reasons.

Because there is discretion afforded to a bank in dealing with nonperforming assets, regulators pay a great deal of attention to how banks deal with nonperforming loans, often demanding that banks make additional write-downs. Delaying write-downs or charge-offs can easily lead to an incorrect valuation of the bank's financial condition, because the value of its loans will be overstated. Overstating the value of loans negatively affects the bank's earnings capacity and the size of its equity capital. This could hinder its ability to support operations and absorb future losses, and would be misleading to the shareholders.

2.4.4 Provision for Loan Losses and Loan Loss Reserves

As we will see in later sections, particularly in Chapter 5, the bank's entire underwriting process focuses on making a prediction about the borrower's likelihood of defaulting. Even though the bank thoroughly analyses all the loans it underwrites, circumstances can change so that what was initially considered to be a good, high-quality loan becomes a nonperforming loan. Banks know this and expect a reasonable level of losses on the loans they make. To compensate for the *expected* loan losses, banks price their loans accordingly: The interest rate and other fees the borrower pays for the loan are calculated to compensate for the risk the lender undertakes, including the potential loan losses the bank would suffer if the borrower defaults. That is why higher-risk borrowers pay a higher interest rate to the bank.

Another approach a bank can use to manage the effect of loan losses is to create a loan loss reserve in its balance sheet. Through provisions in their income statements, banks set aside part of their earnings to cover the losses they expect to suffer from bad loans. The **provision for loan losses** reduces the bank's income and creates a **loan loss reserve** on the balance sheet that reduces the value of the loans recorded on the bank's balance sheet. The loan loss reserve is also referred to as an "allowance for loan losses" or a "credit loss reserve."

EXAMPLE

Using the income statement example in Section 2.2.4, earnings before taxes were USD 25 million. When the bank makes a provision for loan losses, the bank's earnings are directly reduced. If the bank decides to make a USD 2 million provision for loan losses, it reduces its earnings by the amount of the provision.

Earnings before provision for loan losses	USD 25 million
– Provision for loan losses	USD 2 million
= Earnings after provision for loan losses and before taxes	USD 23 million

Banks pay taxes on earnings after the provision for loan losses is calculated.

There is an important difference between the provision for loan losses and the loan loss reserve. *The provision for loan losses is recorded in the income statement of the bank and affects the earnings of the bank. The loan loss reserve is recorded on the balance sheet of the bank and affects the value of the bank's assets.*

The provision for loan losses can be general or specific. A *general provision for loan losses* is used to build loan loss reserves over time and is not motivated by the nonperformance of any one individual loan. General loan loss provisions can be used to:
- Offset the losses associated with any loan the bank has made, without having to identify a specific loan that is nonperforming, or
- Allow the bank to smooth its earnings over a period of years.

During good times, banks generally perform well, experience infrequent defaults, and generate high earnings. Stability coupled with high earnings allows banks to make loan loss provisions as a part of their normal business operations to ultimately bolster the bank's loan loss reserve in anticipation of an economic downturn. Banks actually budget for losses on loans each year based on historical experience and business judgment. When actual loan losses start accumulating, usually during weaker economic times or recessionary environments, the loan loss reserves can be used to absorb some, if not all, of the losses the bank will suffer. Since the bank made provisions for potential loss in previous years, the loan losses will reduce the loan loss reserves first, not the earnings of the bank. Because of this, losses are not recognized in that year's income statement unless the accumulated loan loss reserves are depleted that year and additional provisions have to be made. In effect, by maintaining an appropriate loan loss reserve, the bank is able to smooth its earnings.

Many banks aim to have a general loan loss reserve range between 1.5 and 2% (loan loss reserve ratio) of the value of their loans. Regulators pay close attention to the size of the loan loss reserve as inadequate provisions for loan losses can hurt the bank's equity capital during economic contraction, when banks need the most protection to withstand potentially sizable losses.

EXAMPLE

Revisiting our previous example, FirstBank, will allow us to demonstrate the impact of a general provision for loan losses. The bank decides to keep about 2% of the total value of its loans as a general loan loss reserve on its balance sheet. The bank records the value of its loans at USD 890 million. Since the balance sheet records the loans at the value they expect to repay, the USD 890 million is the value that the bank expects to be repaid. The gross value of the loans the bank has made is USD 908 million, including the 2% loan loss reserve of USD 18 million.[2]

Figure 2.12 shows the detailed balance sheet of FirstBank taking into consideration the loan loss reserves for the different loan types.

Figure 2.12   Different loan types and loan loss reserves

Assets in million USD	Amount		Liabilities in million USD	Amount
Cash		10	Short-term deposits	300
Government bonds		100	Long-term deposits	250
Loans to local government, total	194			
– less loan loss reserve	4			
Loans to local government, net		*190*		
Loans to SMEs, total	204			
– less loan loss reserve	4			
Loans to SMEs, net		*200*		
Loans to large corporations, total	510		Short-term financing	200
– less loan loss reserve	10		Long-term bonds	150
Loans to large corporations, net		*500*	Equity capital	100
Total		**1,000**	**Total**	**1,000**

---

2. Total amount of loan = $\dfrac{\text{Net amount of loan}}{1 - \text{Loan loss reserve ratio}} = \dfrac{890}{1 - 2\%} = 908$

Loan loss reserve = Gross amount of loan * Loan loss reserve ratio = 908 * 2% = 18

A *specific provision for loan losses* is a reserve made in anticipation of a loan loss that can only be used to offset the losses associated with one specific loan. The accounting steps and results for handling a specific loan loss reserve are the same as for those for a general loan loss reserve.

EXAMPLE

When FirstBank recognizes that the loan to Mega Construction is nonperforming, FirstBank can make a specific provision for loan losses against that loan. If the bank believes that of the USD 5 million loan, only USD 4 million will be recovered, it can make a provision of USD 1 million in the income statement. This provision will reduce the net income of the bank and affect the equity of the bank as well.

The USD 1 million loan loss provision will increase the loan loss reserve of the bank. This increase in the loan loss reserve reduces the net value of the loans (assets) recorded on the bank's balance sheet by USD 1 million. As a result of the specific provision, the net value of the Mega Construction loan on the bank's balance sheet is USD 4 million.

2.4.5   Loan Loss Reserves and Loan Losses

The loan loss reserves a bank builds up over the years and holds should be sufficient to offset future charge-offs the bank is expected to encounter. When a bank writes down or charges off a loan, the loan loss reserves are reduced first. Since the provision for loan losses has previously reduced income (and reduced equity), there is no immediate impact on the bank's assets and the bank's equity.

EXAMPLE

FirstBank's loan loss reserves for large corporations at the beginning of the year were USD 10 million. Its total loss reserves were USD 18 million, but for simplicity, the example only focuses on the loan loss reserves for large corporate loans. For further simplicity, there are no other transactions that would affect these particular loan loss reserves (i.e., all other loans perform contractually). The transactions affecting Mega Construction as described in the example in Sections 2.4.3 and 2.4.4 would be recorded as the following:

1. During the year, the bank added USD 2 million to the loan loss reserves as a general loan loss provision.

Beginning balance for loan loss reserves	USD 10 million	
+ provision for loan losses (income statement)	USD 2 million	(1)
Ending balance for loan loss reserve	USD 12 million	

2. Mega Construction, a home builder that has been materially impacted by the softening real estate market, is largely incapable of divesting its already built property inventory and has not been able to raise sufficient funds to make its loan payments as scheduled. The bank has already made a specific reserve of USD 1 million against this loan.

Beginning balance for loan loss reserves	USD 10 million	
+ provision for loan losses (income statement)	USD 2 million	(1)
+ provision for loan losses (income statement)	USD 1 million	(2)
Ending balance for loan loss reserve	USD 13 million	

3. After the bank decides to make a specific reserve of USD 1 million against this loan, FirstBank decides to write down the loan to the value the bank expects to recover of USD 4 million.

Beginning balance for loan loss reserves	USD 10 million	
+ provision for loan losses (income statement)	USD 2 million	(1)
+ specific reserve for the Mega Construction loan	USD 1 million	(2)
− write-down of the Mega Construction loan	USD 1 million	(3)
Ending balance for loan loss reserve	USD 12 million	

Since the bank has already made a prior specific provision for the losses on the Mega Construction loan, the effects of writing down the loan will not impact the bank's assets and equity.

4. The materially weakening economic conditions necessitate that the bank charge off the remaining USD 4 million balance on the Mega Construction loan.

Beginning balance for loan loss reserves	USD 10 million	
+ provision for loan losses (income statement)	USD 2 million	(1)
+ specific reserve for the Mega Construction loan	USD 1 million	(2)
− write-down of the Mega Construction loan	USD 1 million	(3)
− charge-off of the Mega Construction loan	USD 4 million	(4)
Ending balance for loan loss reserve	USD 8 million	

What is important to recognize is that the charge-off reduces the loan loss reserves, and the net effect on the bank's balance sheet (assets and equity) of the charge-off of this loan depends on the amount of reserves built up over the years. If the loan loss reserves are sufficient to absorb the losses, there may not be any balance sheet effect as the charge-offs reduce the loan loss reserves that the bank has accumulated over the years.

EXAMPLE

The effects of the charge-off on the loans are recognized as follows.

1. After step 1 in the previous example—USD 2 million in loan loss provisions on the income statement of the bank—the proportion of the balance sheet that relates to the Mega Construction loan looks as follows:

Loans to large corporations, total	510 million
– Loan loss reserve	10 + 2 = 12 million
Loans to large corporations, net	498 million

    The value of loans decreased by the USD 2 million general provision to the reserves.

2. After step 2 in the previous example—the USD 1 million specific reserve—the proportion of the balance sheet that relates to the Mega Construction loan looks as follows:

Loans to large corporations, total	510 million
– Loan loss reserve	12 + 1 = 13 million
Loans to large corporations, net	497 million

    The net value of loans decreased by the additional USD 1 million specific provision made to the reserves.

3. After step 3 in the previous example—the USD 1 million write-down of the loan—the proportion of the balance sheet that relates to the Mega Construction loan looks as follows:

Loans to large corporations, total	510 – 1 = 509 million
– Loan loss reserve	13 – 1 = 12 million
Loans to large corporations, net	497 million

    The net value of loans did not change as the specific provision against the expected loss of Mega Corporation was used to offset the write-down of the loan.

4. After step 4 in the previous example—the USD 4 million charge-off of the loan—the proportion of the balance sheet that relates to the Mega Construction loan looks as follows:

Loans to large corporations, total	509 – 4 = 505 million
– Loan loss reserve	12 – 4 = 8 million
Loans to large corporations, net	497 million

The net value of loans did not change as the built-up loan loss reserves were used to offset the effects of the write-offs.

FirstBank charged off the USD 5 million loan. The net effect on the bank's balance sheet is only USD 1 million as the USD 5 million loss only partially affects the assets. Due to the general and specific loan loss provisions made by the bank, the USD 5 million loss on the Mega Construction loan is absorbed in two steps:
1. The assets of the bank fell by USD 1 million, from USD 498 million to USD 497 million.
2. The loan loss reserve fell by USD 4 million from USD 12 million to USD 8 million.

As the net effect on the balance sheet is USD 1 million; this is also the net equity effect for the bank that this transaction generates.

The loan loss reserve is also impacted by any recoveries the bank makes on previously charged off loans. Although a bank has written down or charged off a loan, it does not mean that the bank ceases its efforts to recover the loss it has suffered. Any recovery will be added to the bank's loan loss reserves, effectively replenishing the reserves. If recoveries are large enough to cover all the expected and unexpected credit losses the bank were to suffer, the bank could opt not to make any additional provisions for loan losses.

EXAMPLE

Continuing with FirstBank's example, we now look at the effect of a potential recovery on a charge-off. In the previous examples, FirstBank first wrote down and then charged off Mega Construction's USD 5 million loan (steps 1 to 4 above). Due to changing conditions, the bank was able to recover USD 2 million of the USD 5 million loan. The effects of the recovery in step 5 are as follows:

Beginning balance for loan loss reserves	USD 10 million	
+ provision for loan losses (income statement)	USD 2 million	(1)
+ specific reserve for the Mega Construction loan	USD 1 million	(2)
− write-down of the Mega Construction loan	USD 1 million	(3)
− charge-off of the Mega Construction loan	USD 4 million	(4)
+ recover on the Mega Construction loan	USD 2 million	(5)
Ending balance for loan loss reserve	USD 10 million	

The use of provisions for loan losses and loan loss reserves offers banks a great deal of flexibility in managing the effects of loan losses. Bank management can decide to build up a substantial loan loss reserve over time that can reduce the potential negative effects of loan losses. Loan loss provisions reduce earnings, but, in turn, the potential impacts of loan losses on the bank's equity can be reduced.

Banking Regulation

Chapter 3 introduces bank regulation and outlines the impact regulations have on bank operations. This chapter discusses why banks need to be regulated, what regulatory processes are in effect, how international cooperation helps shape bank regulation, and what role deposit insurance plays in banking stability. Chapters 1, 2, and 3 together provide a comprehensive foundation for the remaining chapters.

Chapter Outline

- 3.1 From Liquidity Crisis to Bank Panics
- 3.2 Foundations of Bank Regulation
- 3.3 International Regulation of Bank Risks
- 3.4 Deposit Insurance
- 3.5 The Road Ahead

Key Learning Points

- When a bank lacks the funds to repay its depositors on demand, the bank is in a liquidity crisis. The mere rumor of a liquidity crisis could lead to a bank run—when a large number of depositors demand a return of their deposits from one bank simultaneously. If a bank run spreads to other banks, there is contagion that has the potential to spread further panic and runs on other banks.
- Bank regulation seeks to ensure that banks are operated prudently, that non-systemic risk is reduced, and that there are systemwide support mechanisms to assist banks and provide stability before they reach a crisis. Bank regulation achieves these objectives using two main tools: licensing, the granting of the right to operate a bank, and supervision, regulatory and recurring monitoring of the bank's operations and activities.

- The Basel Accords are the international regulatory frameworks that govern the activities of banks. The two Basel Accords acknowledge that the risk of the bank's assets and operations is related to, and can be minimized by, a minimum regulatory capital standard. In the Basel II Accord, this minimum regulatory capital covers credit, market, and operational risks.
- Deposit insurance provides protection for depositors in case banks suffer a liquidity crisis and is intended to reduce both bank runs and panics by reducing the incentives for depositors to withdraw funds from a bank.

Key Terms

- Balance sheet
- Bank for International Settlements
- Bank panic
- Bank run
- Basel Committee
- Capital adequacy
- Capital ratio
- Contagion
- Credit mitigation techniques
- Deposit insurance
- Explicit deposit insurance system
- Financial stability
- Illiquidity
- Implicit deposit insurance system
- Insolvency

- Lender of last resort
- Licensing
- Liquidity crisis
- Market discipline
- Monetary stability
- Nonsystemic risk
- Off-balance sheet
- Pillars 1, 2 and 3 of the Basel II Accord
- Regulatory supervision
- Regulatory capital
- Risk-weighted assets
- Spillover effect
- Systemic risk
- Tier 1 and Tier 2 capital

Banking Regulation

3.1   FROM LIQUIDITY CRISIS TO BANK PANICS

Banks play a crucial role in the economy by offering payment services and providing credit. Because any disruption to the banking system could have widespread effects on businesses and people, all governments regulate banking. It was not always so, however. In fact, up until the early 20th century, there were still parts of the world where banking was unregulated; anyone able and willing to open a bank could do so without any qualifications, hindrance, or permission. However, such an uninhibited banking environment was unstable—bank failures were common—so, over time, governments began to regulate banks actively.

3.1.1   Liquidity Crisis and Bank Runs

When a bank makes a large number of loans that borrowers cannot repay, the bank's liabilities (deposits and borrowings) could exceed the bank's assets, rendering the bank insolvent. As it relates to a bank's (or a company's) balance sheet, **insolvency** means that its liabilities exceed its assets—it has zero or negative equity. While this implies an inability to repay creditor claims when they become due, it does not mean that an insolvent bank may not be able to raise cash to meet depositor withdrawal needs. However, since the fractional reserve banking system allows banks to retain only a fraction of their deposits on hand as cash, insolvency problems can be magnified. This problem can be particularly acute if the bank experiences severe defaults.

Without adequate liquidity, a bank may have insufficient cash readily available to pay its depositors' claims when they come due. While a bank may have assets that could be sold or leveraged to raise cash, it may not always be possible to do so in a timely fashion. This inability to make payments when they are due is termed **illiquidity**, and can lead to a **liquidity crisis**. A liquidity crisis, in turn, can lead to a bank run, as described in the following example.

EXAMPLE

An increasing number of AlphaBank's borrowers have failed to repay their loans at all or in a timely manner. This has placed a severe strain on the bank's liquidity position. For the last two months, AlphaBank has depleted its cash reserves to make payments to its depositors and bondholders because the cash it received from its borrowers fell short of what was required to pay out in new loans and deposit withdrawals. Suddenly, AlphaBank found itself in the position that its available cash reserves were insufficient to pay its creditors' interest payments when due. Moreover, AlphaBank found that the credit markets it occasionally tapped for funds are no longer available. Since the bank does not have the funds available to make its payments and cannot borrow the funds, the bank finds itself in a liquidity crisis. As a result, its depositors and creditors are at risk of not receiving their funds when due.

The only option AlphaBank has to raise cash to pay the depositors is to sell off its assets—loans and bonds—to other banks. However, such a sale would likely be at prices below the value at which the loans were recorded. Selling the loans to another bank at a loss would exacerbate the bank's worsening financial position—further erode its equity position (see Section 2.3)—and increase the likelihood of balance sheet insolvency. This puts AlphaBank in a "no win" situation because if information about its position became public it would add to concerns about the bank's stability, potentially causing even more depositors to attempt to withdraw their funds. Whether the original problem is real or not, the unexpected and excessive demand for withdrawals would position AlphaBank for possible failure since it has no viable, timely alternatives other than to appeal to its customers for patience while it attempts to arrange for some immediate cash or capital infusion from other institutions or investors. Alternatively, the bank could look to merge its business with a partner. Unfortunately, all these alternatives take time, which works to AlphaBank's disadvantage.

If no solution is found and the bank fails to raise sufficient funds to continue its operations, the bank may collapse, potentially wiping out the depositors' funds in the bank. Such a collapse could have widespread ramifications for other banks, the availability of credit, other businesses, and the economy.

A liquidity crisis in one bank can cause a minor, often local, economic decline. Fear that one bank does not hold or cannot obtain sufficient cash to meet depositors' demands to withdraw their funds raises the risk of a **bank run**. A bank run occurs when a large number of depositors at one bank simultaneously demand a return of their deposits. Since banks are not required to hold all their deposits in cash—they lend out a considerable part of the deposits—then a run on a bank could lead to a liquidity crisis. The expanding demand to withdraw deposits usually feeds upon itself regardless of whether the underlying reasons for the bank run were based on fact or rumor.

When a solvency or liquidity crisis is limited to one bank, then that crisis is generally considered **nonsystemic risk**. In a nonsystemic crisis, one bank's unique circumstances precipitate the crisis, the conditions and circumstances do not apply to other banks, and one bank's crisis is not expected to have a widespread effect. The issues resulting from the crisis will generally be limited to that bank's customers or its local economy.

EXAMPLE

In May 1984, Continental Illinois National Bank in the United States suffered a run on its deposits, which, in turn, prompted the largest bank bail-out in U.S. history at that time. The run was started by rumors that the bank was heading for bankruptcy over poor credit risks, particularly from loans assumed from Penn Square Bank, which had collapsed in 1983. Nonperforming loans at Continental had risen to USD 3.3 billion by April 1984.

Continental Illinois was particularly vulnerable because it relied heavily on short-term financing. Short-term financing is very sensitive to both market interest rates and the short-term investors' perception of the bank's financial safety. It is an elusive financing source. As long as the investors were satisfied that the bank would repay these short-term loans, they were willing to lend to Continental Illinois. Suddenly the bank found that investors did not renew their short-term loans at maturity and that overseas depositors, concerned about the rumors, had begun to shift their deposits away from Continental. Following failed attempts by the bank to arrange a rescue package with a consortium of 16 other banks, Continental's domestic depositors also began to withdraw their funds.

The global nature of the Continental Illinois funding base and the bank's size (at the time it was the 7th largest bank in the United States) made it imperative for U.S. regulators to step in to stop the run and prevent it from spreading to other U.S. banks. The cost of this rescue: U.S. regulatory agencies, with a consortium of banks, assumed the liability and risks for USD 3.5 billion in Continental Illinois debt. In the case of Continental Illinois, therefore, regulators acted to prevent a nonsystemic crisis from spreading to other banks and becoming a systemic crisis.

3.1.2 Bank Panics

Even the rumor of a liquidity problem at one bank can spread quickly and cause depositors at other banks to rush to withdraw their funds. Thus, a problem that exists at one bank can spread to multiple banks. If unchecked, this process can grow into a **bank panic**, when depositors from multiple banks simultaneously seek to withdraw their deposits.

This type of situation can put an entire banking system at risk. Effectively, a multiple and concurrent run on banks, or a bank panic, is an example of a **systemic risk**. Systemic risk is the risk of the collapse of the entire banking system or financial market. A systemic crisis would have very wide-ranging effects. It is very probable that the effects of a severe bank panic and the accompanying instability in a regional financial system would cross country borders and adversely affect the banking systems of other countries.

Also, the failure of a major, globally active bank or the negative effects of a material decrease in asset prices (such as home values), or a bank panic in one country can create shocks that can spillover into other countries. Even upon hearing about a crisis, there is potential that depositors in other countries could become nervous about their deposits. The term for this transference of concern or **spillover effect** between countries (or even markets) is an example of **contagion**. Extreme financial events or economic stress, whether a contagion or a bank panic, raises systemic risk for the banking system. Systemic risks can impart significant negative effects across many industries and countries and are likely to have widespread negative consequences for bank employees, customers, shareholders, and, ultimately, the economy. For small and developing countries, foreign deposits are often a critical source of capital and their withdrawal—as a response to contagion or rumors of contagion—can have devastating effects on these economies.

EXAMPLE

A recent example of a bank run leading to a potential bank panic is the near collapse of the Icelandic banking system. The three major Icelandic banks—Kaupthing, Glitnir, and Landsbanki—grew very aggressively after the deregulation of the Icelandic financial sector in 2001. As Iceland is a small and geographically isolated country with roughly 320,000 inhabitants, the desire for an aggressive growth could not be supported by the domestic market. Consequently, these banks rushed to establish branch networks around Europe. As the banks established operations outside of Iceland, they became heavily reliant on the interbank market, or loans between banks, and not deposits. At the end of July 2008, it was estimated that these three banks had foreign debt in excess of EUR 42 billion compared to Iceland's gross domestic product, or GDP, of EUR 8.5 billion.

In early September 2008, after the collapse of Lehman Brothers, a U.S. investment bank, the market for short-term loans between banks, the interbank market, froze. This change in the funding markets adversely affected the Icelandic banks' ability to secure the necessary funding to keep their widespread international banking networks adequately funded. The Icelandic banks experienced increased liquidity and financing concerns as they lacked access to deposits and a more permanent funding source.

Then on September 29, 2008, the Icelandic authorities announced that the smallest of the three largest banks, Glitnir, would be partially nationalized. Glitnir was about to face repayment of USD 750 million in short-term debt (EUR 600 million), funds that Glitnir did not have, nor was it able to raise.

The decision to partially nationalize Glitnir had effects on both Kaupthing and Landsbanki. Nervous depositors, both in Iceland and in other European countries where the Icelandic banks had a presence, started withdrawing funds. The coverage in the media was also particularly negative. Several Icelandic banks had a presence in the United Kingdom through subsidiaries. The fact that the Icelandic banks owed more than the Icelandic gross domestic product was widely emphasized, particularly in light of the potentially substantial bailout costs. In the ensuing days, as the word spread about the banks' problems, the Icelandic economy was shaken, the value of its currency tumbled and interest rates increased. This had a ripple effect on all the foreign operating subsidiaries of the Icelandic banks. They all experienced significant and unprecedented withdrawal requests. The fear arose that the widespread collapse of Icelandic banking so soon after the collapse of Lehman Brothers would lead to a global financial meltdown. Moreover, due to the size of a potential government bailout of the Icelandic banks, rumors circulated that the country itself would face bankruptcy.

Early on October 7, Landsbanki was nationalized to protect its depositors. The same day, Icesave, an online bank operated by Landsbanki in both the United Kingdom and the Netherlands, suspended withdrawals. On October 9, the day after British and other European banking regulators closed down the local branches of some Icelandic banks, the Icelandic government started to shut down and nationalize Iceland's major banks. After the shutdown, the Icelandic banks continued their operations but under government ownership. The bailout costs were substantial—the equity alone of the newly nationalized banks equaled approximately 30% of the Icelandic gross domestic product. The Icelandic government sought and received emergency funding from other governments. The aid package is estimated to be around EUR 9 billion from the International Monetary Fund, European Union, Nordic countries, and elsewhere.

Here, we introduced four concepts that are key drivers for banking risks and regulation. A bank run on a single bank is a nonsystemic risk. If an individual run is neither avoided nor managed properly, its effects could become systemic and lead to a panic among other banks. Bank panics, as the Icelandic example shows, can lead to contagion. The relationship between these concepts is illustrated in Figure 3.1.

Figure 3.1 **From bank run and nonsystemic risk through bank panic and systemic risk to contagion**

Term	Definition	Risk Type	Definition
Bank Run	A large number of depositors on one bank suddenly and simultaneously demands withdrawal of their deposits	Non-systemic risk	A risk that only affects one bank (local effect)
Bank Panic	A bank run that spreads and causes bank runs at other banks	Systemic risk	Risk of the collapse of an entire banking system or financial market.
Contagion	Shocks that have broader spillover effects into other regions, countries or markets		

3.2   Foundations of Bank Regulation

Avoiding a run on a bank is a chief concern not only of a bank's stakeholders, including management, its shareholders, customers, and employees, but also of bank regulators and various agencies and authorities in charge of managing the economy. Effective bank regulation reduces systemic risk by addressing nonsystemic risks and making sure that individual banks operate prudently and do not fail. The objective of regulation is to institute adequate supervision of individual banks to reduce the chance that runs on individual banks will happen and escalate to systemwide bank panics, contagion, and economic crises.

3.2.1   Regulatory Objectives

To avoid the devastating economic effects of bank failures and to ensure a stable banking industry in well-functioning financial markets, banking and financial regulators actively aim to meet the following objectives:

*   *Ensure that banks are operated prudently.* Regulators set rules that give banks incentives to follow strict operational standards and to avoid risky loans. Regulators also impose capital requirements on the bank, requirements that take into account the risk inherent in the bank's activities.
*   *Reduce systemic risk.* Regulators and bank supervisors, through examinations, inspections, and regulatory audits, monitor banks on an individual basis. In these examinations, the bank supervisors focus on identifying nonsystemic sources of risks that can increase the possibility of a bank run. Usually banks with low equity and regulatory capital levels, risky loans, internal managerial problems, weak earnings, and limited funding sources receive additional regulatory monitoring.
*   *Implement systemwide support mechanisms.* These mechanisms reduce the impact of a possible bank run by offering deposit insurance that insures each depositor's money (see Section 3.4 for a detailed discussion on deposit insurance). Other approaches include reserve requirements and access to various liquidity support systems in the banking system. Ultimately, the country's central bank or monetary authority can act as the "lender of last resort" and may step in to offer temporarily emergency liquidity support to weak but otherwise viable banks (see Section 3.2.3 for a detailed discussion on the lender of last resort).

3.2.2   The Regulatory Process

Bank regulation is a complex process and generally consists of licensing and supervision. The first component, licensing, sets certain requirements on those who want to start a new bank. The second component, supervision, provides for the monitoring of banks to ensure that they are in compliance with regulations.

Licensing

Licensing provides license holders the right to operate a bank. The licensing process is specific to the regulatory landscape of the country and/or state where the bank is located and operates. **Licensing** involves an evaluation of an entity's intent and ability to observe the regulatory guidelines that will govern the bank's operations, financial soundness, and managerial actions. The process is ordinarily somewhat cumbersome and expensive, which, although not intentional, tends to weed out entities that might not be as dedicated to making the longer-term commitment required to obtain the license and operate a bank. When regulators are satisfied that the owners and managers of a newly established bank have fulfilled all their requirements, the regulators will grant the bank a license to operate.

Regulatory Supervision

The second part of regulation is an extension of the license-granting process and consists of the supervision of the bank's activities by a government regulator. **Regulatory supervision** ensures that the operations and functioning of the bank comply with the regulatory guidelines that banks are obliged to follow when they receive their license. Supervision also monitors for and attempts to resolve deviations from regulatory standards.

Regulatory supervision varies, depending on the type of the institution, and is at the discretion of regulatory authorities. Bank supervisors subject riskier banks to more invasive supervision. Some regulatory agencies or regulatory supervisors require a physical inspection of the records, operations, and processes of regulated banks, while other regulators simply evaluate reports submitted by the banks. Complying with regulatory requirements is often resource consuming and expensive to banks, but it is, quite simply, a cost of doing business.

Examples of banking regulators and supervisors include the Federal Reserve System in the United States; the Financial Services Authority in the United Kingdom; the Federal Financial Markets Service in the Russian Federation; and BaFin, or Bundesanstalt für Finanzdienstleistungsaufsicht in Germany, among others.

3.2.3   Stabilization: The Lender of Last Resort

Liquidity and solvency are as relevant today as they were in the 19th century when the current banking system in industrialized countries took form. Early regulators sought solutions to solvency crises at individual banks before these crises transformed into widespread bank panics, and determined that the regulators had to play a role as the lender of last resort. The central bank, as the **lender of last resort**, helps maintain the stability of the financial system by providing emergency funds to banks undergoing solvency or liquidity problems.

EXAMPLE

At the time the Icelandic banking sector collapsed in October 2008, the Icelandic banks had wide branch networks in Europe in such as the United Kingdom, the Netherlands, Luxembourg, Switzerland, and Scandinavia. The collapse of the three major Icelandic banks also severely affected their European branch banks. For instance, Kaupthing, the largest Icelandic bank, had operations in Sweden—Kaupthing Bank Sverige AB. The day before the Icelandic authorities closed down Kaupthing, the Swedish central bank —as the lender of last resort—extended emergency funding to the Swedish subsidiary of Kaupthing. According to the Swedish authorities, the Swedish subsidiary of Kaupthing was still solvent, and the funding—EUR 520 million—was extended simply to allow an orderly shut down of that bank.

Governments hope to ensure the efficiency and resiliency of the financial system. **Financial stability** is the extent to which financial institutions and markets are able to mobilize savings to provide liquidity. In the first example of the Icelandic banking crisis in Section 3.1.2, the actions of the Icelandic government (providing capital support through nationalization of Glitnir in September 2008) were designed to maintain financial stability in both Iceland and countries where its banks operated. This support, while substantial, was limited given the considerable disparity between the asset size of the Icelandic banks and the Icelandic economy. Ultimately the bailout of the Icelandic banks depended on the coordinated action of regulators from different countries as illustrated by the previous example.

Monetary stability is the extent to which the value of money is maintained (i.e., low and stable inflation). One of the many roles that central banks play is to maintain stable prices by reducing inflation to an "acceptable" range, usually considered to be in the range of 2 to 3% per year. Central banks achieve this by setting interest rates and controlling the amount of credit and money available in the economy. Discussion of the specific mechanisms by which central banks achieve monetary stability is beyond the coverage of the material here. Monetary stability should not be confused with financial stability; although they can often exist together, they are not necessarily "fellow travelers." For instance, very high inflation in a country—a sign of monetary instability—tends to disrupt the financial stability of that country. Starting in 2007 (and continuing in 2009), developed countries have suffered from a financial crisis, which has caused shorter, yet very significant, periods of financial instability. Well-functioning markets suddenly froze and established banks failed. Notwithstanding this unprecedented financial instability, monetary stability—a stable inflation rate—was maintained in these countries, and in several of them, inflation rates actually declined (deflation).

3.3   INTERNATIONAL REGULATION OF BANK RISKS

For a long time, banking regulation was national. That is, governments and their regulatory agencies developed rules and banking supervisory guidelines specific to the country's needs. Regulatory rules differed significantly between countries. Not until 1988, when the Basel I Accord was released, did international banking regulations take shape. Both the Basel I and the Basel II Accords outline regulatory guidelines for international banks' operations and risk management.

3.3.1   Bank for International Settlements

The Bank for International Settlements, BIS, established in Basel, Switzerland, in 1930, is the principal center of international central bank cooperation. The BIS acts as:
*   A forum to promote discussion and policy analysis among central banks and within the international financial community
*   A center for economic and monetary research
*   A prime counterparty for central banks in their financial transactions
*   Agent or trustee in connection with international financial operations[1]

After the end of the Second World War, the BIS focused on cooperation among banks, first by implementing and defending the international exchange rate system and then by managing it. The BIS has always performed "traditional" banking functions—gold and foreign exchange transactions—for the central bank community, as well as trustee and agency functions. The BIS has also provided or arranged emergency financing to support the international monetary system when needed.

BANKING IN FOCUS

The collapse of Herstatt Bank (in German, Bankhaus Herstatt) and its effects on the international financial markets—particularly on the foreign exchange market—highlighted the close interdependence among international banks around the world. Herstatt Bank was a mid-sized West German bank active in the foreign exchange market. For a long time, the foreign exchange market was a relatively small and stable market, but it changed dramatically after 1973.

In 1974, Herstatt Bank collapsed after German supervisors withdrew its banking license. Unfortunately, the supervisors did not wait for the close of business to shut down the bank, but acted at lunchtime in Germany. Their timing had international ramifications. Herstatt was engaged in foreign exchange trading, where it was buying and selling foreign currency, mainly German marks. In accordance with custom, Herstatt Bank's counterparties had paid the bank in the morning local

---

1.   The BIS profile, July 2008.

time, roughly six hours ahead of New York, for the foreign exchange transactions that Herstatt was engaged in. When the regulators closed the bank in Germany at lunchtime, or noon, New York banks were not yet open. The counterparties, who made the payments to Herstatt bank in Frankfurt during the morning, expected that they would receive funds in exchange for their foreign currency in their New York accounts in the afternoon. Herstatt Bank was closed at lunchtime Frankfurt time and Herstatt's U.S. bank, aware that Herstatt had been shutdown, subsequently suspended all dollar payments on the parent bank's behalf. When the New York markets opened later in the day, Herstatt's clients were unable to access their exchanged funds. There followed a chain reaction that severely impacted the global payments and settlements system. In the three days following Herstatt's closure, the gross amount of funds transferred among banks for the purpose of payments and settlements fell by approximately 60%. Since then, settlement risk has commonly been called "Herstatt risk."

In the aftermath of the failure of Herstatt Bank, the central bank governors of developed BIS-member countries established the Basel Committee on Banking Supervision, also referred to as the **Basel Committee**. The committee's goal was to foster cooperation in regulating the activities of international banks. As noted, the failure of Herstatt Bank produced major problems for banks making international payments, particularly foreign exchange transactions. To reduce the chance of such an event happening again, the Basel Committee set out to improve international banking supervision.

The BIS provides the facilities for the Secretariat of the Basel Committee in Basel. The secretariat has a small staff of experienced banking supervisors from member institutions. The Secretariat provides administrative help for the committee and its subcommittees and is available to provide guidance to supervisory authorities in all countries.

3.3.2   The Basel Committee

The Basel Committee is a forum for regulatory cooperation between its member countries on banking supervision-related matters.[2] Representatives of the central banks and banking supervisors are the committee members. It is not a global supervisory authority: Both the reports and recommendations issued by the committee lack legal force. Instead, the committee formulates broad banking supervisory standards (such as the Basel Accords) develops guidelines for both banks and regulators, and recommends statements of best practice.

The committee encourages the development of common banking regulatory and supervisory approaches for internationally active banks. It seeks to instill guiding regulatory principles without attempting to micromanage member countries' supervisory approaches. An overall objective of the committee's work has been to close gaps in international supervisory coverage in pursuit of two basic principles:

---

2.   Belgium, Canada, France, Germany, Italy, Japan, Luxembourg, the Netherlands, Spain Sweden, Switzerland, the United Kingdom, and the United States.

1. Every international bank should be subject to supervision.
2. The supervision should be substantial enough to ensure compliance.

To achieve this, the committee has issued several comprehensive documents since 1975 that seek to improve both regulatory understanding and the quality of banking supervision for international banks. More recently, it has acted as a source of domestic legislation or banking supervision in the European Union (EU). In the EU, the Basel II Accord (explained in further detail below) was adopted, largely unchanged, as the basis for domestic banking and financial services supervisory legislation. This has led more and more countries outside the Group of 10 (known as the G10)[3] and EU countries[4] to either adopt or consider adopting Basel II as a basis for their respective banking legislation and regulations for domestic and international banks.

The Basel Committee advanced two accords and one amendment. The timeline of these accords is set out in Figure 3.2. These documents are directly relevant for regulating the capital needed to balance the risks of internationally active banks. The accords are closely related to one another and reflect the development and increased sophistication of current-day finance and banking. The committee has also undertaken consultative activities.

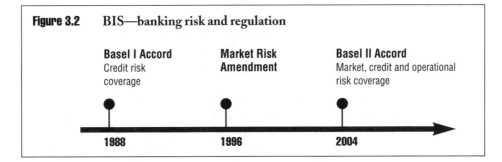

Figure 3.2   BIS—banking risk and regulation

Basel I Accord Credit risk coverage	**Market Risk Amendment**	**Basel II Accord** Market, credit and operational risk coverage
1988	1996	2004

3.3.3   The Basel I Accord

The Basel Committee recognized an overriding need to strengthen the international banking system's ability to withstand shocks. The committee also sought to level the competitive playing field by standardizing national capital requirements. Lower capital requirements, or higher leverage, mean that the bank can use more debt to finance the loans it makes, which reduces the cost of funds and increases profitability. At the time, international banks in Japan were required to maintain less capital—or were allowed to operate with more leverage—than banks domiciled in other countries,

---

3. As of 2008, there are 11 G10 countries: Belgium, Canada, France, Germany, Italy, Japan, the Netherlands, Sweden, Switzerland, the United Kingdom, and the United States.
4. Austria, Belgium, Cyprus, Czech Republic, Denmark, Estonia, Finland, France, Germany, Greece, Hungary, Ireland, Italy, Latvia, Lithuania, Luxembourg, Malta, Netherlands, Poland, Portugal, Slovakia, Slovenia, Spain, Sweden, and the United Kingdom.

giving the Japanese banks a competitive edge. In December 1987, the committee published a consultative study supporting a proposed system for the measurement of capital. The document is commonly referred to as the Basel I Accord. It was approved by the governors of the central banks of the G10 countries, Spain, and Luxembourg and was released to banks in July 1988.

The capital measurement system provided for the implementation of a common framework for capital assessment as a function of the riskiness of assets.

The Accord introduced a system to help banks better assess their level of risk across all assets. The system established risk weightings based on the perceived relative credit risk associated with each asset class. The idea was to generate a risk identification system to make it possible to compare different types of banks and the different types of assets they held. To derive a balance sheet weighted by risk factors, each instrument, loan, or debt is grouped into four broad categories depending on its perceived credit risk. Figure 3.3 lists these risk weights.

Figure 3.3	**Risk weights associated with certain credits**	
Category	**Examples**	**Risk Weight**
1	Cash, loans to governments in OECD[5] countries	0%
2	Loans to banks in OECD countries	20%
3	Residential mortgages	50%
4	Corporate loans, consumer loans	100%

In practice, banks had a multitude of different assets with different characteristics, and the actual weights used could vary according to the principles of the Accord and the discretion of the banking supervisor. This system allowed banks to consider all their assets, categorize each, and then calculate their total **risk-weighted assets (RWA)** as the sum of the absolute value of each asset multiplied by its risk weight. Risk-weighted assets include the bank's loans and securities recorded on the bank's balance sheet and also some commitments not recorded on the bank's **balance sheet**. For example, **off-balance-sheet** items would include financial derivatives, standby letters of credit, and other contingent liabilities that, if ever triggered, could expose the bank to financial risk.

In addition, the Accord created a framework for the structure of bank capital, often called eligible capital. The Basel Committee considers equity capital as the preferred element of eligible capital for a bank. However, for **regulatory capital** purposes, most banks could hold capital in two tiers:

- *Tier 1,* core capital, is primarily the bank's equity.
- *Tier 2,* supplementary capital, mainly includes reserves and provisions as well as hybrid capital instruments and subordinated debt. Tier 2 capital was restricted to

---

5.   The Organization for Economic Cooperation and Development (OECD) is a group of 30 developed countries with a democratic government and a market economy.

be at most 50% of total regulatory capital.

Finally, the Accord also set a minimum capital requirement of 8% for the ratio of risk-weighted assets to regulatory capital. The ratio of the risk-weighted assets (RWA) to the regulatory capital of the bank is called the **capital ratio** or **capital standard**. Tier 1 capital is usually the equity of the bank; Tier 1 and Tier 2 capital, with some adjustments, usually equals the regulatory capital. The minimum capital standard of 8% was to be implemented by the end of 1993. **Capital adequacy** is achieved when an institution's capital ratio meets or exceeds the minimum capital standard. The Accord's common framework for capital was progressively introduced in virtually all countries with active international banks.

EXAMPLE

Suppose BetaBank currently holds the following assets:
1. EUR 1,000 million loan to UK government (OECD)
2. EUR 300 million loan to international bank in Germany (OECD)
3. EUR 700 million mortgage portfolio
4. EUR 800 million corporate loan portfolio

The following Figure 3.4 shows the calculation of the risk-weighted assets for BetaBank.

Figure 3.4   Calculation of risk-weighted assets for BetaBank

Description	Size (EUR million)	Risk Weight	Risk Weighted Asset (EUR million)
Loan to UK government	1,000	0%	0
Loan to international bank in Germany	300	20%	60
Mortgages	700	50%	350
Corporate loans	800	100%	800
		Total RWA	**EUR 1,210**

Thus, assuming the country in which BetaBank operates uses the Accord's 8% minimum capital requirement, BetaBank's minimum capital required is EUR 96.8 million (= EUR 1,210 million * 8%). Therefore, to meet the Basel I capital requirement, BetaBank must have at least EUR 96.8 million in Tier 1 and Tier 2 capital. To meet the regulatory requirements, at least EUR 48.4 million has to be Tier 1 capital.

The Basel I Accord was the first international regulatory attempt to link the risks a bank takes to the bank's equity. Over the years both regulators and economists have found that prudently operated banks are characterized by higher capital ratios, take fewer risks, and suffer losses less frequently. And, the more equity the bank has, the greater the cushion the bank has to absorb potential losses (see Section 2.2 on the role of the bank's equity).

3.3.4   The Market Risk Amendment

Banking changed dramatically after the original Accord was introduced. Due to largely other regulatory changes (deregulation) that allowed banks to have greater self-determination in how they conducted their activities, banks became broad-based providers of financial services. Because trading activities in banks began playing a more significant role, the Basel Committee in 1996 issued the Market Risk Amendment, formally titled Amendment to the Capital Accord to Incorporate Market Risks. The Amendment focused on the effect of a bank's positions in various market-traded financial assets—foreign exchange, debt securities, equities, commodities, and derivatives.

The risks arising from trading positions in bonds, equities, foreign exchange, and commodities were separated from credit risk calculations and assigned to a new risk category—market risk. The Amendment allowed banks to use their own systems for measuring market risk, subject to banking supervisory approval, and the capital required to cover that risk was based in part on how effective their models had been at measuring the bank's market risk. In particular, the Amendment allowed banks to use value at risk (VaR) models to measure market risk capital requirements. VaR then was a new methodology for measuring risk; it has since evolved to become a cornerstone of financial risk management. Chapter 6 will further delve into the VaR methodology.

Subsequently, the Market Risk Amendment was incorporated into the Basel II Accord. Further details will be discussed in Chapter 6.

3.3.5   Weaknesses of Bank Capital Requirements in Basel I Accord

The 1988 Accord was intended to evolve over time. In 1991, the Accord was amended to provide a more precise definition of general provisions against bad debts that are included in general loan loss reserves. Since 1991, general loan loss reserves have been included as capital for purposes of calculating capital adequacy.

However, as implementation and use of the Accord progressed, it became evident that Basel I was too simplistic to address the activities of complex banks. For instance, according to Basel I, banks that lent to companies with a very good credit standing were obliged to hold exactly the same amount of regulatory capital as banks lending to companies with poor credit standing. But banks could charge higher interest on loans to companies with poor credit standing. Thus, the Basel I Accord provided banks— inadvertently—with the incentive to underwrite loans to companies with lower credit ratings. These credit ratings are provided by credit-rating agencies that routinely evaluate the creditworthiness of a wide range of borrowers. (Section 4.4.2 discusses credit rating agencies more.) A higher credit rating, such as an AAA rating, indicates a lower risk of default than a CCC-rating. Since AAA-rated borrowers offer lower interest rates than CCC-rated borrowers, this structure provided banks fewer incentives to underwrite loans to companies with good credit ratings. (Figure 5.11 summarizes the various credit ratings and their interpretation.) While the purpose of the Accord was to reduce the overall risk of internationally active banks, these incentives actually encouraged banks to underwrite riskier loans.

Another concern with Basel I was that it did not recognize the benefits of credit mitigation techniques. **Credit mitigation techniques** help banks reduce the credit risk associated with loans through the use of collateral and loan guarantees. Although certainly not the intent, the Accord did not provide banks with the appropriate incentives to use credit mitigation techniques. Under the Accord, banks could employ these techniques but not receive any capital relief.

EXAMPLE

GammaBank is evaluating a EUR 100,000,000 loan request from Bear Inc. Bear Inc has fallen on hard times and has a CCC credit rating. The company has some undeveloped—and otherwise unencumbered—land worth EUR 125,000,000 that it can use as collateral for the loan. Since the value of the collateral (see Section 4.4.5 for additional details on collateral) exceeds the value of the loan, GammaBank is confident that even if the loan becomes non-performing, Bear Inc can sell the land and repay the loan. Since there is collateral and the value of the collateral exceeds the value of the loan, this loan is relatively safe. Yet, GammaBank will be charged a risk weight of 100% towards the 8% regulatory minimum capital, notwithstanding the existence of collateral.

The Accord also did not recognize the benefits of diversification for credit risk reduction; a bank that lends to the same type of customer in the same region faces greater credit risk than a bank that lends to a diverse group of customers in the same or different regions of the world.

The committee initiated the Basel II Accord in an attempt to correct the drawbacks and inadvertent consequences of the Basel I Accord.

3.3.6   The Basel II Accord

In 1999, the committee issued a proposal for a new capital framework to replace the 1988 Accord. The new accord proposed to connect capital requirements more closely to the actual risks incurred by a bank. It also aimed to broaden the risks banks considered when calculating their minimum capital requirements. The new accord proposed approaches that would accommodate banks' differing complexities in their operations and businesses. Most importantly, it sought to provide incentives for banks to develop more sophisticated internal risk management systems that reduce non-systemic risk in the banking system. From a regulatory perspective, the new accord would provide banking supervisors with enhanced powers to redress weaknesses in individual banks.

In 2004, after lengthy consultations, a new capital framework, Basel II, was introduced. It consists of three pillars, shown in Figure 3.5.

- *Pillar 1.* Sets minimum capital requirements designed to improve upon the standardized rules set forth in the 1988 Accord. These minimum regulatory capital requirements should reflect the three major types of risk that a bank faces: credit risk, market risk, and operational risk. The approach in Basel II cures some of the arbitrariness or coarseness in Basel I. Under Pillar 1, banks can choose from different alternatives of varying complexity to calculate their minimum regulatory capital requirements. Basel II also represents the first attempt to assign a regulatory capital charge to the management of operational risk.

- *Pillar 2.* Complements and strengthens Pillar 1 by establishing a prudential supervision process. It covers all the risks in Pillar 1 and adds some other considerations:
  - The calculation by the bank of the amount of economic capital, the amount of capital a firm will require to survive during times of distress to cover Pillar 1 risks. Economic capital is discussed extensively in Chapter 8.
  - The creation of a governance structure within the bank to ensure internal supervision and oversight from the board of directors and senior management.
  - The evaluation, by the banking supervisor of the bank's own risk profile level and the processes the bank used to determine that level.

- *Pillar 3.* Outlines the effective use of market discipline as a lever to strengthen disclosure and encourage sound banking practices. **Market discipline** is public disclosure of a bank's financial condition to depositors and other interested parties, allowing these to assess the condition of the bank. It relates to transparency of the bank and its activities. Disclosure, or transparency, is the degree to which a bank or any company reveals its assets, liabilities, and/or inner workings. Disclosure affords the market—other banks, depositors, and borrowers—a better picture of the bank's overall risk position and allows the bank's counterparties to price and deal appropriately.

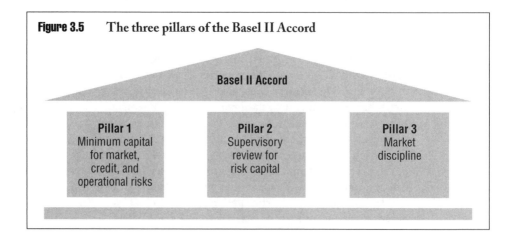

Figure 3.5   The three pillars of the Basel II Accord

The three pillars are intended to reinforce each other in an approach designed to strengthen the safety and soundness of the global financial system. The complex regulatory framework has two overarching objectives:

1. Improve how regulatory capital requirements reflect underlying risks
2. Address the effects of financial innovation that has occurred.

3.3.7   Adopting Basel II

When a country incorporates the Basel Accord into its banking regulatory and supervisory framework, it must do so by adjusting it to its own laws and regulations. Most members of the Group of 10 (G10) have adopted the Accord by incorporating the requirements into their respective national laws and/or regulations with some amendments and adjustments. The Basel Committee worked closely with the European Union in developing the new Accord. As a result, the Basel II Capital Accord has become the basis for the EU regulatory framework and has been implemented across EU countries through EU's Capital Requirements Directive (CRD) and other directives. The European Union has adopted the CRD through an EU-wide legislative process. A new organization, the Committee of European Banking Supervisors (CEBS), has been created to ensure that Basel II is applied, interpreted, and implemented uniformly across all 25 member states.

A study by the Financial Stability Institute (FSI) reported that out of 115 countries in Africa, Asia, the Caribbean, Latin America, the Middle East, and Eurasia (not counting EU countries), a vast majority of countries are planning to implement parts of Basel II. Of course, different countries will have different approaches to implementing these Accords. The decision to implement the Basel II Accord in a country is motivated by several factors.

*   The relative success being enjoyed by banks that use risk-based capital
*   The desire of many bank supervisors across the world to move toward risk-based regulation
*   The desire of many countries to enhance the reputation of their banking system

Different countries have different banking industry structures and specific rules and regulations that govern their business activities. The Basel II Accord takes these country-specific differences into consideration by allowing the national bank regulators and supervisors in countries that adopt the Accord to customize certain Basel definitions, approaches, or thresholds that they plan to adopt when implementing the proposals. Implementation of rules and regulations subject to a country's decision are to be based on domestic market practice and experience and consistent with the objectives of the Basel II Accord and its principles.

EXAMPLE

In determining the risk weights of loans secured against commercial real estate, the national regulators have the national discretion to allow a 50% risk weight for certain loans that meet particular requirements although the Basel II Accord sets out that loans secured against commercial real estate have a 100% riskweight.

3.4 DEPOSIT INSURANCE

One of the tools that ensures the safety and soundness of the financial system is deposit insurance. **Deposit insurance** is a promise by a government or an insurance system that, in the event of a bank failure, bank depositors will receive back the deposits they made with that bank.

Deposit protection is generally limited to a certain amount of the deposits held at each bank. In the United States, deposit insurance protection is currently and temporarily limited to USD 250,000. Prior to October 2008, when the coverage was temporarily raised to the new limit, the coverage was USD 100,000. In the third quarter of 2008, many governments around the world decided to guarantee all or significant amounts of customer deposits in their country's banks temporarily. Their intent was to provide some security in response to the credit crisis and avoid runs on banks and bank panics. For instance, Finland upped its deposit insurance coverage to EUR 50,000 until the end of 2009; prior to this increase, the coverage was EUR 25,000.

EXAMPLE

Currently, the Financial Services Compensation Scheme in the United Kingdom covers bank deposits up to GBP 50,000. Mr. Smith has GBP 55,000 deposited with VegaBank, a bank that has failed. After the bank failed, the deposit insurance agency reimbursed Mr. Smith GBP 50,000 and the remainder, GBP 5,000, was not reimbursed. Deposits that the deposit insurance system is not able to repay may be fully or partially repaid later if the failed bank has sufficient funds to repay some or all the deposits that exceed the deposit insurance coverage. In the end, the GBP 5,000 that the deposit insurance did not cover may not be a total loss to Mr. Smith.

The motivation for deposit insurance is to help prevent the risk that a bank run will grow to a broader bank panic. Knowing that their deposits would be repaid fully or in most part even if the bank were to fail means depositors have fewer incentives to withdraw their funds from an institution even when there is news that the institution is about to fail. As noted above, deposit insurance reduces bank runs, bank panic, and contagion.

EXAMPLE

Let us revisit the example of AlphaBank from Section 3.1, and change the story by introducing deposit insurance. AlphaBank is rumored (correctly or not) to have made an extraordinary number of bad loans that have led to losses. This rumor concerns depositors but doesn't motivate them to withdraw their deposits from the bank because of the deposit insurance system covering all customer deposits with AlphaBank. In reality, AlphaBank has suffered very material losses on its loan portfolio and is close to being insolvent. It also has exhausted all its reserves and sources of cash. However, the existence of the deposit insurance has kept the bank from failing and reduced the risk of a bank run.

3.4.1   Deposit Insurance Coverage

Historically, deposit insurance was voluntary and was offered by insurance companies, banks, and governments. Banks that wanted to participate in these deposit insurance systems were able to market this added protection against the failure of the institution to existing and potential depositors. Consequently, these banks were able to secure financing at relatively lower costs than banks that did not offer deposit insurance coverage. Despite the advantage of lower financing costs to banks, few deposit insurance systems were popular, and many were severely underfunded, meaning the deposit insurance provider did not have sufficient funds available to repay the depositors in case of widespread bank failures. Many of the voluntary deposit insurance systems exhausted their assets during poor economic times when multiple banks failed. This original combination of voluntary participation and poor funding reduced the effectiveness of deposit insurance.

During the Great Depression in the United States starting in 1929, bank runs grew into a bank panic and lead to widespread bank failures. As a result of sweeping legislation, in 1933 the United States created the world's first comprehensive, compulsory, and explicit deposit insurance system. Under this system, which continues to exist today, the Federal Deposit Insurance Corporation (FDIC), an independent agency, provides protection for deposits in United States banks.[7] Protection is subject to certain limits, constraints, and caps, but in effect a large proportion of deposits in the United States are protected against a bank's failing. This approach has been espoused by deposit insurance systems around the world. The FDIC regularly examines the safety and soundness of the banks it insures to determine the bank's capitalization and overall financial health. The decisions they make based on the bank examinations, in a sense, are the same as an underwriting activity for a bank and lead to a determination of the premium the bank will pay to the FDIC for deposit insurance. The FDIC has become one of the principal bank supervisors in the United States.

---

7.   The United States has several government agencies that provide deposit insurance to the different types of banks. The chief deposit insurance agency is the FDIC.

BANKING IN FOCUS

Deposit insurers set a deposit insurance premium that is the annual levy banks pay on their deposits to receive deposit insurance coverage. The U.S. system sets the premium in relation to the risk of the bank. Consequently, the FDIC considers the following:

- *The relationship between the bank's risk weighted assets and equity.* The FDIC divides banks into three groups, *well-capitalized* where the risk-weighted assets and capital exceeds 10%; *adequately capitalized*, where the risk-weighted assets and capital exceed 8% but not 10%; and *undercapitalized* where the ratio of risk-weighted assets and capital does not exceed 8%.

- *The overall health of the bank.* In the United States, the FDIC jointly with other regulators and supervisors examines each bank on a regular basis. Based on these regulatory examinations, the bank is assigned to a risk group. Supervisors examine the bank's capital, asset quality, management quality, earnings, liquidity, and sensitivity to market risk to assess the degree of risk the bank assumes. The higher the risk the bank takes—the more risky loans it under-writes, the more weaknesses the regulators find—the higher supervisory risk rating it has. By examining each bank that receives deposit insurance coverage, the agency sets the appropriate level of insurance coverage that reflects the risk of the bank's overall assets to ensure that the loans the banks made and the bonds and other investment the bank bought are safe.

At the end of 2008, well-capitalized U.S. banks that belong to the lowest supervisory risk rating (the lowest overall risk of operations, loans, and investments) pay between 5 and 7 basis points (bp) of deposits for insurance coverage per year. A *basis point* is one-hundredth of one percent, or 0.0001. A bank paying 7 bp of deposits in deposit insurance premium would pay USD 7 for each USD 10,000 in deposits.

Undercapitalized banks that belong to the *highest* supervisory risk rating group (the highest overall risk of operations, loans, and investments) pay 43 bp of deposits for insurance coverage. Other factors may adjust these deposit insurance assessment levels, but at the core the difference in deposit insurance premium between risky and prudent institutions can be substantial.

EXAMPLE

Both PrudentBank and RiskyBank have USD 1,000 million in deposits. While PrudentBank is well-capitalized and holds the lowest supervisory risk rating, RiskyBank is both undercapitalized and holds the highest supervisory risk rating. PrudentBank pays 5 bp in insurance, or USD 500,000, while RiskyBank pays USD 4.3 million. The difference in premium, USD 3.8 million reflects the higher risk of RiskyBank.

3.4.2 Deposit Insurance Around the World

At the end of 2008, there were 100 countries with deposit insurance systems in operation, and 19 countries with deposit insurance systems that are pending, planned, or under development.[8] Several countries have multiple deposit insurance systems. For instance, Austria has five different deposit insurance providers. There are also deposit insurance systems that cover multiple countries.

Many countries have adopted the FDIC's approach to deposit insurance, making participation in deposit insurance programs compulsory for all banks and financial institutions that accept deposits from the public. Insurance can either be provided by a government agency or through private insurance companies. These approaches are different, but ultimately all seek to protect depositors in case of bank failure.

Deposit insurance coverage varies across countries. In most countries, retail customers' deposits are protected at the expense of commercial customers. The reason for this two-tiered approach is that commercial customers are generally believed to be more sophisticated than retail customers and maintain multiple banking relationships that reduce their overall risks if one bank should fail. Also, regulators consider commercial depositors to have the capability to assess the possible risk of a bank failing.

EXAMPLE

According to the latest data available, the deposit insurance system of Serbia and Montenegro in 2003 covered deposits of banks in that country up to RSD 5,000 (Serbian Dinars), the equivalent of USD 87 at the then-prevailing international exchange rate between the RSD and the USD. This was the lowest deposit insurance coverage in the world at that time. At the same time, the Dominican Republic, Thailand, Turkey, and Turkmenistan all provide unlimited coverage for deposits. As of October 2008, the countries within the European Union have coverage of at least EUR 50,000.[9]

While there are 100 countries that have *explicit* deposit insurance systems in operation, there are several countries that provide *implicit* deposit insurance coverage. An **explicit deposit insurance system** is where the government, through an agency, has created a deposit insurance system to guarantee deposits. Such a system relies on regulation through the government or a dedicated agency, banking and other legislation, and active involvement of regulators as well as a law that explicitly states the coverage limits of deposit insurance, the assessment of deposit insurance premia, and regulatory rules. An **implicit deposit insurance system** is a system where the government has not created a specific agency providing deposit insurance, but has stated its willingness to guarantee deposits when so needed.

8.   International Association of Deposit Insurers, Country System List dated May 1, 2008.
9.   "Deposit Insurance around the World: A Comprehensive Database," by Asli Demirgüç-Kunt , Baybars Karacaovali, and Luc Laeven (World Bank and CEPR), World Bank Policy Research Working Paper 3628, June 2005.

EXAMPLE

In the early 1990s, Sweden suffered through a major banking crisis. At that time Sweden had neither an explicit nor implicit deposit insurance system. In the early days of the crisis, it became clear that due to the substantial losses many banks suffered from speculative real estate lending, which was the cause of the crisis, most banks would not have been able to withstand a run and the system would soon be engulfed in a bank panic. As the signs of a bank panic became more evident, the Swedish government sought to avoid it by stating its readiness to guarantee all bank deposits. This implicit guarantee reduced the incentives for bank runs and was successful in averting widespread bank panic and bank failures. Later, the government created an explicit deposit insurance system.

3.5   THE ROAD AHEAD

Chapter 1 introduced the banking industry in terms of the services and functions it provides and its pivotal role in economic development. In the second chapter, we focused on the financial information banks provide, the financial management of banks, and the treatment of loan losses. This chapter started by examining how systemic risk can quickly cripple a bank and ultimately hurt an economy. The importance of a stable banking industry motivated the need for banking regulation to ensure that banks are properly operated and managed. With the globalization of the banking industry, international banking regulation based on the Basel I and Basel II Accords has developed. These initiatives have become the cornerstones of banking regulation globally. In the next four chapters, we consider the core risk types of the Basel Accords—namely, credit risk, market risk, and operational risk—and highlight the methods for calculating regulatory capital requirements associated with each, as defined in Pillar 1 of the Basel II Accord. Chapter 8 considers Pillars 2 and 3 by reviewing the roles of supervisory review and market discipline and the relationship between economic capital and regulatory capital.

Credit Risk

T his and the following chapter provide a comprehensive introduction to credit risk: Chapter 4 focuses on credit risk and credit products and Chapter 5 explains the analysis of credit and the management of credit risks. This chapter addresses credit risk by focusing on three related topic areas. The first section introduces credit risk by defining and explaining the source of credit risk. The following sections provide a detailed overview of lenders and borrowers. The final two sections introduce the characteristics of credit products and discuss features of specific credit products used for retail and commercial lending.

Chapter Outline

- 4.1 Introduction to Credit Risk
- 4.2 Lenders
- 4.3 Borrowers
- 4.4 Characteristics of Credit Products
- 4.5 Types of Credit Products

Key Learning Points
- One of a bank's core risks is the possibility that borrowers will not repay their loans on time, or at all.
- Lenders distinguish between retail and commercial borrowers and tailor products to meet each group's unique financial needs.
- Loan products can be characterized by maturity, repayment method, loan use, the different types of security the borrower needs to provide the lender (collateral), or the restrictions the borrower must agree to in order to obtain the loan (covenants).
- There is a wide variety of credit products, and similar products can be used to meet both retail and commercial borrowing needs.

Key Terms

- Agricultural loans
- Asset conversion loans
- Asset-based lending
- Automobile (car) loans
- Balloon payments
- Banker's acceptance
- Cash flow-based loan
- Collateral
- Commercial mortgages
- Commercial paper
- Commitment fee
- Committed facilities
- Compensating balances
- Consortium
- Corporate borrowers
- Cost of funds
- Counterparty risk
- Covenants
- Credit rating agencies
- Credit risk
- Default
- Facility fee
- Factoring
- Fixed interest rate loan
- Floating interest rate loan
- Home equity credit
- Investment banks
- Investment grade rating
- Leasing
- Level amortization
- Line of credit
- Loan-to-value, LTV, ratio
- Maturity
- Mortgage
- Noninvestment grade rating
- Note NRSRO
- Principal
- Project, or infrastructure finance
- Public borrowers
- Recovery risk
- Residential mortgages
- Retail borrowers
- Revolving lines of credit
- Securitization
- Sinking-fund amortization
- Small and medium enterprises, SMEs
- Sovereign borrowers
- Syndicated loans
- Uncommitted facilities

Credit Risk

4.1   INTRODUCTION TO CREDIT RISK

Credit risk encompasses various components that, in combination, offer the bank a way to measure the probability a borrower may default on a contract—a debt, loan, or similar promise to perform—and how much value is likely to be recovered in the event of a default. **Credit risk** is most simply defined as the potential that a borrower, or counterparty, will fail to meet its obligations in accordance with agreed terms. **Default** is the failure to repay or meet existing obligations.

EXAMPLE

Growth Inc. provides goods and services that customers pay for after they receive the goods and services. The company provides the goods and services because it is confident its customers will make the payment when it is due. However, receipt of the payment is uncertain until it is actually made. Growth Inc. has taken on the risk that its customers may not honor their obligations. This is credit risk. In order to minimize its credit risk, Growth Inc. must evaluate its prospective customers in advance, determine if they are likely to honor their obligations, and decide to provide goods and services or not.

Counterparty risk is a common reference to the risk that another party to a contract or agreement will fail to perform under the terms of the agreement. This could mean the failure to provide promised goods or services, a refusal to provide promised loan facilities, or the failure to pay amounts owed.

EXAMPLE

On June 30, AlphaBank and BetaBank entered into an agreement that contained the following terms:

Lender:	BetaBank
Borrower:	AlphaBank
Amount:	USD 150 million
Term:	3 months from July 15
Interest rate:	5%

BetaBank has incurred counterparty credit risk. Specifically, BetaBank's counterparty credit risk is that AlphaBank will not repay the USD 150 million under the terms of the agreement. Conversely, AlphaBank has also accepted a counterparty credit risk: that is, the risk that BetaBank may be unable to honor its agreement to lend funds on July 15.

This example illustrates that in its most basic form, credit risk arises between two parties when there is a contractual obligation for one party (the lender) to provide funding to the other party (the borrower) in exchange for promised future payments.

Earlier sections provided several examples of defaults, including how a default affects the bank's assets, liabilities and equity (Section 2.2), and how banks seek to mitigate the effects of default through loan loss reserves (Section 2.4).

4.2   LENDERS

As discussed in Chapter 1, banks facilitate financial intermediation, the process by which one group in need of capital borrows funds from another group that has excess capital available for investment. In arranging this transfer of capital between the two groups, the bank uses deposits to finance the loan. Intermediation is critical to promoting economic development. Banks accept deposits from one group (depositors) and use those funds to provide credit products to another group (borrowers). Granting credit facilities (i.e., loans) creates risk. Banks accept this risk as a regular cost of business. Essentially, banks are in the business of managing risk. Banks continually attempt to expand their ability to manage all types of risks and, in particular, have gained considerable experience with credit risk analysis. Banks routinely evaluate their experiences and incorporate the lessons learned into their business practice by modifying existing or adding new policies and procedures that mitigate credit risk. Despite these efforts, recent events in the banking sector highlight how challenging credit analysis and credit risk management can be.

Banking is essential to both the retail and the wholesale markets. There are thousands of local, regional, and global banks that offer a variety of products and services to meet the retail market's (individual customers, shops, and small- and medium-sized businesses) needs. In the wholesale market (lending to other banks, large corporate entities, and large global institutions), only the larger banks are able to offer a diverse enough product range to meet the needs of the customers. Figure 4.1 describes the two major banking sectors.

Figure 4.1	Major types of banks
Retail Customers include: • Individuals / Shops • Small businesses	**Wholesale Customers include:** • Other banks / Large corporations • Large global institutions

Local and regional banks provide traditional and commercial banking operations such as lending to businesses, making loans to individuals, and accepting deposits. Examples of regional banks include Fifth Third Bank in the USA, Bank West in Australia, Raiffiesen Bank in Central and Eastern Europe, and Abu Dhabi Commercial Bank in the UAE. Global banks such as HSBC, ANZ, JPMorgan Chase, and the Royal Bank of Scotland are well placed to undertake both commercial banking and investment banking activities.

4.2.1   Investment Banks

Investment banks often act as an agent or financial intermediary to companies. Although they may have their own brokerage operations, provide investment advice to their customers, and provide loans and credit to commercial customers, their core activity is to arrange equity and debt—loans, bonds, and other types of credit—financing on behalf of their corporate customers. Investment banks typically do not accept deposits from customers or provide loans to retail customers, and they are not directly regulated by bank regulators in most cases, unless the investment bank is part of a bank that is otherwise regulated by bank regulators.

In late 2008, most of the world's largest investment banks, including Goldman Sachs and Morgan Stanley, converted to banks regulated by the government. The change was considered necessary in order to allow these entities to increase their capital by collecting customer deposits. Given the severity of the global financial market turmoil of 2008, it would appear that the investment banking model that existed in the United States since the mid-1930s is becoming obsolete in a globally connected and capital intensive financial world.

4.2.2   Credit Rating Agencies

Although technically not lenders, **credit rating agencies** (CRAs) play one role that is similar to lenders: they evaluate the creditworthiness of various borrowers. The difference between credit rating agencies and lenders is that the CRAs do not lend money.

CRAs evaluate the creditworthiness of borrowers and publicly traded debt and assign credit ratings to borrowers and the debt instruments they issue. Ratings are intended to provide an independent assessment of a borrower's general creditworthiness based on a wide array of risk factors. Ratings on individual debt instruments incorporate the creditworthiness of the issuer with relevant instrument-specific risk factors.

The ratings range from the highest credit rating—typically AAA or Aaa indicates a very high ability to repay the loan—to the lowest credit rating—typically C or D suggests the bond is about to default or is in fact in default. **Investment grade ratings** are generally from AAA/Aaa to BBB/Baa, and **noninvestment grade ratings** generally fall in the BB/Ba to C/D range. Table 5.11 contains a detailed description of the various ratings.

Single-letter ratings—such as AAA, BB, or C—represent the distillation of material information including quantitative, qualitative, and legal data about the borrower and communicate the results of the ratings process to the public. Credit analysis by CRAs is similar to the credit analysis process described in Section 5.2; CRAs examine the borrower's fundamental and vital characteristics including the borrower's industry, prospects for growth, risks, threats, and weaknesses. A particular concern for many borrowers is the potential of a materially adverse impact from an unexpected and unfavorable regulatory action such as reduction of subsidies—operating and development grants, funding assistance, tax deductions, and credit support—provided by government entities to business.

In the United States, some CRAs, called Nationally Recognized Statistical Rating Organization (**NRSRO**), are regulated. These credit rating agencies meet the regulatory requirement of the U.S. Securities and Exchange Commission and issue credit ratings that financial institutions can use for various regulatory purposes. Figure 4.2 lists the NRSROs as of December 2008. The SEC acts as the regulator for the NRSROs. To access financial markets, borrowers typically seek a rating from either one of the major international NRSROs (Standard and Poor's, Moody's, Fitch, DBRS) or from a regional NRSRO. Most of the NRSROs are paid a fee by the rated borrower. This is known as the *issuer-pays* model. Egan-Jones is an example of an NRSRO that is paid by investors for its ratings, an *investor-pays* model. Both models are under review due to their performance relating to the credit crisis that began in 2007.

Figure 4.2   **List of current NRSROs (as of December 2008)**

- A. M. Best Company
- Egan-Jones Ratings Company
- Japan Credit Rating Agency, Ltd
- Moody's Investor Service
- Realpoint LLC

- Dominion Bond Rating Service, Ltd
- Fitch Ratings
- LACE Financial
- R&I, Inc.
- Standard & Poor's

Ratings agencies evaluate different criteria for the different borrower types. For instance when rating sovereign borrowers (Section 4.3.3), ratings agencies analyze a country's ability and willingness to repay a debt and consider pertinent and substantive information on the economic and fiscal strength of the country and the stability and viability of the political and social system. This approach would differ if the CRA was analyzing a company issuing debt whose repayment depends on revenue generated from manufacturing goods or services provided in an emerging market country.

EXAMPLE

During the global financial crisis that started in 2007, many CRAs came under criticism for not catching quickly enough the material adverse changes in the financial products that they rated. CRAs were accused of making significant errors of judgment or being subject to conflicts of interest in their ratings of complex financial products. Most of the criticism was directed toward CRAs because certain parts of highly complex financial products were rated AAA when, in fact, these issues were major contributors to the crisis and were subsequently downgraded or defaulted.

In recent years, CRAs have started to assign *recovery ratings* to individual instruments issued by low-rated firms (e.g., firms with high probability to default on their debt). This is an attempt by the CRAs to quantify **recovery risk**, the value a lender to these low-rated firms might expect to suffer on an obligation in the event of default. This approach effectively separates default risk from recovery risk.

4.3 BORROWERS

Both retail and wholesale banks differentiate between different types of borrowers based on a variety of factors, including size and financing needs. On the retail side, one broad distinction is typically drawn between individual borrowers and small business borrowers. On the wholesale side, however, the differentiation tends to be more complex.

4.3.1 Retail Borrowers

Retail borrowers include consumers (individuals) who borrow money to purchase homes, cars, and other goods (in many countries, consumers also borrow to finance education and similar expenses). Generally, consumers with high income, low levels of debt, and solid loan repayment records are considered less risky borrowers, but a borrower's rating ultimately depends on a variety of criteria.

In today's banking environment, retail banking has become a commoditylike business. Most banks now group their retail borrowers into relatively homogeneous risk groups based on standard criteria. This process allows banks to analyze repayment and default characteristics based on standardized borrower characteristics. One aspect of this process is credit scoring, which allows the common characteristics of loans and borrowers to be grouped and analyzed. Scoring in groups enables loans and borrowers to be dissected and analyzed by various layers to assess more accurately a portfolio's probability of loss. Standardization and credit scoring allow the assessment process to be completed more cheaply, making relatively small loans profitable. It has also facilitated **securitization**, the bundling or packaging of portfolios of loans, against which debt instruments can be issued. Securitization is covered in more detail in Section 5.3.2.

4.3.2   Corporate Borrowers

Corporate borrowers include companies ranging from small local companies to large global conglomerates (see below). Each has different financing needs, and each should be analyzed on a stand-alone basis. Depending on the ease of access to capital (public markets, banks, private funding), companies may borrow capital or raise equity to finance growth and generate income. When borrowing, companies typically repay their obligations from the cash generated from the growth. Companies with steady profits, low debt levels, and solid management are considered to be less risky and are offered relatively better contractual terms for their borrowings. Corporate borrowers are frequently differentiated by their size and global reach. The main differences are listed in Figure 4.3.

- *Local companies.* These companies are generally referred to as **small and medium enterprises (SMEs)**. SMEs are usually smaller corporate entities such as partnerships, sole proprietorships, owner-operators, mom-and-pop shops, and other small businesses. SMEs are generally privately or closely held and have a straightforward legal structure. Annual sales are generally below USD 1 million, EUR 750,000, or GBP 500,000, but business size does differ across institutions and regulatory frameworks.[1]

- *Regional companies.* Regional companies are commercial businesses, generally who are larger SMEs, and include chain stores, gas stations, and restaurants, with sales between USD 1 and 100 million (EUR 750,000 and 75 million, GBP 500,000 to 50 million). Some would fall into the definition of SMEs according to the Basel II Accord. Further, their business activities usually expose them to one or more local markets or provide general exposure within a region. The legal and ownership structure of these businesses can be more complex, with multiple owners, several subsidiaries, and locations in different legal jurisdictions.

- *International companies.* International companies conduct their business across country borders but generally limit their activities to a certain region around the globe (e.g., Western Europe, the U.S., and Canada). They may also be "listed" or publicly traded companies on a stock or other similar exchange or may be large, privately held businesses that operate in different countries. International companies can have sizable annual sales (often in the billions) and will need to borrow regularly from banks to finance their activities and growth.

- *Universal companies.* These companies are generally considered global conglomerates with exposures around the globe. They typically manage their businesses by being constantly aware of global business considerations and pressures. Most are publicly traded on an exchange. Examples would include Siemens, Mitsubishi Heavy Industries, Lafarge, BP, Royal Dutch/Shell, and General Electric. All are considered institutional borrowers by banks and demand unique consideration for their financing needs. Hedge funds, international banks, and global insurers are also considered universal companies and institutional borrowers.

---

1.   Definitions of SMEs and corporate sizes vary widely. For instance, the Basel II Accord in its Annex 5 defines loans to SMEs as loans to corporations with reported annual sales of less than EUR 50 million.

Figure 4.3   An overview of the differences between borrower types

Borrower	Capital Needs	Ownership Structure	Operations	Financial Sophistication
Local companies	Small needs and simple loan products.	Simple ownership structure (proprietorships, partnerships, or closely held and family-based corporations).	Limited operations at one location with fewer than 50 employees.	Limited. Relies heavily on one bank for financial advice and solutions to financial problems.
Regional companies	Substantial needs met by a combination of simpler loan products.	Several partners or corporations with multiple owners. May have some subsidiaries. May be publicly traded on a limited or regional scale.	Operations focused on one or a couple of closely related business at several locations, possibly including international operations. Employs several hundred people.	Some financial experience and understanding. Ability to evaluate what combination of loan and other financial products would best fit their needs. Often have multiple banking relationships.
International companies	Large, varied, and complex needs that require a range of simple and more complex loan products.	Publicly traded with a large number of owners (shareholders). Several subsidiaries around the world.	Focused on multiple businesses worldwide. Employs several thousand people.	Highly sophisticated. Employs staff that focus on finding optimal financing alternatives for the company. Multiple banking relationships, with one lead bank.
Universal companies	Large, varied, and complex needs that require a wide range of simple and complex loan products as well as other innovative financial products.	Publicly traded at several exchanges with a large number of owners (shareholders). Multiple subsidiaries around the world.	Multiple, possibly disparate businesses worldwide. Employs tens of thousands of people.	Very sophisticated. Employees in different parts of the world focusing on finding optimal financing options. Multiple banking relationships in several countries support the financing of the business.

4.3.3   Sovereign Borrowers

Sovereign borrowers are governments that raise capital through bonds or direct borrowing generally from the larger global banks. Amounts raised are often used for large capital investments (better roads, railways) or to finance government spending. Governments often use tax revenues to repay these loans.

In general, CRAs review sovereign borrowers just as any other debtor. It should be noted, however, that not all countries ask to be rated by a CRA, and CRAs may provide ratings on sovereigns and private borrowers without their asking. Credit review of sovereigns includes their ability to deal with internal as well as global economic, political, interest rate, and commodity changes. Most sovereigns that ask to be rated would consider themselves investment grade (see Section 4.2.2) prior to engaging a rating agency.

Unfortunately, over the years, there have been a number of sovereign debt-related defaults following the issuance of a credit rating. Figure 4.4 provides a timeline of some recent sovereign defaults.

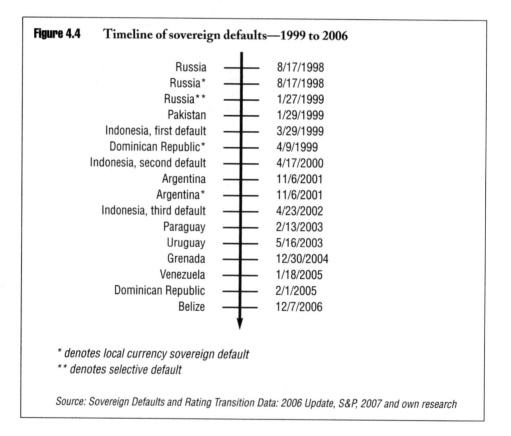

Figure 4.4   **Timeline of sovereign defaults—1999 to 2006**

Russia	8/17/1998
Russia*	8/17/1998
Russia**	1/27/1999
Pakistan	1/29/1999
Indonesia, first default	3/29/1999
Dominican Republic*	4/9/1999
Indonesia, second default	4/17/2000
Argentina	11/6/2001
Argentina*	11/6/2001
Indonesia, third default	4/23/2002
Paraguay	2/13/2003
Uruguay	5/16/2003
Grenada	12/30/2004
Venezuela	1/18/2005
Dominican Republic	2/1/2005
Belize	12/7/2006

* denotes local currency sovereign default
** denotes selective default

Source: Sovereign Defaults and Rating Transition Data: 2006 Update, S&P, 2007 and own research

Like corporations, sovereigns can expect their debt creditworthiness to be subject to upgrades as well as downgrades. The underlying analysis of the credit risk sovereigns represent, however, would be based on criteria different from what is used for corporations. Additionally, sovereigns should always be analyzed when considering counterparty creditworthiness. Oftentimes, a sovereign's credit rating will serve as an implicit ceiling on the credit ratings for firms in that country.

4.3.4   Public Borrowers

Public borrowers are primarily state, provincial, and local governments (municipalities) and their subentities (e.g., water and sewage commissions, airport authorities, public hospitals, and school districts). Amounts borrowed at this level are normally used either for investments (streets, water supply) or general spending. Since most local governments have the ability to generate cash by taxing their constituencies, public loans are considered relatively low risk. Nevertheless, there have been times when strong local governments have defaulted on their loans. Supranational institutions such as the European Investment Bank, Asian Development Bank, European Bank of Reconstruction and Development, World Bank, African Development Bank, Inter-American Development Bank, and Islamic Development Bank are also classified as public borrowers.

4.4   CHARACTERISTICS OF CREDIT PRODUCTS

There is a wide variety of loan types. All were developed to meet specific business needs of different borrowers' unique situations. The following section describes basic lending facilities and their differences. To understand which type of lending facility is appropriate for a borrower, lenders must understand the details of the borrower's financial status, especially how it relates to existing and anticipated conditions in the local, regional, or international marketplaces. Chapter 5 provides additional details on corporate credit analysis.

There are a number of ways a credit product can be classified:
- Maturity
- Commitment specification
- Purpose
- Repayment source
- Collateral requirements
- Covenant requirements
- Repayment characteristics

While not exhaustive, this list sets the stage to understand the complexity of the lending process and the unique nature of most loans. We explore each of these characteristics in detail next.

4.4.1   Maturity

Credit needs range over different time periods, with the loans made to meet those needs generally classified by maturity. **Maturity** simply means the date the final payment on the loan or other financial instrument becomes due. For instance, a loan of a maturity of one year must be repaid in full within one year.

For business, regulatory, and accounting purposes, banks usually distinguish between three maturity bands for lending: short, medium, and long term. Descriptions of the different maturity ranges or maturity bands are given in Figure 4.5. As noted in the table, loans within a particular maturity band tend to have similar uses and characteristics. For example, medium-term lending is usually cash flow based or asset based. With **cash flow-based lending** the quality and sufficiency of the cash being generated by the company over the period is paramount. **Asset-based lending** is secured by corporate assets such as accounts receivables, inventories, or certain property or equipment (see Section 4.5.2).

In the last few decades, there has been an increasing shift toward the establishment of long-term strategic banking relationships between banks and their borrowers. Banks support these relationships by increasingly offering longer-term loans to meet a borrower's credit needs (needs that previously were fulfilled by short-term borrowings). Having diverse facilities helps to cement a bank's corporate relationships, retain customers for the longer term, and contain competition from other banks. It also means that, despite a borrower's deteriorating credit condition, a bank may be obligated to fulfill lending commitments made to it at a much earlier time. Proper credit analysis, therefore, must take the time horizon (the maturity) of a loan commitment into consideration.

The business motivation to distinguish among the three maturity bands is to allow the bank to group loans of comparable maturity. Grouping creates efficiencies by allowing banks to manage loans within the same maturity band similarly. Banks seek to have a balance of maturity bands in their assets (loans and securities in their portfolio) to correspond to the maturity of their liabilities (deposits and other borrowings). Part of this process is managed by the bank's treasury department within its ALM function. From an accounting perspective, the maturity bands allow the bank to classify the various loans as short-term or long-term; banks use different accounting treatments for short-term and long-term loans. Most medium-maturity loans, for accounting purposes, are treated as long-term loans. From a regulator's perspective, a loan grouping reflects regulatory concerns and allows supervisors to assess more readily how closely the maturity of the bank's assets matches the maturity of the liabilities.

Figure 4.5   Short-term, medium-term, and long-term lending

Category	Short-Term Lending	Medium-Term Lending	Long-Term Lending
Maturity Range	Less than 12 months	1 to 5 years	More than 5 years
Typical Use	Used for temporary or seasonal financing needs	Generally used for ongoing financing of investments in machinery and equipment or facilities for short-term projects, but not major capital expenditures. This type of financing can also meet cyclical needs as investments of this nature are not expected to generate cash within a short period.	Provides finance for a company's long-term needs. Typically, this credit type will finance the construction of larger capital-intensive projects or major capital expenditures. The cash produced by the new equipment, product, or activity is the primary source of repayment.
Example	A toy manufacturer expects to increase its borrowing needs during the early summer as the company buys raw materials and builds its inventory for the end-of-year holiday season. The money borrowed is then repaid from the cash collected when the goods are sold.	The toy manufacturer also needs to purchase machinery and equipment for the manufacturing process. These assets will have an expected life of 3 to 4 years and contribute to finished goods. Purchase of these assets increases manufacturing capacity, but the funding of the machinery will require matching funding over a 4-year period, either asset based or cash flow based.	As the toy business grows, the company decides to build a new manufacturing plant in a different part of the world. Building a new factory and buying new machinery is a considerable expansion, and to finance this expansion, banks usually will offer long-term financing to be repaid from the revenues generated from the expansion or derived from the new equipment.

The maturities also deliberately correspond to the way corporations choose to finance their businesses and generally include a mix of short-term debt (to be repaid in less than one year), medium-term debt (to be repaid in less than five years), and long-term debt (to be repaid over more than five years).

EXAMPLE

The third pillar of the Basel II Accord mandates what disclosures banks must make to the public, financial markets, and regulators. Disclosures are designed to provide the market and potential counterparties to the bank with an accurate and information picture of the bank's overall risk position. The chief intent behind transparency is to provide counterparties with information they need to price transactions accurately and deal appropriately with their counterparties. Disclosures to the public and regulators are common and often contain a great deal of detail about the bank. Typically, banks disclose the value of loans that mature within various maturity bands, such as within 3 months, up to 1 year, up to 3 years, up to 5 years, up to 15 years, and beyond. These broader disclosures allow counterparties and regulators to better assess the bank's sensitivity to interest rate changes and how these interest rate changes affect the bank's banking book (Section 2.2.1).

4.4.2   Commitment Specification

Banking facilities are further classified as committed or uncommitted.

- *Committed facilities are characterized by formal loan agreements, usually for one year or more.* **Committed facilities** earn a margin for the bank above its own cost of funds and include a facility fee, a commitment fee, and a fee for the amount of the loan the bank has actually extended to the borrower, whether or not the borrower uses the full amount of the loan. The amount of the loan not yet taken by the borrower is referred to as an *undrawn commitment.* The **cost of funds** reflects the prevailing interest rates in the market, the bank's own cost to secure the funds to be lent, and a margin to cover the costs of asset transformation. The **facility fee** is a fee charged by the bank for simply putting the loan into place all the aspects of the program that allows the borrower to borrow the funds if and when needed. The **commitment fee** is the fee the lender charges a borrower for its commitment to make available a line of credit and to guarantee that a loan may be available to the lender at a certain future date, even though the credit in question is not being used at that particular time.

- *Uncommitted facilities are less formal arrangements but often include a facility letter stating that funds would be made available on demand but solely at the lender's discretion.* **Uncommitted facilities** provide a general framework for the terms of the lending without noting the specific contractual terms of that agreement, such as the amount of the loan or its duration. There may be different contractual terms depending on when the facility is used. Uncommitted facilities are short term in nature (often *on demand* or *overdrafts*). Uncommitted facilities are generally cheaper than committed facilities and priced on a margin above the bank's base rate. There may also be an arrangement fee charged at each renewal of the uncommitted facility.

Figure 4.6 outlines the differences between standard bank facilities. A **banker's acceptance** is an example of an uncommitted facility. A banker's acceptance is similar to a postdated check, except that once the bank "accepts" the draft, it becomes obligated to disperse the funds on the date they become due.

A **line of credit** is considered a short-term uncommitted facility. With a line of credit, the borrower is preapproved to draw from the bank funds up to a specified amount on demand. The borrower repays, in whole or in part during the term of the letter of credit, the full amount plus any interest due when the letter expires. The borrower may or may not ever use the credit line, but is charged by the bank for making it available.

Both lines of credit and banker's acceptances are generally considered short-term methods of financing characterized by a three- or six-month time horizon.

Figure 4.6   **Committed and uncommitted facilities**

Uncommitted Facility
- Less formal arrangement
- At lender's discretion
- Usually short term in nature
- Often "on demand"
- Generally cheaper than a committed facility
- *Example: line of credit*

Committed Facility
- Formal loan agreement
- Lender is legally bound to extend the credit to the borrower when the borrower so requires
- Usually for one year or more
- Borrower charged to ensure loan is available at future date
- *Example: mortgage loan*

Banks can also generate income through compensating balances. When a bank extends a committed or an uncommitted facility, it may require the borrower to deposit certain amounts of money with the lending bank for the duration of the loan commitment. These funds are referred to as **compensating balances**. What this arrangement does is to provide the bank with funds to be used for other purposes, allowing it to earn a return on those funds in excess of the costs of the services being provided by the borrower. The borrower may also receive a credit for the compensating balance through an offset of the fee for the banking facility.

Compensating balances serve several functions:
- They serve as collateral in case the borrower defaults.
- They reduce the bank's interest expenses. Since the deposit usually carries a very low interest rate, sometimes as low as zero percent, it allows the bank to secure additional deposits effectively at a very low cost, providing the bank with cheap financing through low-cost deposits. Borrowing at a low rate and lending at a higher rate increase the bank's potential earnings.

- Compensating balances also indirectly increase the interest the borrower pays to the bank and are consequently considered as a charge to the borrower in the same nature as interest is charged for the extension of a loan.

EXAMPLE

GammaBank has extended a five-year, USD 1,000,000 loan to Growth Corporation. The loan carries an interest rate of 10% per year; in the first year, the bank would receive USD 100,000 in interest income. However, the bank requires Growth Corporation to deposit 5% of the amount borrowed into an account with the bank that pays 0% interest. Thus, the bank effectively only lends USD 950,000 to Growth Corporation, but receives USD 100,000 in interest, which can be calculated as an effective interest rate of 10.53%. Taking this example even further, Growth Corporation will also be charged an additional fee by the bank to set up the loan facility. In this case, GammaBank lent the funds to Growth Corporation and charged Growth Corporation 10% interest on the loan, earned 10.53%, and collected set-up fees. Additionally, the bank can channel the USD 50,000 in deposit to generate additional revenue.

4.4.3   Loan Purpose

The use of loan proceeds can vary widely and can impact a lender's credit decision. A loan used to finance inventory, to purchase equipment used in the production process, or to address some other type of working capital need may be viewed as facilitating the normal course of business or perhaps making possible the exploitation of a perceived strategic opportunity. Typically, there is little credit quality decline inherent in these transactions. Loans, however, can also be used to buy back stock, to finance a leveraged buy-out, to pay a dividend, or to fund other shareholder-friendly activities. These loans are typically considered riskier, as they tend to benefit shareholders at the expense of creditors.

4.4.4   Repayment Source

Another way to distinguish between the different loan types is to consider how the borrower generates funds to repay the loan.

Asset conversion loans, also known as self-liquidating loans, are loans that are repaid by converting the asset that is used to collateralize the loan into cash. The assets used for this type of loan are typically inventory and work in progress (partly completed job[s]). The asset conversion loan is normally considered short-term or temporary financing with the asset later being sold on credit terms or cash that ultimately will be used to repay the loan. Note that these loans are different from asset-based loans in that the asset used as collateral is being sold to repay the loan versus being used simply as collateral for the loan. Agricultural loans (see Section 4.5.1) are asset conversion loans.

EXAMPLE

The small swimwear manufacturer from the previous example decides to build a new manufacturing plant. To finance the plant, it borrows from GammaBank against the property itself (mortgage). To purchase machines and other equipment used for manufacturing, the company pledges these as collateral.

With *cash flow-based loans*, a bank provides funds that are repaid with the cash flow from the company's operations. With *asset-based loans*, a bank extends a loan after a specific asset or a combination of assets are pledged as collateral, or security (see section below on collateral), to cover the loan. Collateral for this type of loan typically includes inventory, machinery and equipment, leases, furniture and fixtures, or other tangible assets.

EXAMPLE

The small swimwear manufacturer from the previous example decides to build a new manufacturing plant. To finance the plant, it borrows from GammaBank against the machinery used to manufacture swimwear as well as against the property itself (mortgage).

4.4.5   Collateral Requirements

Assets pledged by a borrower to secure a loan are called **collateral** (or security). Collateral is used by the bank to safeguard its capital and acts as insurance in case the borrower cannot repay its loan. In the event of default, the bank has the option of accepting the collateral as full or partial repayment of the loan's principal, accrued interest, fees and costs, and expenses. As such, collateral plays a major role in a bank's lending policies—it reduces the potential loss the bank can suffer when a borrower defaults. Collateral can come in many forms. Cash is the most obvious and most secure form of collateral since it is already liquid. Property is the most common form of collateral but is unpredictable because its value fluctuates with market conditions and the lender may or may not have access to it. Mortgage lending uses real estate as the collateral for the loan against the property (Section 4.5.8).

EXAMPLE

GammaBank lends money to a customer to buy a house, and the customer agrees to put the house up as collateral. If the customer does not make loan payments as scheduled, the bank would take legal action to become the owner of the house. Assuming the bank prevailed, it would then attempt to sell the house and use the proceeds to repay the loan. Here, the house serves as collateral for the mortgage loan.

Although the borrower gives the bank the keys to the house because he or she cannot repay the loan, the borrower may still have a legal obligation to repay the debt. The bank may be able to sell the collateral, but the borrower could continue to remain liable for any amount that the bank does not recover on the loan when it disposes of the home according to the rules laid out either in the loan agreement or the laws regulating this process.

From the bank's perspective, the collateral should mitigate (or eliminate) the effect of the borrower's default. Historically, it was a good bet that the value of the collateral would turn out to be greater than the amount of the loan. However, that assumption was proven to be inaccurate in recent years, particularly during the global credit crisis that began in 2006 and that has resulted in material losses for banks around the world. When a home is worth more than the loan, the borrower is less likely to simply "walk away" from the property, abandoning both the property the borrower owns and the borrower's contractual obligation to make payments on the mortgage. Rationally, walking away from a house that is worth more than the mortgage does not make sense. However, if the home is worth less than the loan itself, the borrower could have an incentive to walk away from the property and hand the keys over to the lender, assuming that walking away from the property extinguishes the debt that the borrower owes to the lender fully and completely. However, to preclude this from happening, lenders include in their agreements with the borrowers provisions that extend the liability of the borrower to any proportion of the loan that the bank has not been able to recover from selling the collateral—the property. The bank's ability to enforce these claims may be complicated if the borrower declares bankruptcy, in which case relevant bankruptcy laws must be considered.

EXAMPLE

Expanding on the previous mortgage example, GammaBank lends USD 250,000 to the customer to buy a house valued at USD 300,000. This would indicate a loan-to-value (LTV) ratio of 83% (USD 250,000/USD 300,000). Generally, the LTV ratio serves as one indicator of default likelihood: The higher the LTV ratio, the higher the risk of possible default (the customer has less to lose by "walking away"). In this example, if the customer does not make payments on the mortgage and walks away from the loan, the bank then becomes the owner of a property valued at more than the loan. The borrower may give back the keys, but this does not mean he or she is no longer responsible for the debt in certain jurisdictions. The borrower could be liable for any amount of the loan not recovered by the bank in the resale of the home plus any expenses incurred by the bank to take back the home from the borrower (in the United States, this process of taking back the home by the bank is called foreclosure) and to resell it. Walking away from the property even when the loan is valued less than the property could be a loss to the borrower.

The bank also has to consider the changes in the value of the collateral and must ensure that the collateral will retain as much value as possible in the event of default.

EXAMPLE

Continuing with the previous mortgage loan example, initially, the LTV was 83%. Due to a decline in the value of the property, the value has dropped to USD 225,000. The borrower still owes USD 250,000 on the loan and the LTV has increased to 111%, indicating increased risk of default. The USD 250,000 loan is collateralized with a property valued at USD 225,000. The borrower now has more of an incentive to "walk away" from the USD 250,000 loan. If the borrower decides to simply give up and not make any further loan payments, the bank will foreclose on the property and become the legal owner, even though the property is worth less than the loan. In that case the bank would sell the property and seek to recover the difference between the proceeds it receives from the sale of the property and what is due on the loan from the defaulting borrower. The borrower could remain liable to repay that proportion of the loan that the bank has not been able to recover from selling the property. The extent of the borrower's liability even after the borrower walks away from the property and the property is sold ultimately depends on the contract between the borrower and the lender and reflects relevant laws, regulations, and commercial conventions.

The LTV ratio is a very important indicator for lending and credit risk management. Historically, banks very rarely underwrote loans when the LTV exceeded 75–80% unless there was considerable collateral support or the borrower—due to superior financial strength, access to funds, and capital in general—presented limited risk to the lender. Pledges of very high quality collateral, such as government bonds (e.g., U.S. Treasuries or similar) or deposits with the bank, would often make higher LTV ratio loans possible.

LTV serves as a critical benchmark in residential and commercial real estate lending (see Sections 4.5.6 and 4.5.8). Banks and other real estate lenders have long established LTV-based lending rules. Until recently, these rules rarely allowed lending above the 80% LTV threshold that had emerged as a gold standard of lending.

In recent years, however, financial innovation led to the creation of ingenious mortgage products designed to help individuals who could not afford to purchase a home. One of the products was a mortgage with an LTV in excess of 100% and, in certain cases, up to 125%. Essentially, the homeowner could purchase a property for USD 300,000 and finance the purchase with a mortgage of USD 360,000 (an LTV ratio of 120%), allowing the newly minted homebuyer to spend funds (USD 60,000) refurbishing a dilapidated building and improving the value of the home by adding features such as master bedrooms, bathrooms, decks, and landscaped outside areas, including pools. Lenders were willing to extend such highly risky but inventive mortgages because they allowed individuals to acquire homes they otherwise could not have afforded. This approach assumes that home prices never went down, and they counted on the LTV ratio decline to properly collateralize the loan.

The additional funds designated for repairs and improvements were expected to increase the value of the homes and in many cases banks often relied on the home-owner's own labor, called *sweat equity* to make the improvements. Lenders speculated that sweat equity would decrease the very high LTV ratio to a more acceptable range (roughly in the 90-100% range), reducing the inherent riskiness of such highly levered loans. Additionally, lenders expected that homeowners who made considerable invest-ments of sweat equity in their homes would be less likely to default on their loans, assuming this investment would further reduce the risks inherent in these loans.

In the United States and elsewhere, these products became very popular in areas where the real estate prices were high and many individuals were priced out of the market. Because most homeowners used the extra funds to increase the value of the build-ing, these products were reasonably successful. Needless to say, there were homeowners who spent the funds on consumption (new cars, excessive spending, etc.) and did not make home improvement investments. The more aggressive lenders provided these loans to individuals with the expectation that the LTV ratio would decline, not because of investments in the property made by the homeowners, but rather due to the overall appreciation of real estate values. As real estate prices were increasing in areas where prices were already high, many potential homeowners—and lenders—believed that as long as the real estate values were appreciating, it would be an innovative way to "have your cake and eat it too," effectively monetizing on yet-to-be-realized price appreciation.

Lenders went even further and promoted these loans to potential borrowers who were considered to be at high risk of default, termed *subprime*, due to either previous defaults or foreclosures or otherwise inadequate financial strength. Reaching out to this high-risk segment magnified the innate risk of the high LTV mortgages. Now, not only were lenders willing to lend against expected price appreciation on property, lenders were also willing to assume the added risk of a high-risk borrower.

When real estate prices started to collapse in 2006, many borrowers who used high LTV homes to acquire buildings in anticipation of future price appreciation suddenly found the value of the house eroding, causing the LTV to increase to dangerously high levels. Buyers who were now forced to sell their homes to cover their mortgage indebtness were not able to sell their property in a rapidly deteriorating housing market at a price that exceeded their investment, the original purchase price plus value-increasing improvements. In many cases, the houses would only sell with significant price concessions. Lenders became understandably very nervous and began to restrict these high-risk loans. When contractually and legally possible, they started to demand the homeowner reduce their LTV. Many homeowners—particularly those who other-wise carried a high risk of potential default—simply could not comply with the lender's request to bring the LTV values into a more acceptable range. Lacking both the finan-cial capacity and ability to make payments, an increasing number of borrowers were forced to walk away from, default on, their home loan and in some areas the market value of the house might have been 50% of the value of the outstanding loan—an LTV ratio of 200%.

4.4.6   Covenant Requirements

Covenants are one-way commitments or promises by the obligor to honor an obligation. The essential purpose of covenants in the financial marketplace is to attempt to prevent events and/or processes that could result in a potential deterioration in the borrower's financial or business condition.

EXAMPLE

GammaBank requires the borrower—a construction company—to build no more than 10 houses on a tract of land. The reason the bank may require such a covenant is if it is concerned that the company would overextend itself and then be unable to repay the loan.

A NOTE ON BANKRUPTCY

As noted in the previous examples, it is possible a borrower could simply walk away from a loan and the lender would then become the property/collateral owner. Most countries have a bankruptcy process within their legal systems that the lender must follow in order to take possession and ownership of a loan's collateral. A bankruptcy proceeding is a legal process that requires the lender to follow certain legal rules and procedures in order to become the legal owner of the collateral. Simply missing a loan payment, for example, will not allow the lender to commence a bankruptcy proceeding. The lender in most loan contracts is required to provide a *notice of default* to the borrower and to give the borrower a certain period of time to "cure" the default. Only after these and other procedures are followed will the lender be allowed to go before a legal court to ask for possession of the collateral.

There are two categories of bankruptcies: business and consumer. The rules pertaining to each vary by country with the processes to be followed in each very different. In the United States, business bankruptcies can follow a number of different formats. There are two primary types of corporate bankruptcies:

1. Chapter 11 bankruptcy allows a firm to reorganize its indebtedness under the direction of a court with the objective of allowing the company to remain in business after it "emerges" from bankruptcy with a court-approved plan to repay its debts.
2. Chapter 7 bankruptcy occurs when the firm simply does not have the ability to remain in business and under a court's direction will liquidate its assets and cease to exist.

A consumer bankruptcy is fundamentally different from a business bankruptcy. In most legal systems, the courts will attempt to protect the consumer as much as possible during the process while attempting to develop a plan to allow the consumer to cancel its debts or repay them at a materially reduced percentage of the overall debt outstanding. This differs from most commercial bankruptcy proceedings where the court works with the main objective of protecting the company's debtors.

In either a business or consumer bankruptcy, the resulting consequences to the bankrupt party are usually severe. A Chapter 11 business bankruptcy usually means the company will find borrowers reluctant to deal with it. While the company is in a Chapter 11-type bankruptcy, it continues its operations and may emerge with a healthier business. After bankruptcy, many business are likely to have difficulty obtaining any type of credit well into the future and, if it is able to do so, the credit facility will be at a higher interest rate. A consumer declaring bankruptcy will find it virtually impossible to obtain credit in the near future, will have to wait years to be considered for a loan by a lender, and will have to demonstrate an excellent payment record between the bankruptcy and the loan application.

In other parts of the world, the bankruptcy process for businesses more closely resembles Chapter 7 proceedings. The company under bankruptcy proceedings is managed by a trustee on behalf of the court to the benefit of the creditors. The trustee seeks to pay off all the company's liabilities by selling all its assets and redistributing the proceeds to the creditors following a strict order of priority. The creditors who have the highest order of priority receive payments first. These creditors usually include the employees for unpaid salaries and wages, the government for unpaid taxes and fees, and those creditors that hold a security interest—collateral—in the company's assets. Generally, the higher the order of priority or the better the collateral, the more likely it becomes that the creditor will get paid.

Covenants are a control mechanism and typically restrict or affect the borrower's ability to manage its business. For example, as a condition of loan approval, a lender may require that the borrower agree to establish a board committee consisting of individuals possessing certain skill sets to oversee a specific project for which a loan is given.

Covenants may also include additional features such as caps on dividend payments to shareholders or limits on owner and management compensation. Covenants may also restrict other corporate actions and may prevent a company from disposing of certain assets or to require the company to purchase particular assets.

EXAMPLE

After suffering significant losses, Fly-By-Night Airline was forced to arrange for a credit facility through its banks that would allow it to meet its cash flow needs. The borrowing (credit) ceiling was set at GBP 350 million, and covenants were agreed to by the airline as a part of the financial deal. The lender required the covenants to monitor the progress of the company to ensure that company management's decisions would not compromise the value of the lender's investment.

One of the covenants allowed Fly-By-Night to pay dividends to its shareholders only if the company could achieve eight consecutive profitable quarters. Another covenant linked the amount of the credit facility to the airline's assets, which, at the time of the agreement, were valued at GBP 450 million. One year later, the covenant that linked the airline's assets to what it could draw on from the credit facility became an issue when it was determined that the aircraft it owned were worth about GBP 50 million less than originally estimated because of an over-supply of planes in the marketplace.

Fly-By-Night's borrowing line was reduced from the original GBP 350 million to GBP 300 million.

However, throughout the year the airline also reported losses of approximately GBP 10 million each quarter. Because the losses reduced the airline's assets, its borrowing ability, as defined under the covenant, fell even further, to around GBP 260 million. Because of the banks' covenants, Fly-By-Night's continued losses reduced its ability to obtain necessary funding. Fly-By-Night's management was unable to secure additional funding to support its operations and was forced to seek financing for its daily operations elsewhere. Given its history, entering into a new credit facility proved to be difficult for Fly-By-Night. With limited options, Fly-By-Night was eventually acquired by a larger airline.

The previous example shows how covenants are an important tool banks use to limit their counterparty credit risk. It is also crucial that the borrower sufficiently understands and thinks through the covenants it enters.

EXAMPLE

Covenants come in many different forms. In late November 2008, the U.S. government provided emergency financing to Citigroup, the bank with the largest assets at that time in the United States. Citigroup held USD 2 trillion in assets at the end of the second quarter of 2008. As a result of the financial crisis, Citigroup was forced to make several substantial write-downs on its equity capital due to considerable exposure to highly complex financial products—collateralized debt obligations or CDOs—that became difficult to value. Problems with valuation originated with the unrealized shortcomings of the complex mathematical models banks designed to value and create the complex financial instruments. A dramatic increase in defaults of both commercial and residential mortgages in the United States signaled the models were failing. Complex financial instruments were built on the cash flows generated by residential and commercial mortgages. The risks in these instruments were packaged in various financial instruments and sold to investors with specific and distinctly identifiable risk appetites. As the credit crisis intensified, real estate prices declined and mortgage defaults skyrocketed. The information necessary to value these complex securities became increasingly difficult to acquire and progressively less reliable. As a result, trading in the complex securities came to a grinding halt, further impeding the ability of the mathematical models to predict or correctly determine the value of the CDOs. Existing models were unable to integrate the material changes in circumstances and market realities. The interdependence between the mathematical models, the ability to trade using the values provided by the mathematical models, and the valuation that required both access to high-quality data and trading information led to an unprecedented and unexpected collapse of the market.

The difficulty in valuing CDOs was in large part the reason Citigroup was forced to make considerable write-downs on these troubled assets—approximately USD 65 billion between the second half of 2007 and the third quarter of 2008—and seek emergency funding from the U.S. government. In November 2008, the U.S. government provided financing to Citigroup in several stages with different parameters: an investment of USD 20 billion in the bank as preferred stock with an 8% dividend and partial protection against the possibility of unusually large losses on approximately USD 306 billion of loans and securities backed by residential and commercial real estate that

Citigroup owns. To receive this financing, the U.S. government demanded that Citigroup comply with covenants that imposed strict restrictions on executive compensation and limited Citigroup's dividend to USD 0.01 per quarter for the next three years.

4.4.7   Loan Repayment

Loan products are also differentiated by the method of repayment. The stipulated payments that borrowers make to the lenders throughout the loan period—from the day the loan is funded until the day the loan is repaid in full—include both the contractual interest payments and the repayment of the amount borrowed, or the **principal**.

Interest rates on loans can be either fixed or floating. In a **fixed interest rate loan**, the interest rate charged on the loan does not change during the maturity of the loan. In a **floating interest rate loan**, the interest charged on the loan is tied to or follows a base rate, set by an independent third party, or an index. The bank will add a charge on top of the base rate or index to earn a profit.

EXAMPLE

On January 1, GammaBank extends a floating rate EUR 100,000 loan with a three-month maturity to Centre Corporation. The monthly interest rate is tied to an index and is set on the first day each of the following three months following the issuance of the loan.

The index on January 1 was 1.25%; on February 1, it increased to 1.50%; and by March 1, it was 1.75%. The monthly interest payments on this loan are as follows:

January	EUR 100,000 * 1%	=	EUR 1,000
February	EUR 100,000 * 1.50%	=	EUR 1,500
March	EUR 100,000 * 1.75%	=	EUR 1,750

Three general approaches are common for repayment: the sinking-fund amortization, the level amortization, and the balloon payment.

Figures 4.7 to 4.9 show the repayment characteristics of a loan with the same principal but using the three principal repayment structures. For simplicity, the loan in the example is a three-year loan with monthly payments (36 monthly payments). The principal is EUR 100,000 and the interest rate is fixed at 5%.

Under **sinking-fund amortization**, Figure 4.7, the borrower pays a predetermined amount of the principal as well as interest on the outstanding balance of the loan. Initially, the payments on simple amortization loans are large, but as the principal is reduced, the interest payment accruing on the outstanding balance is reduced. If the loan is a fixed-rate loan, the proportion of the loan repayment that reflects the interest payments will decline over the life of the loan; if it is a floating-rate loan, the interest payments will fluctuate.

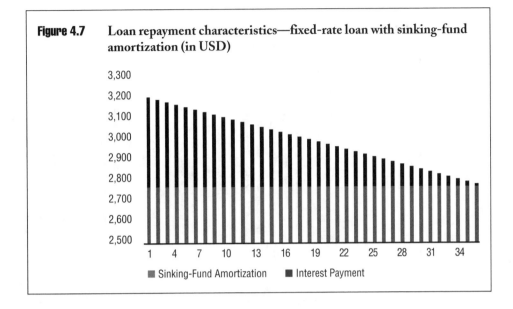

Figure 4.7 Loan repayment characteristics—fixed-rate loan with sinking-fund amortization (in USD)

Under **level amortization**, Figure 4.8, the borrower, at each payment date, pays a predetermined amount of the principal, as well as interest on the outstanding balance of the loan. The payments for a fixed-rate loan do not change over time: the amount to be paid is the same each month, but the proportion of interest payment and principal repayment does change. Initially, the proportion of interest payments is considerably larger than the principal repayment, but over time, the proportion of principal repayment increases. With a floating-rate loan, the interest payments will change as the index or base rate is reset, and the amount to be paid changes, requiring the level payments to change to accommodate the interest rate changes.

The distinguishing feature of **balloon payments**, Figure 4.9, is that there is a large payment at maturity, which usually includes the repayment of the principal. A large balloon payment structure can also include all the accumulated interest on the loan, but the borrower typically pays interest on the outstanding loan periodically and repays the principal fully at maturity. In the floating-rate balloon loans, the payments will be determined by the index and change over time.

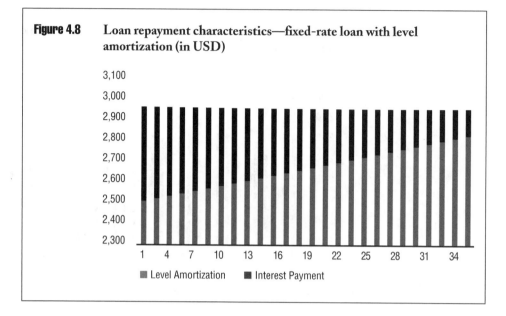

Figure 4.8 Loan repayment characteristics—fixed-rate loan with level amortization (in USD)

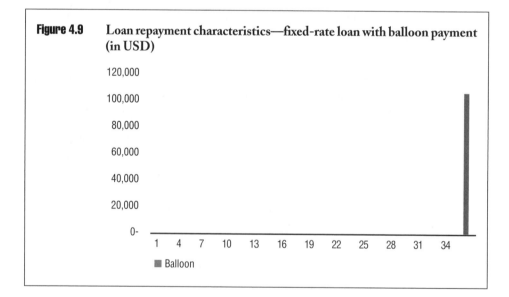

Figure 4.9 Loan repayment characteristics—fixed-rate loan with balloon payment (in USD)

4.5   TYPES OF CREDIT PRODUCTS

This section explains the most common commercial and retail credit products that combine the key credit product characteristics covered in the previous section. The credit products are listed alphabetically.

4.5.1   Agricultural Loans

Agricultural loans support lending for farming and other agricultural production. Clients borrow money to finance the purchase of fixed assets such as land and equipment or to cover their cash-flow requirements for the growing season until the farm has had time to sell its goods. Facilities are generally medium to long term but can also be short term in nature (to finance seed, feed, and cattle for rearing). The type of loans used may range from asset-based to simple revolving facilities.

EXAMPLE

GammaBank provides funds to a farmer for the planting season; the loan is to be repaid after the crop has been harvested and sold. If the farmer delays the sale of crops by storing them in the hopes of achieving a higher market price, the bank would most likely offer additional financing to carry the unsold crops (inventory) over the extended term. Farmers also need to replace or expand upon existing equipment. Increasingly sophisticated, and therefore more expensive, new farming machinery is driving demand for longer-term loans, giving the farmer a longer time period to pay off the loan.

4.5.2   Asset-Based or Secured Lending

Asset-based or *secured lending* involves a bank or commercial finance company lending specifically against the borrower's assets. Commercial bankers will generally lend against inventory (also called stock, stock-in-trade, or items for sale) and receivables (factoring). Asset-based loans generally require a company to be able to repay a loan out of operational cash flow. Thus, the value and marketability of the collateral is important. Asset-based lending can be extended to both commercial and retail customers.

EXAMPLE

Growth Corporation is a small manufacturer, with almost 60% of its assets in receivables and inventory and an additional 35% in fixed assets. It turns to GammaBank to see how it can use its inventory and receivables to raise the financing necessary to support future growth. With sales almost doubling in the last year, Growth Corporation appears to be a strong candidate for asset-based lending. With so much of its assets tied up in inventory and receivables, this company is also a great potential client for factoring. Clearly, factoring is an alternative that GammaBank has offered Growth Corporation. However, to sustain this trend in sales growth, the company is likely to experience serious cash shortages. As with all companies, it must continue to manufacture its products, and it will need cash to purchase the raw materials and pay its employees. Rapidly growing companies also need to provide funding for their investments. Repayment of the loan could be tied to the sale of inventory, one of its largest assets. Asset-based financing would increase the company's interest expense, but it would also provide the cash needed to support sales growth.

4.5.3 Automobile Loans

Automobile or **car loans** come either as **direct automobile loans** that finance the purchase of a car between the bank and the customer in which the bank secures the loan using the car as collateral or as **indirect automobile loans,** which are loans arranged between an automobile dealer and the customer. In an indirect automobile loan, the customer applies for a loan through the dealer, who then forwards the borrower's information to the lending bank. In some instances, this type of loan is thought to allow the borrower (automobile purchaser) the ability to obtain a lower interest rate on the loan if the dealer and the bank have an arrangement. The bank may offer a lower interest rate to customers introduced by the dealer.

Automobile loans are predominately retail loan products. However, in some cases, banks provide fleet financing for companies that need to build up a fleet of cars—such as distribution and transportation companies. In these cases, the financing is considered commercial and is usually priced at a lower rate than a retail or individual automobile loan.

EXAMPLE

To increase its distribution network, Growth Corporation decides to acquire a fleet of vehicles that it finances using a program provided by GammaBank. The bank lends against the vehicles—they serve as the collateral—and instead of committing a large proportion of its cash reserves, Growth Corporation extends the payments for these cars over several years.

4.5.4 Commercial Paper

Commercial paper is short-term, unsecured notes generally issued by large and financially strong companies. A **note** is a bond with very short maturity. The funds are generally used to purchase inventory or manage a company's everyday capital needs. Commercial paper is considered a low-risk or safe investment, and the return on this investment is nominal. The commercial paper market is primarily used by large, publicly traded corporations.

EXAMPLE

A major activity of General Motors Acceptance Corporation ("GMAC") is the dealer and consumer financing of purchases of General Motors' vehicles (indirect and direct automobile financing, respectively). GMAC issues commercial paper to raise the funds that finance the dealers' purchases of inventory and to finance customers' purchases of GM cars from the dealer. This arrangement allows the automobile dealer to finance its inventory of cars while it sells them to consumers; in effect, this is a short-term loan. Short-term notes (or paper) are frequently used by mature companies and purchased by an investor who is interested in earning a nominal but relatively safe return.

4.5.5   Factoring

Factoring is a service that a specialist financial institution or a bank offers to help a company meet its cash requirements and reduce its potential credit losses. There are different types of factoring approaches that can be used separately or in combination. The different factoring approaches all assure the company of earlier receipt of cash payment. The advantage of factoring is that the company is better able to manage its assets, particularly its cash position. The major disadvantage is that the company will not receive the full amount of the money due, as the bank or the organization providing the factoring services charges a percentage of the assets as a fee for providing the service, typically called a *haircut*. The following is a listing of the various types of factoring services available to companies:

- *Maturity factoring.* The bank will effectively take over the company's receivables, work to collect on them, and take a commission from whatever is collected. The company receives the funds when due on the invoice, minus the commission.
- *Finance factoring.* The bank will advance funds to the company using the goods and services to be produced with the funds as collateral.
- *Discount factoring.* The bank will advance funds to the company, usually representing no more than 85% of the receivables, and then take full responsibility for collecting the funds owed.
- *Undisclosed factoring.* The bank will take full responsibility for the invoices due, pay the company up to 85% of that amount, and then appoint the company its agent to collect the invoices. In this arrangement, outsiders do not perceive the company as needing the funding, and it appears as if the company is conducting its business in a normal manner.

Among the various factoring arrangements, different parties are exposed to credit risk if a creditor defaults. If the bank takes over collection on the receivables and assumes full responsibility for the potential losses, then the bank bears the risk of the losses. In this case, the bank has a major incentive to collect the funds.

In the case of maturity and finance factoring, the bank does not assume full responsibility for the potential losses; these losses continue to be borne by the company who sold the receivables to the bank. However, in the case of discount and undisclosed factoring, the bank assumes full responsibility.

In discount and undisclosed factoring, the risk of collecting payment is transferred to the factoring entity. In return, the company selling the receivables ensures its cash flow and eliminates its credit risk at a cost of reducing its potential profitability.

EXAMPLE

This example combines multiple factoring types.

Growth Corporation needs to improve its cash flow and quickly raise cash, so it enters into a factoring relationship with GammaBank whereby, at the end of each month, it agrees to sell its invoices to the bank (representing approximately USD 250,000). The bank agrees to buy the invoices at a 2% discount (i.e., for each USD 100 in invoices, the bank pays the company USD 98). In addition, the bank is willing to offer immediate financing on the invoices by advancing 85% of the amount owed. By selling the USD 250,000 invoices at a 2% discount, the company receives USD 245,000 million, and the bank advanced 85%, or USD 208,250, of the total amount due. The remaining USD 36,750 is paid to the bank for collection services. Selling the invoices improved Growth Corporation's cash flow and, in turn, earned the bank a monthly profit.

4.5.6   Home Equity Credit Lines and Home Equity Loans

Home equity credit allows homeowners to borrow against the value of the property in a way similar to mortgages (see Section 4.5.8 for a discussion on mortgages.) Generally, there are two different types of home equity credits.

Home equity credit lines are personal revolving lines of credit (see Section 4.5.11 on revolving lines of credit) collateralized by the borrower's property. The bank issuing the home equity loan limits the amount of the loan to a certain percentage of the equity the homeowner has in the home. Loan to value (LTV), the ratio of the value of the property to the amount of money borrowed (see Section 4.4.5), is an important analytical tool to determine a home equity loan. The holder may draw down on the home equity loan at any time during its term up to the amount of the line of credit. Interest on the loan is usually tied to a major index such as the U.S. prime rate or LIBOR (London Interbank Offer Rate), plus a set interest percent.

A home equity credit line is different from a mortgage. A home equity credit line allows the homeowner to borrow up to a certain limit that reflects the value of the home and the existing mortgage on the home. These credit lines offer the homeowner the convenience of on-demand financing, essentially tapping the equity built up over time in the home in exchange for cash. Many compare these lines to withdrawing a deposit from the bank.

Home equity loans also tap the equity built up in a home. A home equity loan pays out—up front—the maximum allowable amount determined by the value of the home and any existing mortgages.

Home equity credits—both credit lines and loans—can be secured through second mortgages. In case of foreclosure or default, the first mortgage will first be satisfied from the disposition of the foreclosed property. After the first mortgage has been satisfied, any remaining funds are allocated to the second mortgage. This makes a loan secured by a second mortgage considerably more risky than a first mortgage. Due to this added risk, many lenders restrict the amount borrowed against home equity to 80% of the property's value, less other existing mortgages. The combination of two or more mortgages encumbering the same property may lead to potential problems for the homeowner if payments are not made on the mortgages. Nonpayment of a mortgage starts the foreclosure process, which legally transfers the ownership of the property to the lender to satisfy the unpaid balances on the mortgage in question.

In recent years, particularly in areas where real estate prices appreciated precipitously, many home equity credits were extended above the 80% LTV—up to 100% and even 120%. Some of the problems that lenders experienced when the real estate prices started to erode are similar to those that were described at the end of Section 4.4.5.

4.5.7 Leasing

Leasing allows an individual or a firm (called the *lessee* in leasing transactions) the right to use an asset that it does not own. In exchange for the right to use an asset, the lessees will make regular contractual payment(s) to the lessor. The *lessor* owns the asset and provides the lessee the right to use the asset

Leases are both retail and commercial products. As a retail product, leases are often used to finance cars (automobiles) and other expensive consumer products. Retail leases offer flexibility over the time lease payments may be made and may even offer lower payments that fit with the lessee's ability to pay. For example, the longer the lease term, the lower the payment made on the lease; however, the longer the term on the lease, the more interest payments the lessee will pay.

As a commercial product, leases are widely used to finance expensive equipment. One of the main reasons for this is that leasing does not require the large capital outlay required to purchase the equipment. This approach is especially beneficial to small and/or rapidly growing firms, where access to cash and the availability of capital may be limited.

Many leasing arrangements include a provision that, at the end of the lease, the lessee has the right, but not the obligation, to purchase the leased asset at a price negotiated or set when the lease is first signed. This option provides considerable flexibility to the lessee, and may be particularly useful to finance the acquisition of equipment that does not become quickly obsolete. In those instances, the lessee at the end of the lease simply returns the equipment to the lessor, who then must determine what to do with the "old" equipment. The lessee can then negotiate the acquisition of newer equipment.

EXAMPLE

Growth Corporation has been considering purchasing a new telecommunications and computer network infrastructure system for its rapidly growing operations. Currently, it does not have the cash or the capital to pay for the expense of buying the system outright. Additionally, the company is concerned about the historically rapid decline in the value of communications systems such as the one being considered for acquisition, and the company is not confident that the system will meet its needs several years in the future.

The company faces a choice: It can purchase the communications system outright for USD 150,000 or enter into a lease.

- If the purchase is financed through a loan from the bank, the bank would mandate interest payments as well as the repayment of the principal, of USD 150,000. Depending on the repayment structure, the company could face monthly payments that include both repayment of the loan and payment of interest on the loan. For a three-year loan at 8% annual interest rate, the monthly payments that include both interest payment and principal are around USD 4,700.
- If the purchase is financed through a lease from the bank, the bank would mandate payments that include interest payment as well as partial repayment of the principal. Depending on how the lease is structured, the company could face monthly payments and have the option to purchase the equipment at the end of the lease. If the bank mandates the purchase of the equipment at the end of three years for USD 80,000, then the monthly cash flows at an 8% interest rate would be around USD 2,700.

Figure 4.10 shows the size of the cash flows for both alternatives.

Since the purchase price of the equipment at the end of the lease will include the delayed repayment of the cost of the system, the lease payments are less than comparable payments on a loan. Lower regular cash payments, coupled with the option of buying the equipment at the end of the lease—further delaying the cash outflows—make leases an attractive alternative for a company such as this.

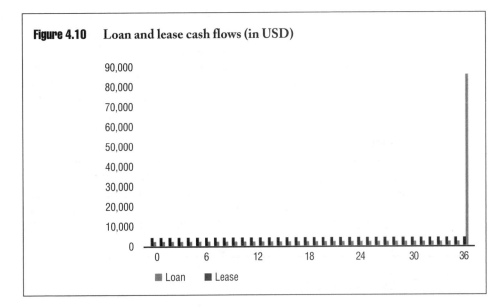

Figure 4.10   Loan and lease cash flows (in USD)

Growth Corporation ultimately decides to lease the communications system from GammaBank for three years. Growth Corporation will have the use of the system for three years and in return will pay a monthly fee to GammaBank. If at the end of the three-year period the communications system does not meet the needs of the company, Growth Corporation does not have to purchase the system and can simply give it back to GammaBank and invest in a new system that better fits its needs. Also, if the system dropped in value, that problem would not be handled by Growth Corporation, but by GammaBank, since it is the bank that owns the equipment. In this case leasing offers a very good business solution, given Growth Corporation's limited access to capital and its concerns about the future viability of the communications system.

In general, there is no ready answer to whether a company or a person should purchase or lease. The factors to consider are numerous and highly individual. Even after a careful analysis, the final decision may rest with the company's or individual's simple business judgment, rather than be the result of a financial calculation.

4.5.8   Mortgages

A **mortgage** is a financial arrangement that enables a borrower to acquire a real estate asset and to use the real estate as collateral for the debt. Mortgages are extended to both commercial and retail customers. The real estate being purchased is used as collateral or "security" for the loan.

Mortgages can be divided into commercial and residential mortgages. **Commercial mortgages** predominantly finance office buildings, factories, and any type of real estate that is used for business or industrial purposes. The main users of commercial mortgages are businesses that consider this as an advantageous source of financing because of the lower rate the bank offers in exchange for applying the real estate being financed as collateral. **Residential mortgages** exclusively finance purchases of residential real estate, such as houses and apartments.

Almost every jurisdiction in the world offers a security interest in real estate that is, or is highly comparable to, a mortgage. Consequently, different jurisdictional areas' legal and procedural rules and commercial conventions determine the extent of mortgage financing.

EXAMPLE

To support its expansion, Growth Corporation's management decided to purchase a new warehouse facility and retail distribution center. GammaBank provides a USD 5,000,000 mortgage to finance the purchase. In exchange for the loan, Growth Corporation pledges the warehouse as the collateral against the loan. Should Growth Corporation fail to make payments on the mortgage, it may lose the facility to the bank.

4.5.9   Overdraft Facilities

Overdraft facilities allow borrowers to borrow funds in excess of those they have deposited into their checking accounts. Overdraft facilities offer a flexible type of financing, but the interest rate is usually significantly higher than other financing options, making it a relatively expensive option. As deposits are received on the account, they are first applied to any borrowed amount outstanding from the overdraft facility. Once the overdraft is repaid, any remaining funds would then be applied to the borrower's account as a deposit. For the business customer, this can be an efficient (but expensive) way to finance short-term business needs. Overdraft facilities are extended to both commercial and retail customers.

EXAMPLE

Growth Corporation arranges a USD 100,000 overdraft from GammaBank to ensure it is able it to meet its regular expenses on a timely basis. There is no specific purpose stated other than to satisfy working investment requirements (this may include the financing of additional inventory and trade receivables, as well as expense items to be found in the income statement). Growth Corporation can draw down on the USD 100,000 at any time but must first use the funds in its checking account; only then will it be able to access the overdraft facility.

Banks, however, have no real control over whether, when, or for how long the funds are used, so they assume a greater risk in providing overdraft facilities than with a conventional loan. This is accentuated when financially stressed borrowers, with access to overdraft facilities, start to use these facilities as a source of financing, which for a number of reasons increases the bank's exposure as well as credit risk. This is an inherent risk of overdraft facilities.

4.5.10   Project, or Infrastructure, Finance

Project, or **infrastructure, finance** funds long-term infrastructure and industrial projects, usually by combining the resources of several banks or other financial institutions to provide the necessary capital. The project itself provides the security for the loans, and the loans are repaid from the cash flow generated from the project.

EXAMPLE

AcmePower Company produces and sells electricity to customers. Its main power plant is fueled with natural gas. BigGas Company wants to sell its natural gas to AcmePower. The two companies agree to build a pipeline from BigGas Company's gas fields to AcmePower's power plant. The pipeline project is expected to cost hundreds of millions of USD. To finance the project, the two companies turn to a consortium led by GammaBank to provide the necessary development funding. The consortium's underwriting analysis concludes that building the pipeline will take several years, with the pipeline's expected life to be several decades. It also finds that the market for Acme-Power is expected to increase over the years and that BigGas's natural gas will be an important part of allowing AcmePower to expand and service its growing market. The banking consortium agrees to tie the loan's repayment terms to the revenues generated from the pipeline when it begins operating and to delay starting repayment of the loan until the pipeline is built and starts running.

4.5.11   Revolving Lines of Credit

Revolving lines of credit are generally provided to businesses with a temporary or seasonal borrowing requirement (these are considered commercial loans). Credit cards and home equity lines of credit are examples of a retail form of a revolving line of credit.

EXAMPLE

Growth Corporation is quickly expanding and wants to be assured that it has the financing to continue this process. It negotiates a USD 1 million three-year revolving line of credit with Gamma-Bank. During the first year, it draws down USD 550,000 of the loan, which it repays, with interest, by the end of the year. Because it has a commitment from the bank for another two years, it can continue to draw down and repay as often as it likes until it either reaches the USD 1 million loan limit, or the three-year maturity period expires. Each time it draws down and repays that amount, the repaid funds become available for borrowing. For example, when Growth Corporation repaid the USD 550,000, the full USD 1 million was again available for it to use.

Credit card lending is an example of revolving consumer loans and is based on preauthorized lines of credit that can be drawn down as the consumer wishes, either through purchases or cash withdrawals. Credit cards, which are used to access the revolving consumer loans, have one of the highest consumer credit growth rates. The rapid increase in credit card debt has been facilitated by the use of EFTPOS (Electronic Funds Transfer at Point of Sale) and ATM (Automatic Teller Machine) in many countries.

EXAMPLE

Credit cards are ubiquitous in modern life. Initially, credit cards were used as a convenience by executives to pay for corporate travel. Having access to credit cards reduced the need to carry large amounts of cash and reduced the likelihood that executives would be robbed. Soon, credit cards migrated to wider use and today offer consumers immediate and instant access to funds.

The bank extending a revolving line of credit has no real control over whether, when, or for how long the funds are used and assumes a greater risk in providing revolving lines of credit than a conventional loan. When financially stressed borrowers, with access to revolving lines of credit, start to draw on their lines of credit, the bank's exposure and credit risk increase. This is an inherent risk of revolving lines of credit, and this risk is similar to overdraft facilities.

4.5.12   Syndicated Loans

Syndicated loans are loans provided to a borrower through the combined activities of several banks. Banks working together to provide the loan are called a **consortium**. Syndicated loans provide capital to companies when the ability or desire of an individual bank to meet the financing need(s) of the company is insufficient. There are a number of benefits to banks for working as a consortium that include but are not limited to:
- Allowing a bank to participate in a lending transaction where it may not otherwise have the opportunity because of the bank's balance sheet or other constraints
- Allowing a bank to reduce its overall risk exposure for the transaction, as any potential loss will be borne by all the bank consortium members

In a syndicated loan, usually one of the participating banks will act as the agent for the transaction on behalf of all the banks, coordinating their efforts to get the transaction done.

EXAMPLE

Big Sky Builders wants to build the world's tallest building to house apartments and offices. The estimated cost of the project is EUR 4 billion. Big Sky does not have the capital to construct the building, so it decided to contact its bank, GammaBank, for a loan. GammaBank analyzes the transaction, considers it a good project with an above-average chance of success, but does not want to finance the project alone. GammaBank arranges a loan syndication with six other banks to provide the capital for Big Sky Builders' project. Each of the banks will participate in proportion to the risk of the transaction it is willing to take. For example, Construction Bank, the leading bank in the consortium, commits to lending EUR 1.5 billion. The other banks in the syndicate provide the remainder of EUR 2.5 billion for the project. The extent of each bank's participation depends on its ability and willingness to contribute. Money Bank is large, so it commits EUR 1 billion, and the remaining five banks provide EUR 300 million each. Because GammaBank arranged the consortium, it receives compensation for the managerial work it undertook. GammaBank will also earn fees from disbursing payments to the borrower, collecting payments from Big Sky Builders, and distributing payments to the six consortium banks.

The Credit Process and Credit Risk Management

Chapter 5 takes a deeper look at credit risk and the credit process. The first half of this chapter describes the steps of the credit process—how banks generate, evaluate, and monitor loans—and the credit analysis process—how banks evaluate the credits. The second half of Chapter 5 explains how banks treat credit risk and discusses the Basel II Accord's guidelines to measure and manage credit risk.

Chapter Outline

- 5.1 The Credit Process
- 5.2 The Credit Analysis Process
- 5.3 Portfolio Management
- 5.4 Credit Risk and Basel II Accord

Key Learning Points

- The credit process contains several sequential steps, including identifying the credit opportunity, evaluating credits, and monitoring credits on an ongoing basis.
- To analyze the borrower's ability to repay, banks engage in a complex credit analysis process that critically assesses the financial position of the borrower using several different methods and sources of information.
- Banks use various tools to reduce the overall risk of their loan portfolios.
- The Basel II Accord provides three primary approaches to measure the capital a bank has to hold against its loan portfolio: the Standardized, the Foundation Internal Ratings-Based, and the Advanced Internal Ratings-Based Approaches.

Key Terms
- Advanced IRB approach
- Asset-backed securities
- Capacity
- Capital
- Character
- Collateral
- Concentration risk
- Condition
- Credit analysis
- Credit score
- Credit-scoring models
- Cyclical financing
- Expected loss, EL
- Exposure at default, EAD
- Five Cs of credit
- Foundation IRB approach
- Internal ratings-based approaches
- Investment portfolio
- Investor
- Loan agreement
- Loss given default, LGD
- Permanent financing
- Portfolio management
- Prime lending rate
- Probability of default, PD
- Ratings-based system
- Recovery rate, RR
- Seasonal financing
- Securitizing assets
- Standardized Approach
- Temporary financing
- Trade receivables

The Credit Risk Process and Credit Risk Management

5.1 THE CREDIT PROCESS

Credit analysis or credit assessment is the process of assessing risk as measured by a borrower's ability to repay the loan. Within the credit analysis or assessment process, analysts also consider possible recovery in the case of default and evaluate the support collateral and other credit support tools that bear on the bank's final decision to develop a creditor relationship. Having assessed the possibility of repayment, the decision to proceed with a loan is then a commercial one: Is the risk of repayment acceptable, given the exposure to the borrower, and do the terms sufficiently mitigate the bank's risk?

Credit assessment is not an exact science, and no one factor, ratio, or other indicator alone determines if a particular loan is a suitable risk. The banking industry has developed numerous methods to help structure the credit process and improve financial results and profitability. Some methods include internal score cards and facility and borrower ratings; cash flow analysis; computer sensitivity models; and external ratings such as those issued by Moody's Investors Service, Fitch Ratings, and Standard & Poor's. Whatever methods are used, credit analysts must balance all the available information and deliver an objective and well-reasoned opinion of the overall risk associated with a particular loan. Figure 5.1 shows the steps involved in the credit process.

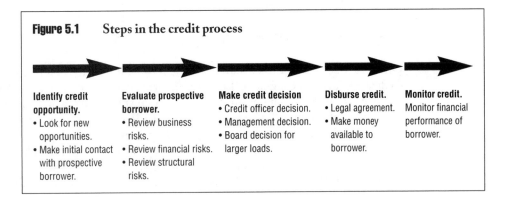

Figure 5.1   **Steps in the credit process**

Identify credit opportunity.	**Evaluate prospective borrower.**	**Make credit decision**	**Disburse credit.**	**Monitor credit.**
• Look for new opportunities. • Make initial contact with prospective borrower.	• Review business risks. • Review financial risks. • Review structural risks.	• Credit officer decision. • Management decision. • Board decision for larger loads.	• Legal agreement. • Make money available to borrower.	Monitor financial performance of borrower.

5.1.1   Identifying the Credit Opportunity

In the credit process, the loan officer or relationship manager initiates contact with the potential borrower. In many banks, the chief function of the loan officer is marketing: to seek out new business opportunities and present them for evaluation.

5.1.2   Credit Evaluation

After a loan officer identifies an opportunity, the officer will gather all required information from the borrower and present it to the credit analyst. The credit analyst then analyzes the creditworthiness of the potential borrower by evaluating the proposed loan type and the potential risks (business risk, financial risk, and structural risk) and then makes a recommendation to proceed with the loan or not and, if so, on what terms (e.g., amount to be lent, the interest rate for the loan, use of collateral or other security, maturity, etc.). The credit analyst's evaluation is often accompanied by qualitative factors, including customer on-site visits, evaluation of the current and the potential for continued business, the availability of collateral to support the credit, and other relevant information.

The credit analyst collects and reviews information about the potential borrower, including:
*   Internal bank records and account performance
*   Historical and current financial accounts (normally data captured in spreadsheets)
*   Management accounts and projections
*   External ratings of the borrower as provided by independent rating firms such as Dun & Bradstreet or similar (smaller businesses), Moody's, S&P, Fitch Ratings (large firms)
*   Company websites and brochures
*   Group structure, ownership, and management information, including information on the board of directors

5.1.3   Credit Decision Making

Often, routine credit decisions are made by the loan officer in conjunction with the credit analyst or by a committee. Loan officers are generally compensated by the number of loans generated. This creates a potential conflict of interest and, therefore, poses a risk when the loan officer makes the loan decision. It is in the interest of a loan officer to underwrite as many loans as possible, potentially ignoring signs that would counter the decision to extend the loan. To guard against this problem, banks implement processes that require all loans to be reviewed by an independent senior manager or credit analyst. Decisions on larger and specialized loans are generally made by senior bank officers or a committee of senior bankers or, in some cases, by the bank's board (the bank's board normally delegates various levels of lending/risk powers to the credit committee and senior bank credit officers).

A core consideration in credit decision making is the pricing of credit—the fees and interest rates the bank charges the borrower. This interest rate may be determined by a loan pricing model that sets the minimum rate the loan should carry and incorporates various pricing factors. Generally, the greater the risk the bank takes when lending to the particular borrower, the higher price—interest rate—it charges. The accuracy of the loan pricing model is essential. In many cases, banks have an extremely narrow margin between the return they earn on loans and the costs of funding, analyzing, and monitoring loans. If the loan is underpriced, then the bank is unlikely to receive sufficient compensation for the risk it assumed. Overpricing the loan has the potential to drive the potential borrower to another lender for the needed funds.

Loan pricing models can be quite complex. Even the simplest of these models take the following factors into consideration:
*   the risk rating of the borrower
*   the bank's underlying funding cost
*   the loan's administrative and processing expenses

The higher the risk of default, the higher the rate the loan should carry. As a result, more-risky borrowers pay higher rates than less-risky borrowers. In many cases, the bank prices the risk in the loan so that as the fortunes of the borrower improve, the price of the loan declines. Some are also structured to penalize borrowers through higher interest rates if their credit quality declines. This type of pricing structure offers the borrower a strong financial incentive and, when correctly used, reduces the risk to the lender. The bank's underlying funding costs reflect the price the bank pays to secure deposits and loans and other bank debt. Maturity and profit margin have considerable influence on the pricing of the loan.

*   Maturity is the date when the principal of the loan must be paid in full. Generally, the longer the maturity of the loan, the higher interest rate the loan carries.
*   Banks profit on the interest rate differential between their assets (loans made by the bank and securities held by the bank) and their liabilities (deposits in the bank and the bank's own debt) (see Section 2.2.4). Both lending and borrowing interest rates are usually set by the market and can be readily captured by an index. In many cases, banks set the price they charge on loans as a markup to an index. The **prime lending rate**—the rate banks charge their best customers—is an example of a common benchmark used as a base rate for a loan with a margin added to enhance risk-adjusted profitability.

Each bank has developed credit decision policies that delineate what types of loans—size, exposure, and business—that need to be signed off or ratified by senior management and/or the bank board committee. Generally, the larger and more risky a loan is, the more likely that the loan passes through several levels of the bank's decision-making hierarchy.

5.1.4   Credit Disbursement

Once the credit request has been approved, the loan agreement is prepared for signature. The **loan agreement** is a legal contract between the bank and the borrower and includes a description of undertakings and understandings, such as the principal, the stated interest rate and its calculation, the schedule of payments and repayments, the use of collateral, covenants, etc. Once the contract is signed, funds are made available to the borrower.

5.1.5   Credit Monitoring

After the credit is underwritten and the funds have been made available to the borrower, the bank continues to monitor the financial performance of the borrower. The contract usually has hard and soft covenants or provisions (Section 4.4.6). An example of a hard covenant is a requirement that the borrower maintains certain key financial ratios throughout the life of the loan. An example of a soft covenant is the requirement that the borrower delivers its financial statements to the lender in a timely manner.

There is a considerable variation with the credit process of banks. Smaller banks may have centralized credit approval, analysis, and administration functions, while others, particularly larger banks, may delegate the authority to a senior banker on a regional level or require that loans in excess of a certain amount be reviewed and approved by a credit committee. Whatever the preferred option or strategy, the key objective is to respond effectively to credit requests swiftly, manage the customer relationship professionally, give good quality service, manage the risks, and engage in an ongoing monitoring of the loan or credit facility.

5.2   THE CREDIT ANALYSIS PROCESS

As previously noted, despite the emphasis on quantitative modeling and vigilance, credit analysis is not an exact science as there is no single formula, ratio, or tool that will determine if a company is an acceptable credit risk or not. Therefore, it is important to follow some basic principles and practices of good lending.

5.2.1   The Five Cs of Credit

The **Five Cs of Credit** provide a basic framework for good lending, which is particularly relevant to small business lending and to the SME sector. Bank financing is the primary option for small or recently established firms, because these firms do not have access to the financial markets—to issue stocks or bonds—in the same way large, established companies with an established financial history do. Figure 5.2 depicts a schematic of the Five Cs.

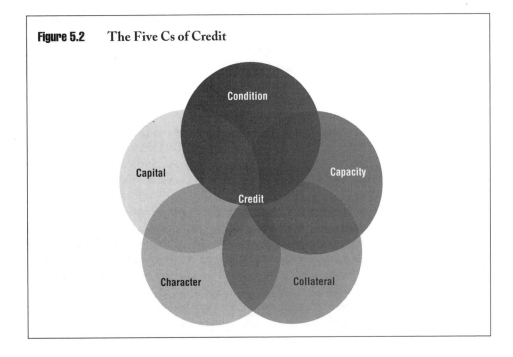

Figure 5.2   The Five Cs of Credit

The Five Cs of Credit: No. 1—Character

In analyzing **character,** the bank seeks to answer the following question: What is the reputation of the company's management in the industry and in the greater business community?

Bankers will always look to lend money to those with immaculate credentials and references. Credit analysts should determine the quality of management's relationship with its employees as well as with its customers and how these relationships are managed through the company's obligations. These characteristics afford insight into management's character.

EXAMPLE

The three owners of Good Impressions Inc., a well-established business, have approached GammaBank for credit. To assess the character of the company's management, the bank analyst would necessarily rely on his or her impressions from interviews of the company's management at the company's premises. The high quality of the products, the generally appealing appearance of the premises, and the good relationship management has with its employees all suggested positive character traits. However, it was subsequently discovered that the company repeatedly overdrew its bank accounts and regularly paid invoices late. The latter two issues should raise the bank analyst's concerns, and the analyst will include this information in the risk analysis. The result of the analysis concluded that doing business with the company would be riskier than originally thought.

Associated with character is management's ability to administer the company's future. Indicators of management capabilities include the level of engagement in day-to-day operations, flexibility in embracing current technologies, understanding prevailing industry trends, and, most importantly, its ability to contain costs and seek efficiencies.

The Five Cs of Credit: No. 2—Capital

When analyzing **capital**, the bank seeks to answer the following questions: How is the company currently financed? What is its level of leverage, that is, the amount of money, or equity, that owners have invested in the business relative to the company's assets? For a discussion on the relationship between assets and equity, or leverage, see Chapter 2.

The relationship between equity and debt is critical, and the higher the level of equity relative to debt, the healthier the company will appear from a credit risk perspective. The lower the leverage or the higher the capitalization of the company is reveals the financial commitment of the company's owners and indicates how much they have put themselves at risk. Particularly in small- and medium-sized businesses where the owner's wealth is very closely linked to the fortunes of the business, it is not only the company's financial statements that receive scrutiny, but also the owner's personal financial standing, assets, and credit quality.

EXAMPLE

In further analyzing Good Impressions Inc., the analyst at GammaBank notes that the three owners of the company have invested USD 250,000 each of their own money into the business—a positive factor. However, the analyst also finds out that collectively the three owners have personally borrowed approximately USD 14 million using their ownership interest in the company as collateral for the loans and are now seeking an additional USD 2 million loan from the bank to support the company's ongoing operations. After taking into account the owners' cumulative capital invested (USD 750,000) and their current borrowings (USD 14 million) using their interest in the company as collateral, the analyst can easily come to the conclusion that the risks of loaning the USD 2 million to the company are too great to move forward with the loan application.

Should a borrower default, a lender loses more than just the funded obligation or capital (principal plus interest). For instance, reputational risk is important because banks have a responsibility to shareholders and are entrusted by depositors to conduct business in a responsible and profitable manner. Significant defaults also use up a disproportionate amount of managerial time, siphoning off scarce resources that the bank's management would prefer to use in business development to manage complex negotiations with the borrowers and other lenders. Defaults could also negatively affect potential borrowers who would be less likely to use a bank with a reputation for foreclosing and forcing customers out of business during tough economic times.

The Five Cs of Credit: No. 3—Conditions

When analyzing **conditions,** the bank seeks to answer the following questions: What is the economic situation in the country or countries in which a company operates, and what are the economic conditions of the industry in which it operates?

The credit analyst must determine what outside risks might cause the company's financial condition to deteriorate.

EXAMPLE

In further reviewing Good Impressions Inc., the analyst at GammaBank discovered that the largest single market for its products is Malaysia, where more than 80% of its sales are made, bringing in nearly 90% of its profits. A business that generates income and cash flow in a currency different from the lender introduces considerable risk. One risk is the potential decline in the value of the Malaysian currency relative to the USD. If Good Impressions Inc. does not reduce (hedge) this risk, the cost of the loan to the company could ultimately be much more than anticipated, perhaps making it so costly that the company would default on either its interest payments or repayment of the loan principal. The analyst making the lending decision must examine the economic conditions under which the company operates (in this case Malaysia and the U.S.) to determine the potential not only for the direct counterparty credit risk it would assume with the company, but also for the risks associated with the company's dealing in a foreign currency and in that particular country.

The Five Cs of Credit: No. 4—Capacity

When analyzing **capacity,** the bank seeks to answer the following questions: How much cash does the company generate, and are the cash flows sustainable, repeatable, and predicable? The credit analyst must evaluate the company's ability to generate sufficient cash flows as well as management's ability to run its operations efficiently and effectively. The credit analyst works from cash flow projections to determine the debt or exposure a company can incur.

EXAMPLE

A bank analyst at GammaBank evaluating Good Impressions Inc. will investigate the sources and uses of the company's income to determine if the company will generate enough funds to repay the loan as well as cover the company's ongoing expenses. The analyst will usually build a quantitative model to attempt to predict the income-generating capacity of Good Impressions. In particular, it is important for the analyst to identify the factors that can easily and rapidly deteriorate, those that would have a negative impact on the future of the business's cash flow, and the business itself. Although income-generating capacity is not the only consideration, it is one of the most important issues to understand thoroughly. Good capacity to generate cash is one of the first and probably the most important factor to analyze.

Financing needs differ from company to company and can be affected by timing, economic conditions, and business circumstances. For some companies, cash flow will follow a stable path, although subject to some predictable seasonal deviations. In those instances, it will be easier to negotiate with a banking institution for a permanent financing facility, as the bank will be better able to judge the company's creditworthiness based on historical information. However, other businesses may experience material cash flow volatility, especially where sales and costs are unevenly matched. In this case, cash flow projections are more difficult, but not necessarily impossible, to project. Business models with random cash flow volatility do not lend themselves very well to establishing a permanent financing facility with a bank because of the risk associated with their cash flows. In these cases, various combinations of temporary financing are usually suggested to the borrower. It is very important to understand a company's cash flow volatility since it may impact the amount or type of financing facility offered by a bank. However, a key factor in the loan decision remains the adequacy and predictability of the cash flows.

Banks distinguish between seasonal, cyclical, and permanent financing. Seasonal and cyclical financing is considered to be temporary financing.

- **Seasonal financing** is usually provided to pay for a substantial increase in inventory and work in progress. For example, seasonal loans may be sought by a swimsuit manufacturer limited to national summer sales or for the purchase of goods by retailers and build-up of inventory by toy manufacturers prior to a peak selling time (e.g., major holidays). Seasonal credit needs are usually quite predictable and follow well-established patterns.

- **Cyclical financing** is similar to seasonal financing , except that the cycle is generally a business cycle rather than a more predictable change in seasons and repayment is more dependent on random changes in the long-term macroeconomic environment in which the business operates. Since banks typically consider cyclical needs to be more difficult to predict, they consider cyclical lending to be riskier than seasonal lending. Another example of cyclical loans are those dedicated loans that support the development and production of a new product with the financing provided incrementally throughout the product cycle.

- **Permanent financing** is usually long-term financing of 15 or more years and is provided in the form of a mortgage (e.g., an individual borrowing to purchase a home with a 30-year mortgage) or bond issuance for a company. Permanent financing is often used for investment in buildings or other types of real estate projects.

Figure 5.3 shows the relationship between asset growth and financing needs. There is a strong relationship between sales and assets and the financing of the assets. As a company grows, its sales, revenues, and assets increase As sales increase, assets increase and companies must finance the increase in assets. However, as sales decline, both assets, and the need to finance them, decline. Part of the increase in assets reflects a permanent increase and includes the new factories, facilities, machinery, and production infrastructure a company has created. It also reflects the increasing level of inventory the company has and corporate receivables that the company collected. A company seeks to finance most of its permanent increase in assets through medium- and long-term financing. Long-term financing needs of these assets can also be met through equity financing.

Growing companies also have temporary changes in assets. Variations in sales and assets are characteristically cyclical or seasonal. Cyclical asset changes reflect the fluctuating fortunes of companies throughout the business cycle. As the economy goes through cycles—expansion, contraction, recession—sales, revenues, and assets are affected. During contraction and recession, sales drop and the need for assets declines. Declining assets reduce the financing needs. During expansion, sales and assets increase and borrowing needs rise. Conversely, declining assets decrease financing needs. To meet the changes in the demand for capital, many banks provide medium-term financing that roughly corresponds to three- to five-year business cycles.

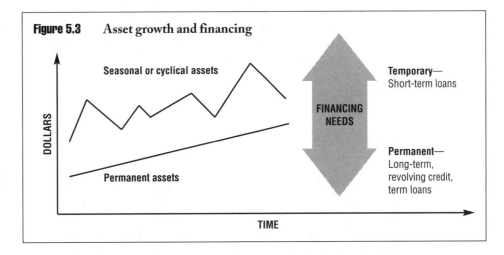

Figure 5.3 Asset growth and financing

Seasonal changes in assets, as shown in previous examples, have shorter-term effects on sales, revenues, and assets. These financing needs are met with short-term loans that have maturity around one year.

Assessing the quality of the borrower's assets is also part of capacity analysis and is particularly useful when the company has significant trade receivables that can be used for asset-based lending or converted into cash after collecting on the receivables.

Trade receivables result from credit sales, where the company extends credit to its customers to purchase its products or services in anticipation of payment. In many small- and medium-sized businesses, a listing of all debtors and the aging of all invoices due from each provides important information of not only what is due and owed to the company but also the company's ability to collect on its debts, implement its policies, and assess whether a buyer is truly creditworthy. In economic downturns, assets could be increasing as customers either use more trade financing or slow their payments. Therefore, asset growth (mentioned earlier as a good thing) needs to be critically analyzed and "good" asset growth differentiated from "bad" asset growth.

Credit analysts also evaluate a company's inventory. Inventory has to be of salable quality reflective of the company's intention to continue business, and, should there be a bankruptcy, the company's assets should be of satisfactory quality to pay debts when sold.

The analyst must also assess the borrower's liquidity. A business that has enough cash is more likely to pay what it owes when payment is due. Illiquid businesses, which can include businesses that are profitable but lack sufficient cash flows, present potential credit risks.

The Five Cs of Credit: No. 5—Collateral

When analyzing **collateral**, the bank seeks to answer the following question: In the event the borrower cannot honor its obligations, what assets does it have that the bank can lay claim to satisfy the debt? Section 4.4.5 discusses the role of collateral.

The analyst should confirm that the company's primary source of loan repayment, cash flow or assets, is, and will be, sufficient to meet all its obligations as they fall due. But, a lender has a responsibility to its shareholders and depositors to ensure a secondary or complementary source of repayment. The secondary source of repayment is other assets owned by the borrower (most commonly referred to as collateral). In the event of a default, the bank should be able to assume control over these assets and organize an orderly sale to satisfy the loan's terms. In loans to lower-rated companies, where the risk of default is greater, the company will typically pledge all of its assets as collateral.

EXAMPLE

In the loan evaluation process, the bank and Good Impressions Inc. discuss what collateral appropriately covers the terms of the loan. The bank and Good Impressions decide that in exchange for the credit to finance the purchase of machinery, that some of the company's machinery is pledged as collateral. At the time the loan was approved, the bank's loan officer was confident that, should Good Impressions default on the loan, the bank could recover the loan by selling the collateral to other companies. Several months after the loan was granted, the business started to worsen. Within a year, Good Impression fell on hard times and was unable to repay its loan, and the bank repossessed the collateral. However, the analyst failed to take into account the fact that Good Impression had several local and international competitors. So, when the bank tried to sell the repossessed machinery, there were no buyers. Eventually, the bank had no choice but to write the loan off, taking a loss on the transaction. The lesson: Always investigate the future value of the assets offered as collateral should they have to be sold in a hurry or in an unfavorable market. In such circumstances, the assets usually will not have much value, if any.

5.2.2   The Credit Analysis Path

The key to a successful credit analysis is to assess accurately the creditworthiness of each prospect. To accomplish this, credit analysts review the key business, financial, and structural risks. These three areas form part of a focused analytical tool referred to as the credit analysis path. The analysis steps are depicted in Figure 5.4.

Figure 5.4   Credit analysis steps and risk

BUSINESS RISKS		FINANCIAL RISKS		STRUCTURAL RISKS	
Macroeconomics Analysis	**Microeconomics Analysis**	**Management Analysis**	**Financial Analysis**	**Type of Borrower**	**Type of Borrowing**
Examples	*Examples*	*Examples*	*Examples*	*Examples*	*Examples*
• Gross Domestic Product (GDP) • Inflation • Demographic trends • Business Cycle • Political Stability • Regulatory Environment • Legal Environment	• Industry Trends • Regulatory Trends	• Proactive or Reactive • Strategy • Motivation • Experience • Integrity • Corporate Governance	• Operating and Financial Position • Financial Disclosure	• Holding Company • Primary Operating Subsidiaries • Secondary Operating Subsidiaries	• Secured • Unsecured • Long-term • Short-term • Subordinated

In the credit analysis path, the focus is to analyze the various risks that may impact the borrower. The overall analysis encompasses business (or macro) risks, financial (or micro) risks, and structural risks. These risk areas overlap as the factors that impact these various areas are closely related and mutually interdependent.

The three areas of analysis are separated into several general layers, or components, and are shown in Figure 5.5.

Figure 5.5   Business, financial, and structural risks

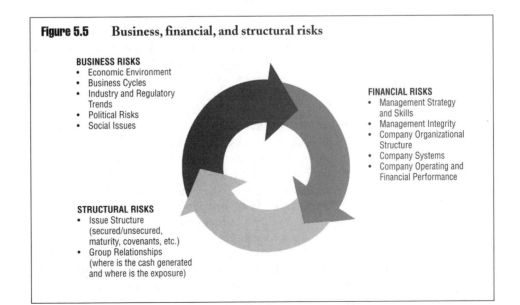

BUSINESS RISKS
• Economic Environment
• Business Cycles
• Industry and Regulatory Trends
• Political Risks
• Social Issues

FINANCIAL RISKS
• Management Strategy and Skills
• Management Integrity
• Company Organizational Structure
• Company Systems
• Company Operating and Financial Performance

STRUCTURAL RISKS
• Issue Structure (secured/unsecured, maturity, covenants, etc.)
• Group Relationships (where is the cash generated and where is the exposure)

The credit analysis path shows that the company's decision-making process will directly impact the risks the organization takes, and that management's decisions are influenced by the industry's macro- and microeconomic trends. The relationship between business risks and structural risks is illustrated in Figure 5.6.

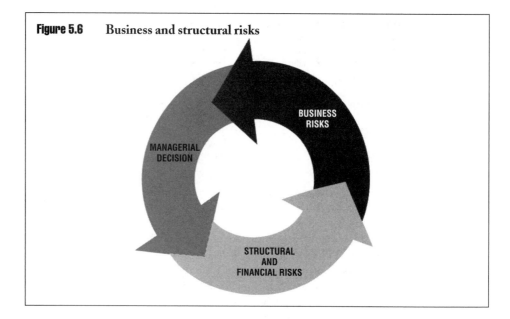

Figure 5.6   Business and structural risks

5.2.3   Business, or Macro, Risks

The business, or macro, risks reflect both the bank's and the borrower's respective environments. Analysis of the bank's operating environment helps management determine the appropriate loan allocation. Banks usually select loans where the risk/return trade-off. In other words, higher returns on loans require the bank to feel comfortable with elevated exposure to default risks and potentially increased exposure to possibly debilitating defaults) offers an appropriate risk-adjusted trade-off. In other words, considering the risks associated with the credit, how does the return offered by the credit provide appropriate compensation to the bank?

Analysis of the borrower's operating environment reflects a market risk assessment. After reviewing the borrower's overall market (i.e., macroeconomic drivers, competitive factors, etc.), the credit analyst is able to determine the borrower's challenges and opportunities. Figure 5.7 shows some of the business, or macro, factors that analysts consider. These macro factors are trends that impact all industries, companies, and firms. There are numerous macro factors; typically, they are likely to include long-term trends:

- Level of economic activity (measured by changes in the global GDP)
- Global changes in inflation (the decline in the purchasing power of money)
- Worldwide price of energy (the price of crude oil, an important commodity that, when refined, powers machinery, etc.)

EXAMPLE

GammaBank evaluated a complex combination of various credits that Libra Corporation has submitted. After analyzing the loan proposal, the loan officer reported that Libra Corporation, a manufacturer of complex and very expensive machinery used in manufacturing, was a global business. It had extensive sales operations in several developing countries. Approximately 80% of its sales were generated from developing countries. Many developing countries where Libra had a significant share of its market were suffering from high interest rates and consequential adverse exchange rate changes, and these adverse economic conditions would be expected to continue in the coming years. Libra's production was concentrated in a few developed countries that had low interest rates and strong economic fundamentals.

In the analysis, the loan officer at GammaBank argued that Libra's management was solely focused on containing the negative effects of short-term market contractions in the developing markets that were caused by high interest rates. Libra's strategy was to provide cheap credit to its customers in developing countries with the expectation that the cheap financing would make their products comparatively more attractive than the products of Libra's competitors. In fact, part of the comprehensive loan package would be used to funnel cheap credit from low-interest-rate countries with strong and stable exchange rates to several high-interest-rate countries with weak and unstable exchange rates. Unlike the bank, Libra was less concerned with the weakening exchange rates and maintained that the additional earnings generated from sales from developing countries would be sufficiently profitable to repay these loans, even if exchange rates would deteriorate further.

Yet, Libra's top management had not taken a comprehensive action to contain the impact that deteriorating global economic conditions may have on all its businesses. Libra, in particular, had not addressed the increasing costs that it incurred due to exchange rate changes, particularly the fact that most of Libra's production was concentrated in developed countries with strong and stable exchange rates, while its sales were concentrated in several developing countries that were suffering from unstable and weakening exchange rates, as well as continuing adverse economic developments, which was slowly eroding sales in these countries. Since management did not contain production costs in the developed countries, due to the weakening exchange rates, the company's costs of production continued to increase to the point that its products' costs were now negatively impacting its ability to retain customers and acquire new ones, both in developed and in developing countries. The component costs of the goods it produced were overly sensitive to negative exchange rate changes (it had overlooked the macroeconomic impact of both the interest rate and exchange rate changes together). As a result, Libra's management was unable to control its deteriorating long-term prospects and increased its risk of losses and the potential of failing. The loan officer recognized a core weakness in Libra's strategy: There was no focus on mitigating the long-term negatives along with reviewing the short-term impact of the increase in interest rates. As a consequence and on the advice of the loan officer, GammaBank did not extend credit to Libra Corporation.

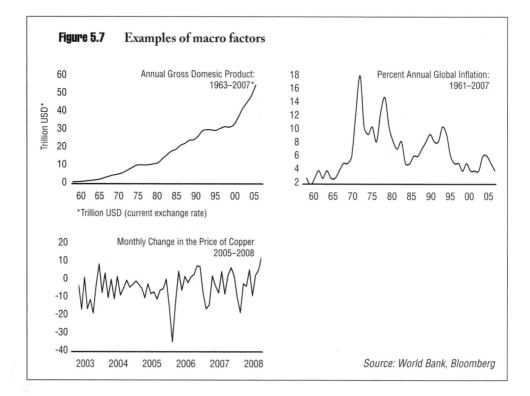

Figure 5.7   **Examples of macro factors**

An analyst's evaluation of the business includes how the client's management team deals with competition. There are a number of ways to analyze competitive forces. It is vitally important to identify and understand how competitive forces can influence the company's risk drivers, which, in turn, will impact its liquidity and solvency. These competitive forces can include government regulation, changes in technology and technological advances, and the environment, all areas where matters can and do change dramatically and quite swiftly. Such changes can prove very costly and can either open up or close down markets.

EXAMPLE

Significant costs can be incurred by companies as a result of unexpected actions taken by others. In 1995, the Shell Oil Company wanted to dispose of its Brent Spar Oil Rig by sinking it into the North Atlantic Ocean. The environmental lobby group Greenpeace opposed the plan and organized a vigorous public protest. The result was a widespread boycott of Shell products. The protest forced Shell to undertake a much more expensive yet more environmentally friendly option. In the end, management was able to handle the matter in a more favorable manner with minimal environmental impact. However, this is not always an option for many companies that might not be able to afford expensive alternatives due to their size, other exposures, or business requirements.

5.2.4   Financial, or Micro, Risks

The financial risk assessment reviews the company's management and especially how it handles the company's operating and financial environment. Credit analysts primarily focus on management strategies and their ability to manage the business in conjunction with an in-depth analysis of the company's historical, current, and pro forma financial statements. The overall assessment and results are then compared to the company's peers. Figure 5.8 shows several financial, or micro, risks that analysis would typically consider. This information reflects comparative factors in a distinct part of the economy affecting only a handful of businesses and could include production, capacity, and sales growth over several years. The following graphs show some micro factors from the airline industry:

- Revenue growth (measured by annual sales growth between 2006–2008 and 2003–2007)
- Revenue per flown passenger mile in 2006 and 2007 (revenue in USD divided by passenger miles flown)
- Airline capacity utilization (average number of hours per day the aircraft are being used)
- Average margin of operations (earnings margin 2002–2006 and 2005–2007)

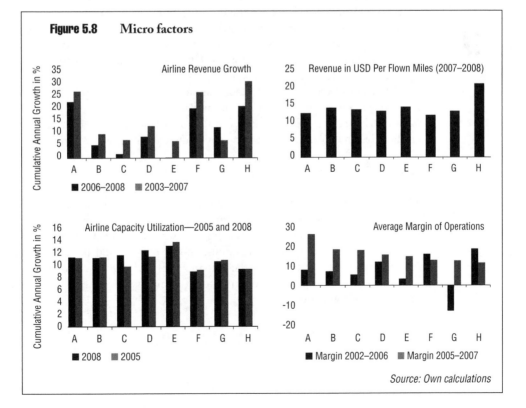

Figure 5.8   Micro factors

Source: Own calculations

It is during analysis of financial, or micro, risks that the credit analysis focuses on the company's credit facilities and how those would relate to the company's future growth prospects and whether they will require a substantial investment in order to sustain future growth. All these factors allow for the relative comparison of the different companies active in the business. In financial risk analysis, the company's operating conditions are important, and the lender must also assess third-party credit and trade references to determine if the company has solid relationships—including payment relationships. This process involves looking at the business partners of the potential borrower to obtain a holistic assessment about how its business relationships are being managed.

Banks, particularly in the United States, use **credit-scoring models** to help in the overall credit assessment process. These models are tools that help predict the probability a loan might default. The probability of default is communicated as a credit score. The **credit score** relates the strength of each borrower relative to all borrowers. The higher the prospective borrower's credit score, the less the chance he/she may default. Credit scores use over 100 different factors in their calculation. Factors included are information about past financial performance payment history; debt capacity; several qualitative factors such as peer analysis; industry review and comparisons; and management, economic, and environment analysis.

Credit-scoring models follow a consistent approach developed from years of experience. Thus, models reduce the cost of credit evaluation and increase the speed and accuracy in the credit decision-making process. They also improve on consistency and accuracy because the results are more "standardized" and can be compared against the results of other prospective borrowers. This allows managers to assess the true quality of their credit loan portfolios better.

More advanced assessment models are used to predict the probability of default for large corporate borrowers. They are similar to credit-scoring models and incorporate financial statement information, but also include quantitative analytics such as data on the price and volatility of the company's publicly traded shares and bonds.

5.2.5   Structural Risk

The analysis of structural risk focuses on loan pricing and mitigation. Covenants and collateral play considerable roles in structural risk assessment. In this assessment, the credit analyst must understand the legal structure of the borrower, the various subsidiaries, intra-company transactions, and ownership and partnership linkages. All are analyzed to better gauge the true financial and potential economic exposure embedded in the proposed credit structure (covenants and pricing are intended to mitigate potential lapses).

5.2.6   Information Sources

There are many different sources of information used in the credit assessment process. A key source is the company's annual report and its audited financial statements. The company's financial statements are usually audited or independently evaluated by outside accounting experts who review the company's financial information to certify it is within a certain country's Generally Accepted Accounting Principles (GAAP) or within International Financial Reporting Standards (IFRS). Accounting principles/standards are part of a company's corporate governance procedures and ensure that all financial information is presented in a uniform way, thus allowing for greater ease of review by the credit analyst.

It is important to note that producing and subsequently providing this information to the credit analyst does not prevent companies from engaging in questionable or fraudulent activities. However, it does serve as a check on the company's management, and an analysis of the audited financial statements provides a reasonable, though not complete, level of comfort to potential investors and bankers alike.

EXAMPLE

Some management teams have allowed questionable financial maneuvers to undermine the financial condition of their overall business that were, unfortunately, not identified by independent auditors. Enron was the top natural gas trader in the U.S. and a leading marketer in wholesale electricity in the late 1990s and early 2000s. In December 2001, Enron filed for bankruptcy, after it was forced to restate its third-quarter earnings of that year to reflect a loss of USD 638 million when it became known that many of the company's financial dealings were entered into in order to mask losses and to make the company's financial position appear sound when in fact it was not. The restatement required Enron to recognize losses associated with off-balance-sheet partnerships—financial relationships that were developed with the objective of keeping certain transactions from appearing in the company's financial reports. Off-balance-sheet activities are an acceptable accounting practice as long as they are appropriately structured, transparent, and appropriately disclosed in the financial statements. In the case of Enron, however, these off-balance-sheet activities were a result of systematically deceptive and fraudulent transactions, where the purpose was to reduce transparency and disclosure.

A basic way to deal with the above issues is to engage in what is commonly referred to as a *SWOT analysis*. SWOT stands for strengths, weaknesses, opportunities, and threats, and is illustrated in Figure 5.9. This is a powerful strategic planning framework to obtain an objective assessment of a company's internal strengths and weaknesses and the opportunities and threats presented by the external business environment in which the company operates. This information, coupled with an in-depth analysis of the company's financial condition, allows for a more objective and accurate determination of the potential borrower's creditworthiness.

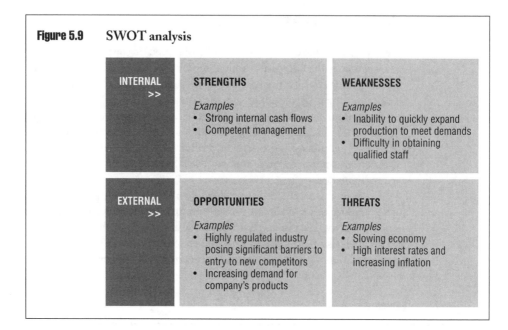

Figure 5.9 SWOT analysis

5.3 PORTFOLIO MANAGEMENT

An **investment portfolio** held by a bank or an individual contains various investments that typically include stocks (equity), bonds, loans, financial derivatives (options, futures, etc.), investible commodities such as gold or platinum, real estate, or similar assets of value. The **investor** is the entity that holds the portfolio and may be a company, a bank, or an individual. **Portfolio management** involves determining the contents and the structure of the portfolio, monitoring its performance, making any changes, and deciding which assets to acquire and which assets to divest. Portfolio managers weigh both the expected risk and return characteristics of individual assets, the performance of the entire portfolio, and the investor's financial objectives in order to find an optimal combination of investments that provides the highest level of return for any given level of risk.

Banks use several approaches to measure portfolio performance and reduce credit losses. The approaches utilize quantitative assessment tools to predict the likelihood of a default and estimate the impact of the default. The following terminology is often used when discussing portfolio management concepts:

- *Probability of default (PD).* The likelihood that the borrower will default.
- *Exposure at default (EAD).* The total exposure the lender could have at the time of default.
- *Recovery rate (RR).* The assumption of the fraction of the asset value that will likely be recovered after a default.

- *Loss given default (LGD).* The actual loss the lender suffers in the wake of a default and is a function of the RR and the EAD.
- *Expected loss (EL).* The loss given default multiplied by the probability of default.

EXAMPLE

In 2005, Libra Corporation arranged a facility to borrow EUR 10 million from International Bank for a five-year period at an annual interest rate of 7%. After two years, Libra has repaid EUR 4 million, but still owed the bank EUR 6 million plus EUR 300,000 in interest. International Bank made the following assessment about Libra Corporation in January 2007:

- If Libra Corporation defaulted in 2007, International Bank's exposure at default (EAD) would be EUR 6.3 million: EUR 6 million in principal and EUR 300,000 in interest.
- International Bank is assuming a recovery rate (RR) in the event of a default in 2007 of 90% or EUR 5.67 million (90% of EUR 6.3 million).
- The actual loss International Bank would suffer (LGD) would be the difference between EUR 6.3 (EAD) and EUR 5.67 (LGD) or EUR 630,000. This equals (1-RR)*EAD.
- The probability that Libra Corporation would default during 2008 was 1% (probability of default—PD).
- Therefore, the expected loss (EL) is EUR 630,000 * 1% = EUR 6,300.

5.3.1   Concentration Risk

As just discussed, banks manage the risks in their loan portfolios by using a variety of risk mitigation methods. One particularly effective method is to ensure that the bank's risks are diversified by geography, industry type, demographics, or other indicators. A diversified loan portfolio reduces the impact of a severe market disruption. An inherent risk in lending is that a bank can become skilled in lending to, for example, one geographical area or to one industry (e.g., tool manufacturers) and will then tend to focus the majority of its underwriting efforts on that area or sector. This can lead to a highly concentrated, or not suitably diversified, credit portfolio. A concentrated portfolio decreases the bank's ability to withstand losses and exposes the bank to **concentration risk**. Concentration risk may be offset to some extent because the bank's expertise in one sector may steer it away from the weakest credits.

By actively managing its loan portfolio, a bank reduces its concentration risk. To decrease concentration, a bank might sell some of its loans to third parties, thereby removing those risks from its banking book. Or it might diversify its portfolio by buying nonsimilar loans from other banks. All such shifts in the banking book can also help to reduce the effects of systematic default.

EXAMPLE

Woodbury Bank, a small rural bank, has made approximately 60% of its loans to area businesses that are all active in or closely related to coal mining. Most of the mining-related companies are well established with very good credit histories. Since Woodbury Bank is closely related to the fortunes of the coal mining industry, bank management decided to reduce its concentration risk and implemented the following plan:

- First, it sold some of its highest-quality loans to banks in a different part of the country. Many of those banks do not have exposure to the mining industry and, interested in their own diversification, wanted to increase their credit exposure to that industry segment.
- Second, it purchased technology-related loans from other banks to increase its exposure to businesses unrelated to mining.
- Third, it started to offer different types of loans. Previously, the bank has not offered any residential mortgage loans at all. By offering residential mortgages, through its correspondent banks, to finance purchases outside the bank's home business area, it expanded its loan portfolio to retail customers and reduced its exposure to its home market.
- Fourth, it started to offer loans to businesses in industries it previously avoided due to weaker credit quality. The new loans, while carrying more risk exposure, effectively helped diversify the risks in its portfolio and increased the portfolio's return—it would earn a higher return on those loans because of their riskier nature.

5.3.2   Securitizations

One technique banks employ to reduce the effects of credit losses is to aggregate, pool, or package assets, usually lower-quality assets, and sell them into the capital markets. This is known as **securitizing assets**. By pooling the assets and their cash flows, then offering a pool with more diversified assets, the bank has a package that becomes more desirable to investors than if the assets were offered individually. These types of assets are referred to as **asset-backed securities** (ABS). Many types of assets can be securitized (e.g., credit cards and leases), as long as they are associated with a cash flow.

Investors purchase securitized assets in order to achieve portfolio diversification. Securitized assets generally provide a fairly predictable schedule of repayments and offer a specified return. A bank would securitize its assets to reduce potentially high levels of risk exposure, including concentration risk, since securitizing the assets, then selling them to third parities, removes them from its books and reduces its capital requirements. Because the securities are sold, banks receive the proceeds from their sale and can then generate new loans or conduct other business with the funds. Typically, the bank will transfer or sell the securitized assets to an issuer who may be affiliated with the bank. The issuer then bundles the assets (mortgages, credit card receivables, etc.) and sells securities backed by them. The anticipated payments on the pool of loans are used to pay off the securities. If the transfer or sale of securities is without recourse (that is, the selling bank is not liable to pay compensation to the buyer in case the loan defaults), this process then decreases the bank's default risk. Figure 5.10 illustrates a securitization process.

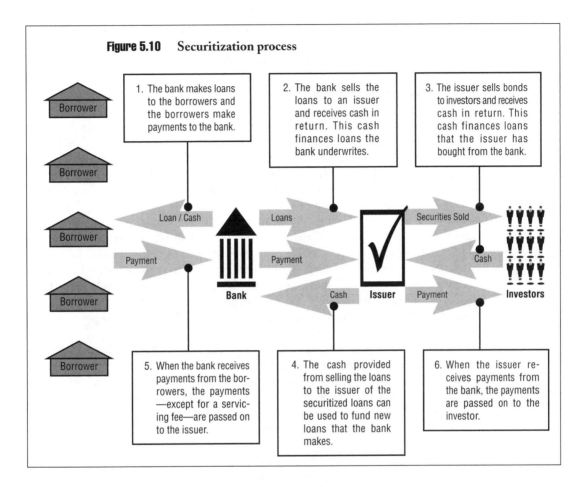

Figure 5.10 Securitization process

1. The bank makes loans to the borrowers and the borrowers make payments to the bank.

2. The bank sells the loans to an issuer and receives cash in return. This cash finances loans the bank underwrites.

3. The issuer sells bonds to investors and receives cash in return. This cash finances loans that the issuer has bought from the bank.

Loan / Cash

Loans

Securities Sold

Payment

Payment

Cash

Bank

Cash

Issuer

Payment

Investors

5. When the bank receives payments from the borrowers, the payments —except for a servicing fee—are passed on to the issuer.

4. The cash provided from selling the loans to the issuer of the securitized loans can be used to fund new loans that the bank makes.

6. When the issuer receives payments from the bank, the payments are passed on to the investor.

Borrower

Borrower

Borrower

Borrower

Borrower

5.4   CREDIT RISK AND BASEL II ACCORD

A key purpose of the Basel I Accord is to determine the regulatory capital for credit risk using a simple credit rating approach (see Chapter 1). Basel II expands on Basel I and, under Pillar 1, requires banks to calculate bank regulatory capital requirements for market and operational risk as well as for credit risk.

To calculate regulatory capital for credit risk, Basel II recommends that banks select one of three approaches that determines their credit risk capital requirements or regulatory capital for credit risk. The three approaches differ not only in their methodology but also in the level of sophistication required of the bank's credit risk processes that support the calculations.

Basel II outlines the following approaches to calculate credit risk capital:

- Standardized Approach—incorporates an external ratings-based approach
- Foundation Internal Ratings-Based Approach
- Advanced Internal Ratings-Based Approach

5.4.1   The Standardized Approach

The **Standardized Approach** evolved from the Basel I credit risk guidelines. In contrast to simple, fixed-risk weightings (a percentage that reflects the risk of a certain asset) assigned to asset types by Basel I, Basel II recognizes that risk weightings for certain asset types, specifically loans to sovereigns (countries), corporations, and banks, need to be more flexible and recommends risk ratings be determined by the external credit ratings assigned to the borrower.

Basel II allows available public credit ratings from credit-rating agencies to be incorporated into the Standardized Approach. Basel II allows risk weights to reflect public credit ratings issued by rating agencies that meet certain standards. In many countries, the usefulness of public credit ratings is limited, as these countries have a relatively small number of public credit ratings available. This effectively limits the application of using public credit ratings to government and large corporate credits (mainly bonds and other publicly traded debt), some banks, and certain government agencies that are large borrowers.

Credit-rating agencies issue credit ratings (see Section 4.2.2). The three best-known ratings agencies are Standard and Poor's, Moody's Investors Service, and Fitch. Figure 5.11 shows the different grades (ratings) used by Moody's, Fitch, and Standard & Poor's. The plus and minus signs following each grade are modifiers indicating relative differences between various issues within the same rating category. A positive or plus sign indicates that the issue is relatively better than the average issue in that rating category. A negative or minus sign indicates that the issue is relatively worse than the average issue in that rating category. These ratings may change as the issuer's credit quality changes. Ratings can also be qualified by rating "watches" and "outlooks" that could provide some forward-looking guidance for a credit analyst.

5.4.2   Internal Ratings-Based Approaches

Basel II Accord's other two approaches to calculate minimum credit capital permit banks to use internally generated credit ratings, provided the ratings are developed on sound financial logic and assigned appropriately. **Internal Ratings-Based (IRB) approaches** share several features but are implemented differently. They are referred to as:

- Foundation IRB Approach
- Advanced IRB Approach

5.4.3   Common Features to IRB Approaches

Both IRB approaches differ from the Standardized Approach by relying on the bank's own information to determine the regulatory minimum capital requirement. The bank's internal processes to assess the creditworthiness of borrowers generate the information to create credit models. Credit models build on common risk factors such as PD, LGD, EAD (see full definitions in Section 5.3), as well as the effective maturity (M).

The difference between the Foundation IRB Approach and the Advanced IRB Approach lies in how the bank's internal models forecast the different risk factors:

*   Under the **Foundation IRB Approach**, a bank is required to estimate only the borrower's probability of default. To verify the PD, the bank must use at least five years of relevant loan performance data from various borrowers. The other risk factors of the credit model (listed above) are provided and determined by the bank's supervisor.
*   Under the **Advanced IRB Approach**, a bank estimates all components of the model. At least seven years of historical data must be used for verification purposes. For all but large corporate exposures, a standard two and a half years may be assumed for maturity, subject to supervisor agreement.

With the Advanced IRB Approach, the bank must estimate all credit risk model components, including data collection, data management, and modeling techniques. The process demands a more sophisticated, and more costly, commitment by the bank.

5.4.4   Minimum Requirements for IRB Approaches

The core requirement is that the bank's complex credit risk measurement, management, and monitoring system should be a ratings-based system. A **ratings-based system** should accurately capture the inherent riskiness of each loan in the bank's loan portfolio and differentiate between individual loan exposures by correctly assessing the inherent riskiness of each loan relative to all the other loans.

All ratings systems build on complex mathematical and statistical models that predict the PD, LGD, and EAD of each loan. Due to the complexity of these models, the sophisticated mathematical methodologies, and the detailed inputs and processes, the model must be well documented so that the regulators can easily validate the model by replicating the model's results.

For a ratings-based system to differentiate risk meaningfully, provide reasonably accurate and consistent estimates of risk, and support lending decisions, the Basel Accord requires banks to develop a ratings system with a minimum of eight *probability of default* rating grades. These should range from very low probability of default (such as the AAA or Aaa ratings or similar ratings by ratings agencies) to very high probability of default (such as the C ratings or similar ratings by ratings agencies).

The criteria for rating definitions should be both plausible and intuitive and result in a meaningful differentiation of risk that is clear both to the employees of the bank and to auditors, regulators, and supervisors. Eight grades are the minimum. Within these eight grades, the system should be able to differentiate even further and become more granular to capture the different shades of credit risk.

The Basel Accord also requires the ratings-based system to be dynamic. A dynamic rating system should immediately reflect up-to-date and relevant borrower information and reassess the credit rating of the loan based on the new information. The rating system should also provide information that allows for continuous reassessment and performance evaluation. Both the bank and the supervisors should be able to evaluate how well the system performs by comparing realized PDs, LGDs, and EADs against those predicted by the model and comparing how well the credit ratings predict defaults and potential changes, such as credit migration over time (e.g., a highly rated credit weakens and drops to a lower rung on the credit ladder from an AAA to an A rating, or a weak credit strengthens and becomes more highly rated, such as a BBB becomes an A rating). Evaluating the performance of the system should lead the bank's risk control unit to modify and improve the system continually. Ongoing monitoring by management and internal auditors is also required.

Ultimately, the ratings should help the bank evaluate each credit exposure (loan), assign each an appropriate rating, and allow for an evaluation of the performance of each exposure relative to all the others the bank has underwritten or is underwriting. They also help to manage more easily the credit risk of the banking book, provide an avenue to quantify exposure, and accurately assess the bank's regulatory minimum capital for credit risk. Moreover, to determine the regulatory capital that the bank should hold against its credit risks, the bank's internally developed ratings-based system should also be used for stress testing. The system must be able to capture not only the deterioration of credit quality of one specific borrower or a group of similar borrowers, but also the effects of economic and industry downturns, market risk events, and weak liquidity conditions.

For a bank to adopt either of the IRB Approaches, it must first demonstrate to its banking supervisory agency that it has been using a broad IRB-compliant system for at least three years. A bank complying with the Foundation IRB Approach must have been estimating the probability of default for at least three years, while banks using the Advanced IRB Approach must also have been estimating their loss given default and exposure at default for at least three years.

Figure 5.11   Credit ratings and their interpretations

	Description	Fitch & S&P		Moody's		Explanation
Investment grade	Highest credit quality —lowest risk	AAA		Aaa		Exceptionally strong capacity for timely payment of financial commitments, which is highly unlikely to be adversely affected by foreseeable events.
	Very high credit quality —low risk	AA	AA+ AA AA-	Aa	Aa 1 Aa 2 Aa 3	Very strong capacity for timely payment of financial commitments, which is not significantly vulnerable to foreseeable events.
	High credit quality —low risk	A	A+ A A-	A	A 1 A 2 A 3	Strong capacity for timely payment of financial commitments, which may be more vulnerable to changes in circumstances/economic conditions.
	Good credit quality —medium risk	BBB	BBB+ BBB BBB-	Baa	Baa 1 Baa 2 Baa 3	Adequate capacity for timely payment of financial commitments but adverse changes in circumstances/economic conditions are more likely to impair this capacity.
Speculative grade	Speculative —high risk	BB	BB+ BB BB-	Ba	Ba 1 Ba 2 Ba 3	Possibility of credit risk developing, particularly due to adverse economic change over time. Business/financial alternatives may be available to allow financial commitments to be met.
	Highly speculative —high risk	B	B+ B B-	B	B 1 B 2 B 3	Significant credit risk with a limited margin of safety. Financial commitments are currently being met, however, continued payments is contingent upon a sustained, favorable business and economic environment.
	High default risk —higher risk	CCC		Caa		Default is a real possibility. Capacity for meeting financial commitments is solely reliant upon sustained, favorable business or economic developments.
	Probable default —very high risk	CC		Ca		Default of some kind appears probable and the issue is vulnerable to worsening in the issuer's conditions.
	Likely default —highest risk	C		C		Default imminent and highly vulnerable to any worsening in the issuer's conditions.
Default	In default	D				Defaulted issue. Payment of interest and repayment of principal have not been made on the due date, or it is highly uncertain that such payment will be made, or the issuer enters in bankruptcy, reorganization, or similar procedure.

CHAPTER 6

Market Risk

T his chapter introduces market risk, the risk of losses on positions held by the bank in financial assets or instruments due to adverse movements in market prices. Banks assume market risk because they trade for their own account, risking their own capital, and hold positions in financial instruments. Failure to manage market risk can have significant direct effects on the bank's profitability and reputation. After exploring the sources of market risk and the trading instruments banks use in their trading operations, this chapter covers various market risk measurement and management considerations, including the approaches outlined in the Market Risk Amendment to the Basel I Accord and the Basel II Accord.

Chapter Outline

- 6.1 Introduction to Market Risk
- 6.2. Basics of Financial Instruments
- 6.3 Trading
- 6.4 Market Risk Measurement and Management
- 6.5 Market Risk Regulation—The 1996 Market Risk Amendment

Key Learning Points
- Market risk arises from the trading activities of banks and is a consequence of movements in market prices.
- Market risk affects all financial instruments and can be general market risk, which reflects the market movements of all comparable financial instruments, or a specific risk, which reflects the risk that an individual financial instrument moves in day-to-day trading.

- The basic financial instruments are currencies, equities, bonds, loans, commodities, and derivatives. Banks can take either a long or a short position in financial instruments.
- The four different types of market risks are equity risk (equities), interest rate risk (bonds and loans), commodities risk (commodities), and exchange rate risk (currencies). To reduce market risk and the impact of market risk, banks can hedge their risk exposures.
- Value-at-risk is a methodology that yields an estimate of potential losses over a certain time period at a specific confidence interval. The estimate this process creates quantifies some of the risk the bank takes.
- The Basel II Accord provides two alternative processes for market risk measurement: the Standardized Approach and the Internal Models Approach.

Key Terms

- Bid-ask spread
- Bonds
- Call option
- Clearinghouse
- Commodities
- Commodity risk
- Coupon rate
- Cross rates
- Currency
- Currency regimes
- Derivatives
- Equity, (shares or stock)
- Equity risk
- Exchange
- Exchange rate
- Foreign exchange risk
- Forward
- Futures
- General market risk
- Hedging
- Interest rate risk
- Internal Models Approach
- LIBOR

- Loans
- Long position loans
- Margin
- Margin call
- Margin requirement
- Market or trading liquidity
- Market risk
- Nominal rate
- Options
- Over-the-counter market
- Position
- Put option
- Risk appetite
- Short position
- Specific risk
- Speculation
- Standardized Approach
- Swap
- Systematic risk
- Trading
- Value-at-risk, VaR
- Variation margin
- Yield curve

Market Risk

6.1   INTRODUCTION TO MARKET RISK

Market risk has two components: a general market risk that affects similar financial assets or financial markets and a specific risk that only affects individual financial assets. **General market risk** or **systematic risk** is the risk of an adverse movement in market prices that is applied across a range of assets.[1] **Specific risk** is the risk of an adverse movement in the price of an individual asset due to factors that only apply to that security or issuer and is not related to the general movement of the markets. The relationship is show in Figure 6.1.

EXAMPLE

When the price of shares issued by Andromeda Corporation declines, the cause of the decline can be due to either an event specific to Andromeda Corporation or an event that impacts the entire market. If the share price declines due to a general worsening of the economic outlook, which significantly depresses a wide range of different share prices in the stock markets, the cause of the decline is attributed to general market risk. However, if the share price declines because of a decline in the business of Andromeda Corporation, then the decline is a result of a specific risk that only impacts the company and its shares.

6.2.   BASICS OF FINANCIAL INSTRUMENTS

Basic financial assets are also called financial products or financial instruments. Banks use financial instruments for trading purposes and to hedge their financial activities. These financial instruments are considered "plain-vanilla" products because they are relatively simple and do not have complex features.

For instance, common stocks and corporate bonds are both considered plain-vanilla financial instruments.

---

1.   Systematic risk should not be confused with systemic risk (see Section 3.1.2), the risk that the financial system may collapse due to a catastrophic event.

Banks trade both plain-vanilla and complex products, with many complex products being able to be broken down into a simpler product(s). New financial instruments usually remix already existing, plain-vanilla instruments into more complex structures, requiring sophisticated pricing and legal structures

6.2.1   Currencies

Most countries (or groups of countries) have their own **currency** (i.e., money). They control its supply through their central bank or a similar institution. For example, the dollar is the currency of the United States, the renminbi is the currency of China, and the euro is the currency of the countries of the European Monetary Union, or Eurozone.

In foreign exchange transactions, one currency is exchanged for another currency. Banking institutions engage in foreign exchange transactions for a wide variety of reasons. For example, they may be conducting operations in more than their home country, requiring that they have cash on hand in a foreign currency to fulfill their obligations in that country.

Exchange rates reflect the relative value of one currency in relation to another currency. For instance, the exchange rate of 1.50 GBP (British pound)/USD (United States dollar) means that for each GBP you receive, you must pay USD 1.50. It also means that for each USD you receive, you must pay GBP 0.67 (= 1.5/1.0).

EXAMPLE

On January 10, GammaBank purchases GBP 1,000,000 for USD—it sells USD to buy GBP. The exchange rate between the GBP and the USD is 1.50; for each GBP, the bank has to pay USD 1.50. To purchase GBP 1,000,000, GammaBank must sell USD 1,500,000.

It is common to refer to the different exchange rates of one currency against other currencies in terms of **cross rates**. Figure 6.1 shows the major exchange rates from September 2008. The table expresses the value of six major currencies against each other and is interpreted as follows: For 1 unit of the column currency, you must pay the amount shown in the appropriate row. So, on that date, one GBP was worth USD 1.8029, CAD 1.8759, EUR 1.2565, and so on. This implies that USD 1 was worth GBP 0.5546 (= 1.0/1.8029); CAD 1 was worth GBP 0.5331 (= 1.0/1.8759); and EUR 1 was worth GBP 0.7959 (= 1.0/1.2565).

Figure 6.1   Foreign exchange rates from September 2008

	USD	GBP	CAD	EUR	JPY	HKD
USD		1.8029	0.9611	1.4349	0.0094	0.1288
GBP	0.5546		0.5331	0.7959	0.0052	0.0714
CAD	1.0404	1.8759		1.4929	0.0098	0.134
EUR	0.6969	1.2565	0.6698		0.0066	0.0898
JPY	106.221	191.5101	102.0914	152.4165		13.6804
HKD	7.7644	13.9988	7.4626	11.1412	0.0731	

Foreign exchange cross-rates, September 29, 2008

There are multiple factors that influence exchange rates. Key factors include inflation rates, political changes and instability, and currency regimes. **Currency regimes** determine to what extent a country or its government manages its currency relative to other currencies. Governments may fix their exchange rates, in which they attempt to keep the relative value of their currency fixed versus another currency or a "basket" of representative currencies, or float their exchange rates, whereby the relative value of the currency is determined by general market forces.

When banks trade currencies with each other, they often act as a broker on behalf of their clients that need to secure foreign currency to pay their bills. Many large multinational banks also actively trade currencies in their own account with other banks with the hope of profiting from exchange rate movements.

6.2.2   Fixed Income Instruments

Two of the most commonly referred to and traded fixed income instruments are loans and bonds. **Loans** and **bonds** are legally binding contracts through which the borrower (also referred to as the issuer of the bond or loan) borrows the principal amount specified in the bond or loan from an investor and in exchange pays a specified amount of interest, usually at regular intervals. The interest rate referenced in the contract is usually referred to as the **coupon rate** or **nominal rate**. This rate may be fixed or floating. For both bonds and loans, the fixed and floating interest rates behave as explained in Section 4.3.

At maturity (i.e., expiration), the borrower repays the principal amount to the investor. The repayment structure of fixed income instruments is similar to the structure discussed for loans in Section 4.4.7. Maturities can range from one day up to 40 years or more. There are bonds that have maturities exceeding 100 years as well as "perpetual" bonds, where the principal amount is never repaid. For a plain vanilla fixed income instrument, the amount of money the borrower receives is set at the day of the bond's issuance and will remain the same and not be affected by changes in the inflation or exchange rates that can happen over the life of the bond or loan. There are complex fixed income instruments that adjust the interest payments, and, in some cases, even the principal payments, to inflation rates.

EXAMPLE

Acme Inc. issues a five-year bond to a group of investors. With the bond, the company borrows USD 100 million at a fixed interest rate of 3% per annum. Each year, the company will make one interest payment of 3% * USD 100 million or USD 3 million to those investors who purchased and hold the bonds in accordance with their ownership interest. Five years from now, the company will make the last interest payment and repay the principal, the borrowed amount, of USD 100 million. Figure 6.2 shows the direction and size of these flows.

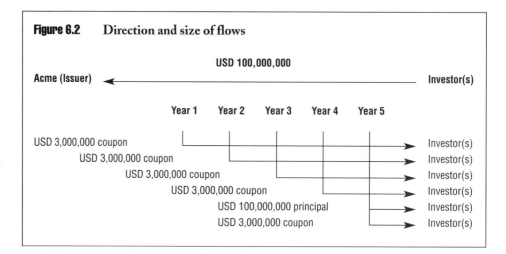

Figure 6.2   Direction and size of flows

One major difference between bonds and loans is that while there has been an active bond market for some time, loans were typically not traded publicly and were usually kept on the bank's balance sheet in the bank's banking book until the loan was paid in full. Historically, banks bought and sold loans to other banks in a limited market to rebalance their respective banking books to achieve their desired portfolio composition. In recent years, however, the market for loans has mushroomed into an active and sizable market, where large banks sell loans they have underwritten, without the intention of keeping these loans on their books, to nonbank investors. Occasionally banks may package groups of loans into what are termed *off-balance-sheet* vehicles or derivative products and then sold to investors. These off-balance-sheet vehicles have formed the basis for many of the credit problems that, starting in 2007, banks have faced. This process, termed *securitization*, was addressed in Section 5.3.

Once issued, most loans and bonds have fixed terms. That is, the coupon rate and the maturity date will not change, and so the size and timing of the loan payments are fixed.

The value of loans and bonds is affected by the interest rate that is driven primarily by three factors:

1. The interest rate of an equivalent risk-free fixed income instrument
2. The creditworthiness of the borrower or default risk
3. The time to maturity

If the interest rate increases, the value of the loan decreases, because for a fixed-rate bond, the fixed value of the future payments is worth less in present value terms. If the interest rate decreases, the value of the loan increases because the fixed value of the future payments is worth more in present value terms. Hence, loans and bonds are interest-rate sensitive instruments, and their value will fluctuate as interest rates change. There are also floating-rate bonds and loans where the interest rate and, consequently, the interest payments mirror an index that reflects the level of interest rates. When rates increase, the interest rate on the bond increases as well, and the value of the bond may remain unchanged. Investors should be careful to understand all the characteristics of the bond they may be considering investing in before actually buying the bond.

EXAMPLE

When the interest rate is 5%, then the value of USD 100 one year from now is not worth USD 100, but only USD 95.24, because investing USD 95.24 at 5% interest will grow to USD 100. Similarly, when the interest rate increases to 10%, the same USD 100 one year from now is only worth USD 90.91, because investing USD 90.91 at 10% interest will grow to USD 100.

In practice, a *risk-free* fixed income product would typically be a government bond, which may be considered to have no credit or default risk. If there is any risk of default, the interest rate must be adjusted with a premium that reflects the risk of default. Currently, U.S. Treasury securities are considered to be one of the safest government bond instruments.

EXAMPLE

Suppose a five-year government bond pays an annual coupon rate of 2%. In order to get investors to accept the default risk associated with the five-year corporate bond discussed in the previous example, Acme Inc. must provide a premium above the 2%, with the size of the premium being a function of the creditworthiness of the company. The more likely investors believe a company is to default, the higher the (interest) premium they will require from the company to invest in its bonds.

The chart in Figure 6.3 is a very simple way of remembering the relationship between interest rates and bond prices.

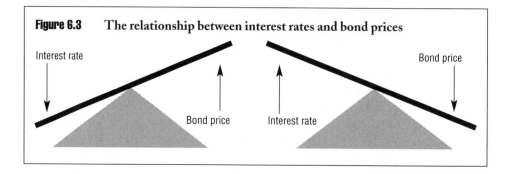

Figure 6.3   The relationship between interest rates and bond prices

The interest rate depends on several factors, including inflation, the general level of economic activity, the political and economic stability of the country where the issuer is located, and time to maturity. In general, the longer the maturity of the loans or bonds, the higher is the interest rate. The explanation is simple: To lend money for a longer time, the lender needs higher compensation for the risk of holding the instrument longer, which increases the level of uncertainty. Linking interest rates with maturity creates a **yield curve**, an example of which is shown in Figure 6.4.

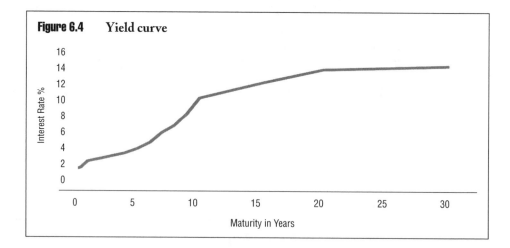

Figure 6.4   Yield curve

Banks trade *bonds* with each other to manage their liquidity, to profit from price appreciation due to changes in interest rates, or to manage their earning assets. Banks trade *loans* with each other primarily when they realign their credit portfolio. Usually, the trading of loans is related to credit portfolio management, particularly as it relates to concentration risk (see Section 5.3).

6.2.3   Interbank Loans

Banks also make loans to each other. Some banks have excess deposits either from unexpected inflows of deposits or because they cannot find suitable loan or investment alternatives for their deposits. These banks sell their excess funds to banks that need them to finance the loans they underwrite or investments they make. Interbank loans can have very short maturities—as short as one day (or overnight). Banks also consider interbank loans to make funds available to their depositors and to manage their liquidity requirements. In many countries, these markets are very active. Like loans and bonds, interbank loans are interest rate sensitive instruments.

Interbank loans are often priced off an index, such the **London Interbank Offered Rate**, or LIBOR. LIBOR is a daily reference rate average based on the interest rates that London banks charge in lending funds to other banks. LIBOR is quoted for numerous currencies and across different maturities ranging from overnight (one day) to one year. LIBOR rates, irrespective of their maturity, are quoted on an annual basis. LIBOR rates can influence the pricing of various types of financial instruments, including loans that banks make.

EXAMPLE

A USD 10 million floating-rate bond issued by Acme Inc. is priced at a 250 bp (2.50%) premium over three-months LIBOR. The interest rate on the floating-rate bond is determined at the beginning of each quarter.

- On January 1, LIBOR is 3.45%; the interest rate on this floating-rate bond for the next three months would be 3.45% + 2.50%, or 5.95%. The interest payment that Acme Inc. will make for the coming the three-month period would then be USD 1,487,500, or USD 10 million * 5.95%/4, as interest rates are quoted on an annual basis.
- On April 1, LIBOR is 2.95%. The interest rate on the floating-rate bond for the next three months would be 2.95% + 2.50% or 5.45%. The interest payment that Acme Inc. will make for the three-month period would then be USD 1,362,500, or USD 10 million * 5.45%/4, as interest rates are quoted on an annual basis.

6.2.4   Equities

Equities, also called **shares** or **stock**, represent a stake in the ownership of a company. The owners of the company are the shareholders, and they participate in the business of the company by voting their shares in support of or against proposals presented to them by the company's board of directors, which the shareholders elect. Shareholders, in most cases, receive dividends from the company's profits. However, some companies do not pay dividends. Instead, they rely on the company's rapidly growing business prospects to entice new stock investors to drive the stock value higher. Examples of these types of companies are technology firms that rarely pay dividends.

Shareholders also gain from an appreciation in the value of the shares: The more successful the company, the better the return earned by the holder and the better the opportunity for the company to grow and earn additional revenues to increase its dividend payments. The price of a share represents the market's perception of a company's current value and the value of its projected earnings. The price of shares will fluctuate as the market adjusts its valuation of the company in response to new information about the company.

6.2.5   Commodities

Commodities are generally homogeneous products irrespective of the geographical or physical market where they are being sold. For example, agricultural products such as corn, soybeans, and wheat, energy products such as crude oil, natural gas, and gasoline, are considered commodities, as are precious metals such as gold and silver.

The price of a commodity is chiefly determined by the supply and demand of the commodity. The rate of change to the supply and demand conditions for a commodity varies widely. For example, a drought in a country's farming region over several months leads to a decrease in corn growth, resulting in a decrease in the number of bushels of corn that would come to market for a prolonged period of time. As long as the demand for corn stays the same or increases, the price of corn due to its limited supply would increase until the supply and demand imbalance disappears. By contrast, within days, a hurricane can close down oil production in the Gulf of Mexico off the coast of the United States, resulting in a decrease in the number of barrels of oil that would come to market over the next week. As supplies are limited, and demand is not expected to change due to these events, the price of oil would also increase until the demand and supply are balanced. These and other factors make commodity pricing inherently complex.

EXAMPLE

Through distillation, crude oil is refined into products such as kerosene and butane. Each of these products is referred to as a specific commodity, and each one of them has its own market and price. Price differences may be determined by such factors as where they were refined and the cost of moving the final product to the user. But, each underlying market price is determined by supply and demand factors affecting the global market for each product.

Banks, through their brokerage units, may trade commodities on behalf of their customers and also for their own account. Commodity trading by banks is neither as common nor important as foreign exchange, fixed income, or equity financial instrument trading.

6.2.6 Derivatives

Over the past 20 years, derivatives have emerged as an integral part of the financial markets. **Derivatives** are financial instruments whose value changes in response to changes in the value of related underlying assets that can also be bought, sold, and traded. Examples of derivative contracts include futures, options, and forward agreements, among others. There are derivatives on currencies, interest rates, equities, and commodities. The main types of derivatives are the following:

- A **forward** is a nontransferable contract that defines the delivery of an asset such as commodities, currencies, bonds or stocks at a specified price, at a specified quantity, on a specified future date. An example of a forward is discussed in Section 6.4.5.
- A **futures** contract is a standardized and transferable contract that defines the delivery of an asset such as a commodity, currency, bond or stock at a specified price, at a specified quantity, on a specified future date.

EXAMPLE

On June 1, Acme Inc., based in Europe, knows that six month later, on December 1, it will have to pay JPY 150 million for goods from a Japanese supplier. On June 1, the exchange rate is 150 JPY/EUR. Foreign exchange futures with a maturity around December 1 also trade at 150 JPY/EUR. To lock in the 150 JPY/EUR exchange rate and to ensure that it will pay EUR 10 million for the goods (JPY 150 million / 150 JPY/EUR = EUR 10 million), it purchases—goes long—futures contracts, equivalent to JPY 150 million.

- **Options** convey certain rights to the buyer of an option. The two main types of options are a call option and a put option:[2]
  - A **call option** gives the buyer the right, but not the obligation, to buy a financial instrument from the seller of the option at a specified time (expiration date) for a specified price, called the strike price.

EXAMPLE

On the exchange, BankDelta buys a call option to buy 40,000 shares in Acme Inc. at EUR 35 per share on the expiration date of March 31. The option is sold to BankDelta by GammaBank. This gives BankDelta the right the buy the shares in Acme Inc. at a known price of EUR 30 per share from GammaBank. GammaBank must sell the shares to BankDelta at that price; in return, GammaBank receives a premium of EUR 1 from BankDelta. As long as the price of shares is less than EUR 35 per share, BankDelta will not exercise the option to buy the shares using the option since

---

2. Other alternative approaches may be used to distinguish between the different types of options.

it will be able purchase the shares in the open market at the lower price. As soon as the share price is greater than EUR 35, it makes sense for BankDelta to exercise the option and buy the shares from GammaBank for EUR 35. If the price of the shares at expiration is EUR 40, BankDelta makes a profit of EUR 5 per share, or EUR 200,000 in total, less the premium paid. This profit also represents the amount lost by GammaBank, which sold the option to BankDelta. In other words, what the buyer of the call option gains, the seller loses, and gains and losses cancel each other out.

The payoff of a long position in a call option is depicted in Figure 6.5. As the price of Acme Inc. shares increases, so does the value of the call option.

Figure 6.5   Payoff call option

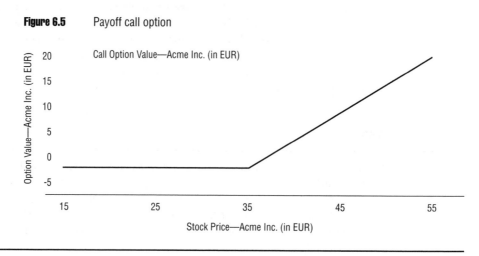

- A **put option** gives the buyer the right, but not the obligation, to sell a financial instrument to the seller of the option at a specified time (expiration date) for a specified price, called the strike price.

EXAMPLE

On the exchange, GammaBank buys a put option to sell 10,000 shares in Acme Inc. at EUR 35 per share on the expiration date of March 31. The put option is sold to GammaBank by BankVega. This gives GammaBank the right to sell the shares in Acme Inc. at a known price of EUR 35 per share to BankVega, who is obligated to buy the shares at that price. In return, BankVega receives a premium of EUR 1 from GammaBank. As long as the price of shares is higher than EUR 35 per share, GammaBank will not exercise the option to sell the shares using the option, since it can sell the shares at a higher price. As soon as the share price is below EUR 35, it makes sense for Gamma-Bank to exercise the option and sell the shares to BankVega for EUR 35. If the price of the shares at expiration is EUR 25, exercising the option is profitable for GammaBank. The profit is EUR 10 per share, or EUR 100,000, less the premium paid by GammaBank to BankVega. This profit also represents the amount lost by BankVega, which was obliged to buy the 10,000 Acme Inc. shares at EUR 35 per share though they are currently worth EUR 25. In other words, what the buyer of the put option gains, the seller loses, and the gains and losses cancel each other out.

The payoff of this transaction is depicted in Figure 6.6. As the price of Acme Inc. shares decreases, the value of the put option increases.

Figure 6.6   Payoff put option

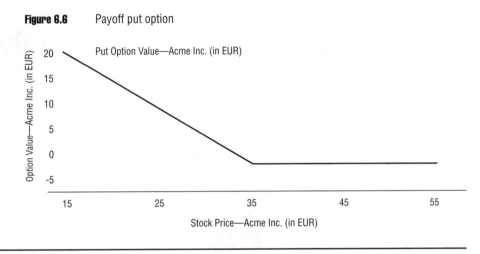

• **Swaps** allow two parties to exchange cash flows with each other at a future date.

EXAMPLE

Acme Inc. obtains a EUR 10 million loan from GammaBank for two years, agreeing to pay a floating interest rate set every three months based on LIBOR + 250 bp. Soon thereafter, the company comes to the belief that it expects interest rates to rise over the two-year period and decides it would be best to "lock in" a fixed rate. GammaBank, however, does not wish to convert the floating rate loan into a fixed rate loan. Acme Inc. can work around this by entering into an interest rate swap with AlphaBank. Acme Inc. agrees to pay to AlphaBank a fixed rate of 5% every three months, calculated on the same principal amount as its loan with GammaBank, or EUR 10 million. In return, AlphaBank agrees to pay a floating interest rate set every three months at LIBOR to Acme Inc. Figure 6.7 shows the direction of the flows between the three entities involved in the transaction:

1. Acme Inc. pays LIBOR + 250 bp to GammaBank
2. Acme Inc. pays fixed 5% to AlphaBank
3. AlphaBank pays LIBOR to Acme Inc.

The payment that changes hands between AlphaBank and Acme Inc. reflects the relative differential between LIBOR and the 5% fixed interest rate on the loan. Acme is now paying

GammaBank a floating interest rate set at LIBOR + 250 bp every three months on the loan, but receiving the same LIBOR-determined interest flow from its swap with AlphaBank. As a result of these transactions, Acme Inc. locked in an annual interest rate of 7.50%.

Figure 6.7   Payment flows in a swap

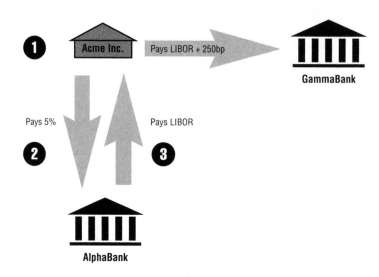

On January 1, LIBOR is 3.45%; the interest rate on this floating rate loan for the next three months would be 3.45% + 2.50% or 5.95%.

1. The interest payment that Acme Inc. will make to GammaBank for the coming three-month period would then be EUR 148,750, or EUR 10 million * 5.95%/4, as interest rates are quoted on an annual basis.

2. The interest payment that Acme Inc. will make to AlphaBank for the coming three-month period would then be EUR 125,000, or EUR 10 million * 5.00%/4, as interest rates are quoted on an annual basis.

3. The interest payment that Acme Inc. will receive from AlphaBank for the coming three-month period would then be EUR 86,250, or EUR 10 million * 3.45%/4, as interest rates are quoted on an annual basis.

The net effect of these three payment streams is
− EUR 148,750 − EUR 125,000 + EUR 86,250 = − EUR 187,500

This net EUR 187,500 payment for every three months equals EUR 750,000 per year, or 7.5% of the EUR 10 million loan. Acme Inc. was able to transform a floating rate loan through the swap into a fixed rate loan, and the company was able to reduce the uncertainty surrounding its interest expenses. Even if LIBOR were to exceed 5%, the interest rate that Acme would be paying would be capped at 7.50%.

Financial derivatives can be used to hedge, in other words, to reduce or cancel, the risk of an unwanted exposure. For example, if a bank wanted to protect itself against an increase in interest rates because it holds a large quantity of bonds in its trading portfolio, it could sell futures contracts equivalent to the portfolio's value, to set up a hedge against a decrease in bond prices. A further example of a hedge will be set out in Section 6.4.5.

6.3 Trading

Banks engage in **trading** operations and buy or sell financial instruments. In some cases, the trading is conducted on behalf of the bank's customers—where the bank acts as a middleman or intermediary—and does not directly risk the bank's capital. In other cases, the trading is done to benefit the bank itself by seeking short-term profits from favorable moves in the market prices. This type of trading, known as proprietary trading, puts the bank's capital directly at risk.

Trading is risky: Prices may not move in the direction the bank expects and the value of the financial instruments may change adversely and hurt the bank. The bank must decide on how much risk it is willing to assume to make a profit, usually referred to as a bank's **risk appetite**. Generally, higher risk implies higher expected return. But higher risk also means that the likelihood of losses increases as well. The trade-off between risk and return is fundamental to any institution. This relationship is shown in Figure 6.8.

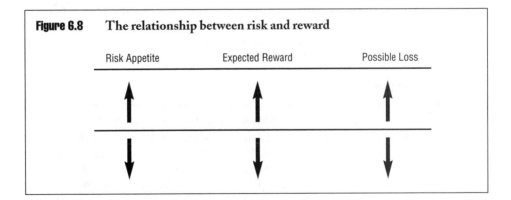

Figure 6.8 The relationship between risk and reward

6.3.1 Fundamental Trading Positions

In financial markets, a **position** refers to the ownership status of a particular financial instrument. There are two fundamental trading positions: The long and the short position. The holder of a **long position** bought the financial instrument and will profit if the price of the instrument goes up or will incur a loss if the price of the instrument goes down.

EXAMPLE

The trading desk of GammaBank expected the price of crude oil to increase in the future from its current level of USD 75 per barrel. To capitalize on this positive price view (increase in price), it purchased 500 crude oil futures contracts at USD 75 per barrel. Several weeks later, the price of crude oil increased to USD 95 per barrel. If GammaBank were to exit from the trade (sell its position) now, it would sell the contracts for USD 95 per barrel and realize a profit of USD 20 per barrel. The bank had a long position in the crude oil contracts and benefited from the price increase in crude oil. However, had the price decreased to USD 65 per barrel, the bank would have lost USD 10 per contract.

The opposite position is a **short position**. The term *short position* has two different meanings, depending on whether the investor/trader is dealing in futures contracts or stock, bonds, or other financial instruments.

The holder of a short position in a commodities futures contract has the obligation to deliver a commodity when the contract expires. Usually, producers of commodities sell short their future production to lock in the price of the commodity in advance. The holder of a short position will profit if the price of the commodity goes down or incur a loss if the price goes up.

In equity markets, if an investor believes that shares of a company are overvalued (i.e., too high) and thinks the price will go down in the near term, the investor can establish a short position by borrowing shares from a broker and then selling the shares. At some time in the future, the investor can buy the shares back and return them to the broker. If the investor sold the shares for more than the cost to purchase the shares, it profits; otherwise, it incurs a loss. This applies to bonds, stocks, or any other financial instruments one sells but does not own.

EXAMPLE

The trading desk of GammaBank expected the price of gold to decrease in the future from its current level of EUR 800 per ounce. To capitalize on this negative price view, it has sold short several hundred gold futures contracts at EUR 800 per ounce. If GammaBank holds onto these futures contracts until they expire, it would be required to deliver the amount of gold that represents the several hundred contracts they sold. Several months later, the price of gold fell to EUR 750 per ounce. If the bank were to exit from the trade and close out its position, it would have to buy the same number of contracts for EUR 750 per ounce. Because GammaBank purchased the gold futures contracts for less than it sold them, it realized a profit of EUR 50 per ounce. The bank had a short position in the gold contracts and benefited from the price decline in the gold upon which the futures contract was based. However, had the price of gold increased to EUR 850 per ounce, GammaBank would have lost EUR 50 per ounce on the deal if it sold its contracts at that time to limit its loss.

Figure 6.9 gives an overview of the relationship between the value of the position and the price change of a long or a short position.

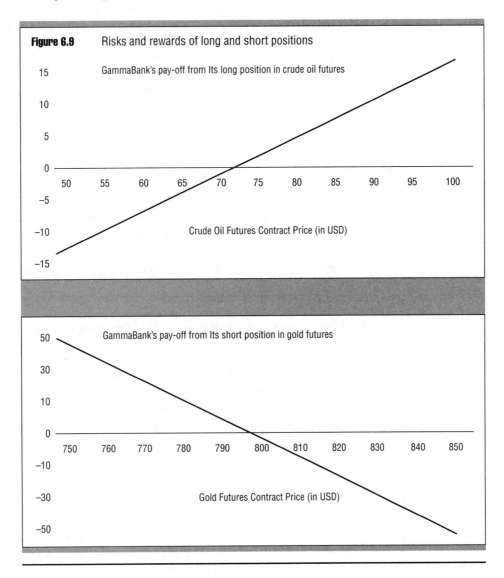

Figure 6.9   Risks and rewards of long and short positions

Speculation involves buying (long position), holding, selling, and short-selling (short position) financial instruments such as stocks, bonds, loans, commodities, foreign exchange, derivatives, or any financial product in the expectation that price fluctuations will generate a profit. Specifically, a bank is not seeking to hedge or protect itself from a price change in a position it already owns, it is simply buying or selling with the hope of earning a profit. The two previous examples using GammaBank also show how speculation in the marketplace works. The bank did not own the actual crude oil or physical gold commodities, it simply bet on the prices of those commodities going up or down. However, if for some reason the bank held either the oil or gold futures contracts to expiration it would have had to purchase the physical oil and gold in the marketplace in order to fulfill its futures contracts obligations.

6.3.2   Bid-Ask Spreads

In buying and selling financial instruments, traders will quote prices at which they are willing to buy or sell the financial instrument. The difference between the buy price (bid) and sell price (ask) is called the **bid-ask spread**.

EXAMPLE

A trader at GammaBank offers to buy stock of Acme Inc. at EUR 10.15 per share, and another trader offers to sell the same stock at EUR 10.25 per share. The bid-ask spread is EUR 0.10.

The size of the bid-ask spread is an indicator of market liquidity: The narrower the bid-ask spread, the closer the buyers and sellers are to placing a true market value on the financial instrument and the more transactional volume or liquidity the market has. This liquidity, referred to as market liquidity, is a very important component of any marketplace, and liquidity is a highly desirable market characteristic that market participants actively seek.

EXAMPLE

Expanding on the above example, unforeseen market events have negatively affected Acme Inc. Virtually all buyers have exited the market for Acme Inc., and interest in its stock has disappeared, resulting in diminished liquidity of, or demand for, its stock. Low liquidity and few buyers contribute to a drop in the bid price from EUR 10.15 to EUR 9.75. The ask price remains the same, EUR 10.25; the bid-ask spread has widened to EUR 0.50.

Note that **market liquidity** refers to the ability to trade in and out of a position without significant price effects. This type of liquidity is fundamentally different from the liquidity that banks must manage on a daily basis: The ability to repay depositors on demand (see Chapter 2).

6.3.3   Exchange and Over-the-Counter Markets

Financial instruments such as foreign exchange contracts, bonds, equities, commodities, and derivatives are traded on either regulated financial markets, called exchanges, or the over-the-counter markets.

An **exchange** is a centralized marketplace where brokers and traders meet and, on behalf of their customers or on their own account, buy and sell standardized financial instruments such as equities, bonds, commodities, options, and futures. For any financial instrument to be traded on an exchange, it must meet both regulatory requirements imposed by the exchange's regulator and listing requirements imposed by the exchange itself. For instance, many stock exchanges impose listing requirements on the listed company regarding the number of shareholders, the stability of earnings, and the size of the company's assets. Futures exchanges list standard contracts that first must be approved by a regulatory body. Any changes to the contract's terms must also be approved.

Historically exchanges possessed a central physical location where trades took place called "trading floors." However, trading floors are being replaced in many markets by pure electronic trading platforms where there is no physical meeting place and brokers execute all transactions electronically, through purpose-built computer systems *(trading platforms)* supporting the exchanges. On these trading floors or in these electronic trading platforms, brokers interact with each other, buying and selling (trading) instruments on behalf of their clients—buyers or sellers—or for their own account. The transactions that the brokers execute, either as agents on behalf of their clients or for their own account, contractually and legally bind the parties to complete the trade as agreed. Moreover, all the trades between the brokers are logged, recorded, and displayed by the exchange. Because both the price and the volume of trades are available and oftentimes prominently displayed on the trading floor or in the electronic marketplaces and are disseminated through price reporting services electronically, exchanges create price transparency that allows market participants to continually price their own holdings of financial instruments.

Whether the transaction takes place on the trading floor of an exchange or in an electronic marketplace owned by an exchange, the parties to the transaction operate according to an agreed set of exchange rules, which in many cases requires clearing their trades and transactions through a "clearinghouse" that is typically affiliated with the exchange. A **clearinghouse**, oftentimes referred as the central counterparty, becomes the buyer to each seller and the seller to each buyer, effectively standing in the middle of the transaction to guarantee the financial performance of the trade as agreed by the parties to the transaction. Each clearinghouse or central counterparty has its own rules, regulations, and conventions, which may differ across the different types of financial instruments that are traded on the same exchange that the clearinghouse or central counterparty clears. However, a clearinghouse typically offers credit support mechanisms, which are supported by the clearinghouse's members and are transparent to the market participants to ensure that the parties to the trade will receive financial compensation if the counterparty to the trade is not able to deliver on the trade as agreed. The different sources of credit support include insurance and collateral, or margin, that the clearinghouse members post with the clearinghouse.

Clearinghouses require their member clearing through the clearinghouses to post collateral or **margin**. (It should be noted that not all brokers are clearinghouse members. Those who are not would trade through a broker member using what is called an omnibus account.) When the broker posts the margin, it provides and transfers to the clearinghouse a high-quality instrument that is both liquid and exhibits low price variability; generally government bonds, such as U.S. Treasuries, or cash deposits serve as acceptable form of margin. The amount of the required margin (**margin requirement**) that the brokers are obligated to post is determined by various material considerations, including the different types of instruments the broker trades on the exchange, the risk of the instrument, and the overall trading volume. The amount of the margin is recalculated at least daily to reflect the trades or other exposures that the broker has, and the broker is required to maintain a margin requirement with the clearinghouse. Were the clearinghouse to deem that the margin posted by the broker is insufficient—due to an adverse price movement in the instruments that the broker trades in or holds, or a sudden, unexpected, and material decline in the value of the collateral provided by the broker—the broker must post additional margin so that the collateral provided reflects the broker's exposure and meets the clearinghouse's minimum aggregate margin requirements. When a broker is required to post additional collateral to fulfill the margin requirements, the notification is termed a **margin call**.

In case the broker fails to deliver on a trade that it has executed at the exchange, for whatever reason, the clearinghouse liquidates the collateral posted by the broker and uses the proceeds from its sale to compensate the broker's counterparty. The availability of and access to collateral significantly mitigates the counterparty credit risk inherent in buying and selling financial instruments. How this compensation is paid depends on the specific financial instrument that was traded between the parties and on clearinghouse rules, regulations, and commercial conventions; it can include some form of financial compensation paid directly to the party that was adversely impacted from the default.

Buyers and sellers who transact as customers through a broker are required to post collateral with their brokers. The amount of the initial margin required to be posted by the broker's customers is determined by the type of financial instrument traded. The margin posted in the customer's account with the broker must meet the minimum margin requirements, as determined by the exchange or clearinghouse. There are brokerages that may insist on higher margin requirements to protect themselves from the risk that a customer may become unable or unwilling to settle the transaction as agreed. It is the margin posted by the brokers' customers that is often used to support the margin the broker posts with the clearinghouse. Additionally, the customers must also meet the required minimum margin requirements imposed by the clearinghouse; the broker has the obligation to maintain the customers margin or issue its own margin call, requiring the customer to replenish the account by providing securities or cash.

In the case of futures markets, the daily profits and losses are added or subtracted from the customer's account (mark-to-market). This adjustment made to the customer's margin requirement based on daily mark-to-market value of the account is called **variation margin**.

While exchanges offer standardized products, price transparency, clear rules that govern the transactions between the buyers and sellers, and collateral support through the clearinghouse, they do not offer the flexibility many sophisticated investors need as such investors must individually structure the trades that they want for hedging or other purposes. These transactions are executed in the over-the-counter markets instead, where both the flexibility and the ability to customize trades and transactions exists.

The **over-the-counter** or **OTC market** does not have a physical location for its marketplace. In the OTC market, the buying and selling of financial instruments takes place directly between the two parties to the transaction through the use of phones or computer networks, with each party directly assessing and taking on the risk of the creditworthiness of the other party to the transaction. Most notably, foreign exchange, derivatives, bond and commodity trading, and some equity trading activities are conducted in the OTC markets. Due to the general need and/or desire in the market to customize instruments and to match as closely as possible the needs and desires of the two parties to the transaction, the OTC market is massive compared to the exchange marketplace.

The use of collateral in the OTC market is not regulated or standardized as it is in the exchange-traded markets. When parties to an OTC transaction demand collateral from each other, they negotiate to determine the size and quality of the specific type of collateral they would be willing to accept to ensure that performance will occur as agreed. In some limited instances, standardized OTC transactions will move to an exchange marketplace for the primary reason of using a clearinghouse to guarantee the transaction. The movements of these transactions to an exchange for this purpose of ensuring counterparty credit is developing rapidly, reflecting the interest from market participants to extend the protection offered by central clearinghouses to OTC transactions.

Figure 6.10 is a general comparison of the OTC and exchange-traded markets.

Figure 6.10   **A general comparison between OTC and exchange markets**

	Over-the-Counter Market	Exchange-Traded Market
Contract terms	Separately negotiated	Standardized
Size of a trade	Parties to the transaction agree on the size.	Set by the exchange, depends on the product and standardized specifications. May need to purchase multiple contracts, depending on how much of the product is required.
Price	Parties determined price through negotiation.	Generally reflects the value market partici-pants trade at. Price is disseminated by price-reporting services.
Legal requirements	Separately agreed and documented between the parties, although form "master agreements" are usually set forth general terms with annexes used to customize the agreement.	Parties agree to abide by the rules of the exchange, which are legally binding.
Transparency	Little if any transparency	Highly transparent
Counterparty risk	Each party determines the risk of its counterparty and limits its transactions according to its own risk appetite for that counterparty.	Exchange clearinghouses guarantee the transaction, eliminating the need to consider the counterparty's risk profile. However, should look at exchange guarantee system to ensure comfort with exchange clearinghouse guarantee system and risk.
Collateral	Individually negotiated and held by the party demanding the collateral.	Broker requires collateral from its customer, which is calculated on the exchange's margin requirements, although the broker may ask for more from the customer than the exchange may require. The broker transfers the margin to the exchange to cover all its customer positions at that exchange. The broker's margin requirement is tied directly to the exchange's margin requirements.

The size of the OTC markets is substantially larger than the size of exchange-traded markets. According to data from the Bank for International Settlement,[3] the daily OTC turnover in April 2007 on the foreign exchange markets, including spot, forward, and swap transactions, averaged USD 3.2 trillion (USD 800 trillion annualized), and the daily turnover of various OTC interest rate derivatives averaged USD 1.7 trillion (EUR 425 trillion annualized).

6.4 MARKET RISK MEASUREMENT AND MANAGEMENT

There are four general market risk categories: Foreign exchange, interest rate, equity, and commodity risk. Market risk can either be general or specific. General market risk refers to adverse change in a market that affects market participants broadly. Specific risk refers to change in conditions that only affect one company.

6.4.1 Types of Market Risk

To better understand the four different types of market risk, this section describes each risk type:

1. **Foreign exchange risk** is the potential loss due to an adverse change in foreign exchange rates and applies to all exchange rate-related products whose positions are valued in a currency that differs from the bank's reporting currency.

EXAMPLE

In August 1998, it was reported that Telekomunikasi Indonesia had incurred a loss of USD 101 million as a result of movements in foreign exchange rates. The losses were due to borrowings of USD 306 million, JPY 11 billion, and FRF 130 million, each of which had been converted into IDR, Indonesia's local currency. The Indonesian government devalued the IDR against major currencies including the U.S. dollar, Japanese yen, and the French franc. The devaluation meant that the bank had to pay more IDR to repay the loans it took out in JYP, FRF, and USD.

---

2. **Interest rate risk** is the potential loss due to adverse changes in interest rates. (As discussed above, the value of a bond will increase if interest rates decrease and decrease if interest rates increase.) Note that the value of fixed income instruments will change if either the creditworthiness of the borrower changes or the risk-free interest rate changes. The potential change to the creditworthiness of the borrower

---

3. Bank for International Settlements, Triennial Central Bank Survey, foreign exchange and derivatives market activity in 2007, December 2007.

is the *credit risk* associated with the loan. The potential change to the interest rate is the *market risk* associated with the loan.

EXAMPLE

In the early 1990s, the treasurer of Orange County in the state of California was responsible for managing a portfolio of USD 7.5 billion belonging to Orange County schools, cities, and the county itself. The treasurer's investment strategy assumed that interest rates would either fall or remain low. This approach worked well until 1994 when interest rates increased. The increases in interest rates drove the value of the county's bond investments so low that in December 1994, the government of Orange County announced that its investment pool had suffered a USD 1.6 billion loss. Subsequently, the county declared bankruptcy. This was stunning news to the markets, as it represented the largest loss ever recorded by a local government authority in the U.S.

3. **Equity risk** is the potential loss due to an adverse change in the price of stocks and applies to all instruments that use equity prices as part of their valuation—for example, derivative products such as futures contracts.

EXAMPLE

Enron, a company in the United States, filed for bankruptcy following an unprecedented accounting scandal that was uncovered in late 2001. Over several years, Enron had accumulated a wide range of energy-related holdings and businesses in the United States and abroad and became a dominant player in the energy business. Throughout these expansive years, the company provided financial information to the shareholders that indicated Enron's growth was robust and that management successfully created a financially stable, strong, and highly profitable company. In reality, however, the company's management used complex, materially misleading, and fraudulent accounting transactions that effectively hid the true financial position of the firm: Its substantial and accelerating losses and sizable liabilities. The deceptive accounting practices involved highly complex and opaque legal transactions that moved Enron's losses to corporations that were affiliated and controlled by Enron. However, due to the structuring of Enron's accounting transactions, their total impact on the company's financial health was not transparent. Enron did not have to disclose this information. Moreover, as Enron's affiliated corporations were not publicly traded, their true financial condition were not disclosed to the public. Only the top executives of Enron were aware of the extent of the deceptive accounting practices.

Since very few individuals outside the top management of Enron were aware of the systematic deceptive accounting practices, the financial markets perceived Enron as a very successful company. Its stock was considered to be a good and safe investment and appreciated considerably over time. By August 2000, Enron's shares were trading at USD 90. Slowly, over the following 14 months, the price of the company's shares started to decline, mainly due to a material weakening in the financial markets.

While the company's management publicly encouraged investment in Enron, as Enron's share prices softened, many executives, who were either directly involved or able to recognize the severity of the misleading accounting statements, began to sell their shares aggressively. By August 2001, the shares dropped to around USD 40. At that time, more and more—previously undisclosed—information came to the market that showed the company's accounting information and accounting practices were systemically fraudulent and misleading. As the true financial situation of Enron emerged, the price of the shares dropped from USD 40 to mere pennies by the time Enron was forced into bankruptcy in December 2001.

4. **Commodity risk** is the potential loss from an adverse change in commodity prices. This applies to all commodity positions and any derivative commodity positions such as futures contracts.

EXAMPLE

Between July 2008 and October 2008, the price of crude oil plummeted significantly. During July 2008, the price of one barrel of crude oil was roughly USD 135-140. These prices were the highest oil prices recorded, and many believed that oil prices would continue to climb during 2008 and could reach USD 160 per barrel or more by the end of the year.

High oil prices are a threat to companies whose business is very sensitive to the price of crude oil. To reduce the price they expected to pay for crude oil later in the year, many energy price-sensitive companies have entered into agreements where they purchased crude oil for delivery in October 2008 at the price prevailing in July 2008, or roughly USD 140 per barrel. For example, if a company in June 2008 purchased 1,000 barrels of crude oil for delivery in October 2008, it paid about USD 140,000. The significant and unprecedented price appreciation abruptly stopped however, and by December 2008, the price of crude oil dropped below USD 50 per barrel. Companies that had entered these contracts with the expectation that the price of oil would stay roughly the same or increase started to receive crude oil worth USD 50 per barrel, yet were paying USD 140 per barrel. The loss of USD 90,000 is entirely due to commodity risk—an adverse change in commodity prices.

The loss to these companies is pure gain to the sellers of crude oil, who held contracts to sell crude oil for USD 140 when the price was USD 50.

6.4.2　Value-at-Risk

To measure market risk in their portfolios, banks commonly use a concept termed **value-at-risk (VaR)**. VaR provides a qualified answer to the question, "How much could we lose in the next day (or week, month, year)?" Formally, VaR is defined as the predicted loss at a specific confidence level (e.g., 95%) over a given period of time (e.g., 1 day). Note that VaR does not provide the worst-case loss, but instead uses a confidence level, generally 95% or higher. With a 99% confidence level, for example, VaR estimates the loss level such that 99% of the time, the actual loss level will be less than that number.

EXAMPLE

GammaBank's risk management team calculates a 1-day, 99% VaR for market risk to be EUR 3 million. This means that there is a 1% chance markets could turn against it and it could lose more than EUR 3,000,000. That also means that there is a 99% chance that losses will be less than EUR 3,000,000 the next day. In VaR terms, its (1-day, 99% confidence level) VaR is EUR 3,000,000.

Calculating VaR involves closely examining current positions and estimating the distribution of possible return values the portfolio could see during the next time period (typically one day for market risk). The graph in Figure 6.11 shows an example return distribution for a portfolio and can be interpreted as follows. The horizontal *X*-axis represents possible gains and losses. Losses would be points to the left of zero and profits to the right. The area under the curve must sum to one. At any particular gain or loss, the height of the curve represents the probability of that gain or loss.

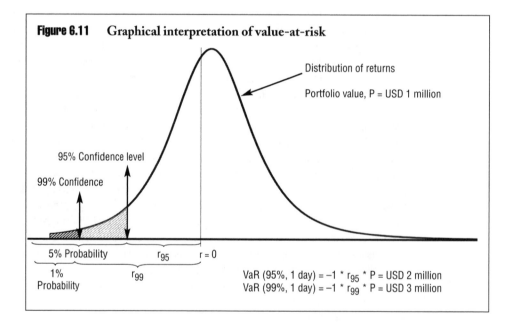

Figure 6.11   Graphical interpretation of value-at-risk

Distribution of returns

Portfolio value, P = USD 1 million

95% Confidence level

99% Confidence

5% Probability r_{95} r = 0

1% r_{99}
Probability

VaR (95%, 1 day) = −1 * r_{95} * P = USD 2 million
VaR (99%, 1 day) = −1 * r_{99} * P = USD 3 million

For GammaBank, the figure above offers a graphical interpretation of its VaR. The line labeled 95% confidence level is at – USD 2 million. The shaded area under the curve to the left of the line is 5%, indicating that there is a 5% chance losses could be greater than USD 2 million. The 1-day 95% VaR is thus USD 2 million. Further to the left, at – USD 3 million, there is a line labeled 99% confidence level. The area under the curve left of that line is 1% of the area below the entire curve and indicates that there is a 1% chance that losses could exceed USD 3 million and that the one-day VaR at 99% confidence level is USD 3 million.

Most of the effort in calculating VaR involves estimating the return distribution, and approaches include the use of common probability distributions—such as the normal distribution, also known as a bell curve, and shown in Figure 6.13—to simulate possible returns and losses. Other approaches also estimate possible returns and losses and include large-scale simulation of randomized potential outcomes and the use of historical return data to predict returns and losses. When implementing a VaR system, risk managers must be cognizant of the different strengths and weaknesses, relative to accuracy and computational effort, of the various approaches.

Given an estimated return distribution—the values that an asset might return—for the current portfolio, the VaR value corresponds to the loss level X such that the probability that losses are less than X equals the given confidence level. In Figure 6.13, the rightmost bar on the horizontal axis corresponds to the 95% VaR.

VaR is a very general concept that attempts to provide a concise snapshot of the current market risk profile of the bank's portfolio. VaR has broad applications in risk management, including market, credit, and operational risk.

VaR as a concept has some shortcomings that are important to emphasize:
*   *VaR is measured with estimation error.* That is, the estimated return distribution is derived from a quantitative model that typically makes simplifying assumptions and is therefore not a precise statement of the range of possible outcomes.
*   *VaR does not give any information about the severity of loss by which it is exceeded.* That is, if the loss amount does exceed the VaR value, VaR does not provide any information about how much greater the loss might be. Risk managers will typically consider a range of confidence levels to understand better the range of possible losses and alternative risk measures such as expected shortfall.
*   *Most importantly, VaR does not describe the worst-case loss but the worst case for a specified confidence level.* This is a point to be emphasized and remembered.

6.4.3   Stress Testing and Scenario Analysis

Although a 99% VaR measure may capture a wide range of all possible outcomes, risk managers must pay particular attention to the remaining 1% of outcomes since these events could cause banks serious financial problems. Stress testing and scenario analysis are important tools of any risk management system that seeks to understand how a portfolio will perform in extreme cases. Given the reliance on modeling, risk measures need to be closely examined and tested against extreme events.

Stress testing considers instances for particular value changes, such as a rapid change in interest rates or equity indices. Scenario analysis evaluates portfolio performance in severe states of the world, either hypothetical or historical.

For example, scenarios that a risk manager may consider for an equity portfolio would be to model and use the U.S. stock market crash of 1987 or the 1997 Asian financial crisis. Other scenarios might be based on natural disasters, wars, changes in political situations—virtually anything that would have a dramatic effect on market prices.

Stress tests are an essential part of risk management and involve a number of supporting activities, such as ensuring that the assumptions underlying each stress test are reasonable. Stress testing has become more important over the years and is now a major part of a bank's risk management activities.

6.4.4   Market Risk Reporting

Communication is a key part of effective risk management, and once risks have been measured, risk reports must be shared with traders, risk managers, senior management, and members of the board of directors. Contents of the risk report typically vary according to the business line and seniority of the users, but most reports include information about trading and balance sheet positions being held by the bank, the reason for the position, where it's being held, the date of its maturity, current profit/loss status, the volatility of the position, and many other factors. Risk reports will also typically provide current risk metrics, including value-at-risk (VaR) values for several confidence levels, stress test results, and analysis of risk by sector, geography, and other factors. Risk reports should allow users to quickly assess the current risk level of the portfolio and identify possible areas of overexposure where risk mitigation may be needed.

The frequency of risk reports may vary according to the user of the information. For example, the most demanding users of market risk information are the bank's traders, who will need real-time risk reports in order to function properly.

6.4.5   Hedging

Banks and individuals hedge in order to reduce or cancel out a risk. When a bank **hedges** a position it currently holds in a financial instrument, the position is matched as closely as possible with an equal and opposite offsetting position in a financial instrument that tracks or mirrors the value changes in the position being hedged. Usually, hedging involves a position in a derivative that mirrors as closely as possible the value changes of the underlying asset.

Hedging is the opposite of speculation. In a speculative trade, the bank chooses to take a calculated risk in the expectation of a positive future return. In a hedging trade, the bank chooses to limit some of the risk exposures it has by sacrificing some, if not all, possible future returns.

While hedging sounds complicated, in fact it is not. In our everyday lives, we all hedge. The simple act of buying car insurance is a hedge against the impact of an accident. In exchange for our payment to the insurance company, it provides insurance. The insurance company promises to pay expenses associated with an accident that we are involved in. What the insurance achieves is simply to reduce the effects of risks that we are exposed to. It is important to remember that the risks still exist; the insurance does not reduce the likelihood that an accident will occur, but, rather, offers financial compensation to us when things go wrong—the undesirable outcome.

Similarly, checking the weather before embarking on a lengthy journey is a hedge against bad weather. We cannot control the weather, but we can, in fact, adjust what we pack for the journey and when we take off on the trip. By adjusting our behavior, we are hedging against the impact of bad weather—the undesirable outcome.

Hedging financial exposures is akin to buying car insurance or checking the weather report. The intended effects are the same—reduce the impact of the undesirable outcome. But the ways financial hedges are created are significantly more complex. The following equity example is a straightforward illustration of hedging in the financial sense. It involves an exposure—the stock or equity—we want to hedge and the "insurance" that we use to hedge our exposure—the put option. For financial hedges, the insurance often involves a derivative. Options are derivatives. The reason we use derivatives to hedge financial exposure is because they derive their value from another asset, usually from the asset that we hedge or an asset that has similar characteristics to the one that we hedge.

For instance, if an investor owns equity in a company, an option would replicate the value of that asset. If the value of the asset increases, the value of the option changes as well; the direction of the change depends on the type of option. As the value of the asset increases, the value of a call option (see Section 6.2.6) increases and the value of the put option (see Section 6.2.6) decreases. Conversely, as the value of the asset decreases, the value of a call option decreases and the value of the put option increases.

To summarize:
- In a long equity position, the undesirable outcome is that the value of the equity decreases; to hedge, a put option should be purchased (long position in a put option) because the value of the put option increases as the value of the stock decreases.
- In a short equity position, the undesirable outcome is that the value of the equity increases; to hedge, a call option should be purchased (long position in a call option) because the value of the call option increases as the value of the stock increases.

The equity example can be extended to more complex situations, but the principles remain the same. The approach can also be extended on interest rate risk—the risk that interest rate changes adversely impact the bank. In most cases, this means that the cost of borrowing—deposits—is greater than the income the bank earns on its loans. This is an undesirable outcome, and the banks use derivatives that reduce this risk.

EXAMPLE

GammaBank has purchased 2,000 shares of Acme Inc. at EUR 30 per share, or EUR 60,000. The bank would like to hedge this equity risk and buys a put option (see Section 6.2.6). The put option on Acme Inc. with three months to expiration and a strike price of EUR 30 has a EUR 3.50 premium. By purchasing 2,000 put options (with three months to expiration and a strike price of EUR 30) for EUR 7,000, the individual has hedged the equity risk for this position over the next three months.

To see this more clearly demonstrated, consider the possible prices of Acme Inc. after three months in Figure 6.12.

Figure 6.12   Value of positions

Price of Acme Inc. in 3 Months (P_{ACME})	Value of Put Option at Expiration	Value of Combined Positions (shares + put options)
< EUR 30	EUR 30 − (P_{ACME})	2,000 * (EUR 30 − (P_{ACME}) + (P_{ACME})) = EUR 60,000
≥ EUR 30	EUR 0	2,000 * (EUR 0 + (P_{ACME})) = EUR 2,000 * (P_{ACME})

If the price of Acme Inc. in three months is greater than or equal to EUR 30, the put options would be worthless—the bank would not want to sell the shares for EUR 30 because the current price is greater than that. However, the shares would be worth EUR 2,000* P_{ACME}, which is greater than or equal to the EUR 60,000 GammaBank paid. If the price of Acme Inc. in three months is less than EUR 30, the bank would exercise the put option and sell the 2,000 shares to the seller of the put option for EUR 30 each for a total value of EUR 60,000. The effect on the value of the position of these changes is depicted in Figure 6.13.

Figure 6.13   Payoff position in Acme stock and put option

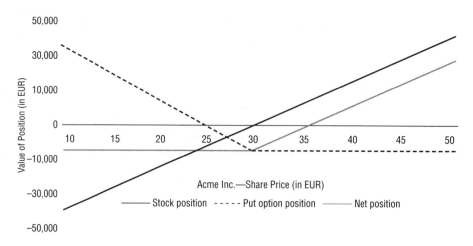

By purchasing the put options, GammaBank has eliminated the possibility of loss from this equity position, assuming that the counterparty does not collapse and exposes the bank to counterparty default. The value of the equity position, no matter how low the equity price drops, will be offset by the increase in the value of the long position in the put option, less the premium paid for the options. Note that for this insurance, the bank paid a EUR 7,000 premium, the cost to hedge this risk. This cost does not change and is not at risk (it cannot increase) and has been incurred by GammaBank and will not be returned to it. This is the out-of-pocket cost of entering into the hedge.

In a similar manner, banks can use derivative products to hedge interest rate risk, commodity risk, and foreign exchange risk. An example of derivatives that reduce interest rate risk is forward contracts.

Derivatives have a wide use in banking and allow a bank to lend/borrow funds at a fixed rate for a specified period starting in the future, thereby reducing the effect changing interest rates have on the interest rate margin. Derivatives, such as the swap described in Section 6.2.6, help borrowers to modify the interest rate on loans they pay.

EXAMPLE

When a bank needs to borrow funds from another bank, its concern is that interest rates will increase, making borrowing more expensive. Conversely, when a bank needs to lend funds to another bank, the concern is that rates decrease, making lending less profitable. In both of these cases, the undesirable outcome is caused by changing interest rates. Through hedging, the interest rate each party may earn is set in advance, so the effects of changing interest rates can be calculated by the bank into its returns.

In a transaction involving forwards, there is no exchange of principal. When the forward contract matures, a cash payment is made for the difference between the rate of the contract and the reference rate, usually LIBOR.

EXAMPLE

On February 1, when one-year LIBOR is 3%, Bank A forward contracts to lend Bank D USD 1,000,000 on April 31 for one year at an interest rate of 3%. No exchange of money takes place on February 1. On April 31, the amount of money exchanged depends on the interest rate that day.

- If one-year LIBOR rates are 2.5% on April 31, Bank A stands to profit because Bank D is obliged to borrow the USD 1 million at the preagreed 3% rate. Bank A's profit on the transaction will be (3% − 2.5%) * USD 1,000,000, or USD 5,000.
- If one-year LIBOR rates are 4.0% on April 31, then Bank A will lend the money at 3%. This means Bank A will lose (4% − 3%) * USD 1,000,000, or USD 10,000. Bank D reduces its borrowing expenses, having to pay 3% for the loan instead of 4.

The gains and losses cancel each other out. In the first example, Bank A gained USD 5,000; that gain equals Bank D's loss. In the second example, Bank D gains USD 10,000; the loss to Bank A is the same. This is the result of using the forward contract and other financial derivatives: transferring risks between the two banks. The objective of the above transaction is to reduce or share risks. In return for bearing certain risks, the companies involved are willing to accept a reduction in their profits.

Reducing the impact of undesirable outcomes is the same as reducing risks. This is the essential objective of hedging.

6.5 Market Risk Regulation—The 1996 Market Risk Amendment

The original Basel I Accord only considered credit risks. In 1996, after consultations with the financial community, the Basel Committee issued the Market Risk Amendment, which was implemented at the end of 1997. Basel II Accord's rules on market risk are largely unchanged from the 1996 Market Risk Amendment. The objective of the amendment was to create a capital "cushion" to balance the negative effects of price movements. Bank trading activities were the primary focus. The bank's trading book refers to the portfolio of financial instruments held by a bank to facilitate trading for their customers, to profit from speculative positions, or to hedge against various types of risk. The Market Risk Amendment created a capital requirement for market risk for:

* Interest rate-related instruments and equities in the trading book
* Foreign exchange and commodities positions throughout the bank

The Market Risk Amendment introduced two methods for banks to use in calculating market risk capital requirements: The Standardized Approach and the Internal Models Approach.

* The **Standardized Approach** is similar to the standardized credit risk approach and consists of instrument-specific risk weights. These weights are applied to all the bank's holdings that are exposed to market risk. The bank's total market risk regulatory capital is the summation of its risk capital requirement across the risk categories of equities, commodities, and currencies.

    This approach uses an arbitrary risk classification; an 8% capital charge is uniformly applied to equities, currencies, and commodities without regard to their actual risk and volatility. Since the risk charges are systematically added up across the different sources of risk, this approach does not account for any offsetting of risks by looking at an entire bank's portfolio or by looking at how well the bank is diversified. This approach tends to lead to a higher regulatory capital requirement, or less "risk-based" capital requirement.

- The **Internal Models Approach** relies on the bank's own internal risk management models and improves on the Standardized Approach. This approach determines the regulatory capital requirement based on the bank's VaR calculations. The bank calculates its 10-day, 99% VaR for adverse changes in interest and exchange rates, commodities, equity, and option prices. Since the VaR is based on the portfolio of the bank's positions, it considers both correlations and portfolio effects across instruments and markets and rewards risk diversification. Thus, banks using this approach to determine their regulatory capital requirements would generally have lower regulatory minimum capital than those using the Standardized Approach.

  In using the internal model approach, the bank's internal risk management models must meet certain regulatory requirements. These regulations also provide banks incentives to improve the accuracy of their internal estimates of the bank's market risk exposure.

CHAPTER 7

Operational Risk

Operational risks are present in virtually all bank transactions and activities and are a major concern of bank supervisors, regulators, and bank management alike. Failing to understand operational risk increases the likelihood that risks will go unrecognized and uncontrolled, resulting in potentially devastating losses for the bank.

Chapter Outline

- 7.1 What Is Operational Risk?
- 7.2 Operational Risk Events
- 7.3 Operational Loss Events
- 7.4 Operational Risk Management
- 7.5 Basel II and Operational Risk

Key Learning Points
- Operational risks are inherent in business and reflect losses from inadequate or failed internal processes, systems, human error, or external events.
- The Basel II Accord identifies five different operational risk events: internal process risk, people risk, legal risk, external risk, and systems risk. These risks are interrelated.
- Operational risk events are characterized by their frequency and impact on the operations of the bank. Banks focus their operational risk management on high-frequency/low-impact risks and low-frequency/high-impact risks.
- Operational risk inventory that collects information on operational risk events can either be top-down or bottom-up.
- The Basel II Accord provides three different approaches to calculate operational risk capital: the Basic Indicator Approach, the Standardized Approach, and the Advanced Measurement Approach.

Key Terms

- Advanced Measurement Approach
- Basic Indicator Approach
- Beta factor
- Bottom-up approach
- Business risk
- External risk
- High-frequency, low-impact, HFLI events
- Internal process risk
- Legal risk
- Low-frequency, high-impact, LFHI events
- Operational loss events

- Operational risk
- Operational risk capital
- Operational risk management
- People risk
- Process mapping
- Reputational, or headline, risk
- Risk analysis
- Risk monitoring
- Standardized Approach
- Strategic risk
- Systems risk
- Top-down approach

Operational Risk

7.1 WHAT IS OPERATIONAL RISK?

Operational risk relates both to problems in the bank's internal processes and to external events affecting the operations of the bank. In recent years, banks have started to address their operational risks, such as fraud and theft, in the same formal manner they manage credit and market risks.

Operational risk is the potential loss resulting from inadequate or failed internal processes or systems, human error, or external events. This definition from the Basel II Accord includes legal risk but excludes strategic and reputational risk.

Over the last 20 years, banking saw an increase in the number of operational risk events that severely impacted both business prospects and profitability. Many events were severe enough to cause catastrophic losses for a bank, far in excess of their capital, such as the collapse of Barings Bank and the demise of Kidder Peabody, once a highly regarded U.S. securities firm. The following is a description of an operational risk event at Barings Bank that erased the venerable bank's capital and ultimately resulted in its collapse.

EXAMPLE

In 1995, Baring Brothers and Co. Ltd. (Barings), headquartered in London, collapsed after incurring losses of GBP 827 million following the failure of its internal control processes and procedures. One of the company's traders dealing on both the Singapore Futures Exchange and the Osaka Securities Exchange had been able to hide losses from his ever-increasing trading activities for more than two years by manipulating trading and accounting records. The trader anticipated an increase in the Japanese stock market and acquired a significant position in Japanese stock index futures. When a devastating earthquake hit the Japanese city of Kobe in January 1995, the Japanese stock market dropped precipitously. This led to considerable losses on the trading positions.

Initial assessments considered this a "rogue trader" incident. However, subsequent analysis revealed that better internal controls could have minimized or prevented the loss. The trader had the authority not only to approve his own trading activities, but also to handle the operational aspects of the very same trades he made. The bank's senior management failed to ensure a segregation of duties between the trader and the operational activities that supported his trading. This fundamental shortcoming resulted in the loss of GDP 827 million, twice the bank's available trading capital. Barings was unable to cover that loss. By March 1995, Barings, including all of its liabilities, was acquired for a nominal GBP 1 by the Dutch bank Internationale Nederlanden Group (ING).

Operational risk events are inherent in running any type of business, not only banks. Banks fully expect that operational risk events will happen, and the more complex the operations of a bank are, the more likely it is there will be significant operational risk events that can affect the bank's profitability. Banks often make provisions in their financial plans for operational losses.

7.2   OPERATIONAL RISK EVENTS

The Basel II Accord considers five broad categories of operational risk events:
1.   Internal process risk
2.   People risk
3.   Systems risk
4.   External risk
5.   Legal risk

These operational risk events are interrelated. Figure 7.1 provides examples for various operational risk events.

Figure 7.1   Operational risk events

Operational Risk Category	Example
External risk	• Events having negative impact that are beyond the bank's control, such as terrorist attacks or natural disasters
Internal process risk	• Failure of the bank's processes and procedures • Inadequate control environment
Legal risk	• Uncertainty of legal action • Uncertainty of rule and regulation applicability
People risk	• Employee errors • Fraud
Systems risk	• Computer, technology, and systems failure • Continuity planning

Additional operational hazards include business risk, strategic risk, and reputational or headline risk.

- **Business risk** is the potential loss due to a weakening in the competitive position of the bank.
- **Strategic risk** is the potential loss due to poor business decisions or incorrect execution of business decisions.
- **Reputational, or headline, risk** is the potential loss due to a decrease in a bank's standing in public opinion.

7.2.1   Internal Process Risk

Internal process risk is the risk associated with the failure of a bank's processes or procedures. In carrying out a bank's day-to-day operations, the staff will conduct business according to prescribed procedures and policies. Corporate policies and procedures include the checks and controls required to ensure that customers receive appropriate service and that the bank operates within the laws and regulations governing its activities. Examples of internal process risk include:

- *Lack of controls*. Failure to audit recorded transactions in and among bank and customer accounts.
- *Marketing errors*. The bank represents that a service includes a specific feature— a checking account that provides free checks for the life of the account that in reality is not actually offered.
- *Money laundering*. Engaging in a transaction or transactions to conceal where money is coming from, whose money it is, and/or where the money is going.
- *Documentation or reporting*. Reports required by the bank's regulators are not accurate or correct; account opening documentation is incorrect or insufficient.
- *Transaction error*. A teller adds an extra zero to a deposit, making it GBP 3,000 instead of GBP 300.
- *Internal fraud*. Intentional behavior on the part of an employee to enrich the employee or the bank at the expense of the customers, clients, or the bank itself.

Errors often occur when a process is unnecessarily complicated, disorganized, or easily circumvented, all signs of inefficient business practices. Reviewing and improving a bank's internal processes to improve operational risk management often enhances the bank's operating efficiency and overall profitability. Similarly, frequently auditing processes and analyzing procedures can reduce internal process risk.

EXAMPLE

At the end of November 2001, UBS Warburg, a Swiss bank, lost an estimated USD 50 million on its trading book due to a mistake by one of its employees. A UBS Warburg trader in Tokyo, Japan, incorrectly sold 610,000 Dentsu shares at 16 yen each, rather than 16 shares at 610,000 yen each. Though the order was questioned by the computerized trading system, an operational failure allowed the trade to go through with the incorrectly transposed amount and price. The computer notification system was not programmed to provide adequate controls.

7.2.2   People Risk

People risk, the risk associated with employee error or fraud, is a common source of operational risk. People risk can occur in every part of a bank, even in the bank's risk management function. People risk is more apt to occur due to:

- *High staff turnover.* Frequent changes in staffing means new people do not have the required background, experience, or training; may not fully understand the processes; and are more apt to commit errors frequently.
- *Poor management practices.* An unclear oversight structure where employees report different risk events to several separate risk functions, and each separate risk function follows conflicting practices, procedures, and policies.
- *Poor staff training.* During the training of new staff, errors are likely to occur, particularly when the trainers themselves are relatively recent hires.
- *Overreliance on key staff.* Gives rise to burnout of overworked staff.

EXAMPLE

A commodities trader received an order to buy "1,000 beans," which is an informal way to say "200 soybeans futures contracts" in the specialized commodities futures trading language used by the exchange participants at the Chicago Board of Trade (CBOT). Each soybeans futures contract traded at the CBOT is for the delivery of 5,000 bushels of soybeans, a common contract size for most agricultural commodity futures traded at the CBOT (1 bushel of soybeans equals roughly 27 kg).

This trader was not trained correctly in trading agricultural commodities and was not aware that an order for "five beans" means one soybeans futures contract for 5,000 bushels in the language the exchange participants used. He mistakenly transmitted not an order to buy 200 soybeans futures contracts—the order he received—but rather, 1,000 soybeans futures contracts, five times as many contracts as needed.

Although various internal control systems signaled that the trade needed authorization from the trader's supervisors, the controls did not prevent the trade. When the trader sought clearance for the trade from the supervisors, they questioned the order. However, the trader overrode the existing control systems, in part because the trader's supervisors were heavily burdened by a broad range of other supervisory and administrative tasks, and did not have time to focus on this issue.

The safeguards that would have prevented the execution of the incorrect trade failed. At the end, the trader established a soybeans futures contract position that was substantially larger than needed. Trading 1,000 soybeans futures contracts on CBOT was such an unusual and significant trade that as the order was executed, the price of these contracts increased significantly. When the internal control systems finally caught the error made by the trader and the decision was made to liquidate the majority of the position, the 800 soybeans futures contracts that had to be sold fetched significantly lower prices than the trader paid for them, causing the trader's employer a sizable loss.

7.2.3 Systems Risk

Systems risk is associated with the use of computer technology and computer systems. All banks rely heavily on computers to support their day-to-day activities. In fact, banks today cannot operate without computer systems. Technology-related systems risk events can be caused by the following:

- *Data corruption.* An electrical surge alters data as they are being processed.
- *Inadequate project control.* A failure to properly plan could affect the quality of a risk report produced by the computer system.
- *Programming errors.* Computer models can be inadvertently programmed to generate inaccurate results.
- *Overreliance on "black box" technology.* This is a problem when users believe that the computer systems' internal mathematical models are correct without considering the problem and its solution from a conceptual or qualitative perspective, and without stress-testing the system adequately.
- *Service interruption(s).* An electrical failure results in not being able to access reports.
- *System security problems.* Computer viruses and computer hacking are increasingly problematic.
- *System suitability.* System hardware might not be sufficient to handle high traffic volumes and crashes or provides inaccurate results.

In theory, the failure of a bank's technology could lead to a catastrophic event, even the bank's collapse. Heavy reliance on technology makes technology failure an important consideration for senior management—banks have invested heavily to ensure that their operations can continue despite technology failure events. This process is called *continuity planning* or *business resumption planning*.

EXAMPLE

The "Year 2000" (Y2K) transition is an excellent example of the banking industry's commitment to continuity planning. Computer programs designed in the 1970s and 1980s stored dates using the last two digits of the year only: The year 1978, for example, would be recorded as "78." In the mid-1990s, banks realized that on January 1, 2000, their computer systems might stop working correctly simply because the new two-digit date would change from 99 to 00 (1999 to 2000).

Considerable investments in reprogramming were made in order to assure business continuity in time for the transition. The media speculated on the potential impacts of the Y2K "bug." For example, on January 1, 2000, would a deposit made in 1999 be credited with 100 years of interest? Or since the current date would change to 00, could it mean that a deposit made in 1938 would stop earning interest? The first of January 2000 came and went without any major Y2K technology disasters—not just in the U.S, where some USD 400 billion was estimated to have been spent in preparation, but even in countries where the problems had been widely ignored.

Though costly, resolving the Y2K bug provided unexpected benefits for U.S. and other banks. To identify and resolve problems before they occurred, banks had first to analyze their internal processes and then establish the relationship(s) across these processes. **Process mapping**, analysis of a business process from inception to completion by identifying and planning all the processes surrounding the activity in detail, unearthed many operational inefficiencies.

7.2.4   External Risk

External risk is the risk associated with events occurring beyond the direct control of the bank. External risk events are generally rare, but when they occur, they can have significant impact on a bank's operations, substantial enough to merit extensive media coverage. Examples of such external events are large-scale robberies, fire, natural disasters, riots, and civil protests. Such events can be caused by:

- Events at other banks, which impact banks industrywide (widespread bank closures, or a bank run)
- External fraud and theft
- Terrorist attacks
- Transport system interruption, which can prevent bank staff from getting to work

EXAMPLE

On September 11, 2001, the 110-floor World Trade Center twin towers in New York City were destroyed by two airplanes that were deliberately flown into them; another airplane destroyed parts of the Pentagon outside of Washington, DC; a fourth plane crashed in the state of Pennsylvania. These acts of terror significantly impacted the financial markets, as the World Trade Center was located near Wall Street, the financial heart of New York City, and many financial institutions had either offices in the destroyed buildings or in buildings nearby that had to be evacuated, either because they were also damaged by debris or for precautionary reasons.

Since the attacks occurred before trading on the major exchanges opened in New York, the stock exchanges did not open for business that day and reopened for trading only on September 17, 2001. When stock market trading started again on Wall Street, equity values declined significantly.

The trading floor of the New York Board of Trade, a commodities exchange, was located in the World Trade Center complex and was destroyed in the attacks. That exchange was able to resume trading on September 17 from a backup facility that it opened after the 1993 terrorist attack on the World Trade Center.

Trading in government bonds halted after the attacks and resumed on September 13, but trading was low as several major government bond dealers had offices in the World Trade Center. One of them, Cantor Fitzgerald (see Section 7.3.2), the market-leading government bond dealer, had its offices in the twin towers and lost all its employees who were working that day. In the immediate aftermath of these attacks, many banks and other financial institutions evacuated their personnel working in New York and elsewhere, causing further disruption in the financial world.

7.2.5   Legal Risk

Legal risk is the risk associated with the uncertainty of legal actions or the application or interpretation of contracts, laws, or regulations. Legal risk varies greatly from country to country; in some cases, legal risk results from unclearly stated laws, which can lead to murky legal interpretation.

Laws passed in the EU or the U.S. often reach across borders and may restrict a bank's international banking activities. With the passing of complex money-laundering, antiterrorism, and customer data protection legislation all around the world, legal risk has evolved as a prominent risk.

EXAMPLE

In December 2003, the United Kingdom Financial Services Authority (FSA) fined Abbey National Bank (Abbey) GBP 2 million for failing to comply with anti-money-laundering regulations. While no actual money laundering had occurred, the bank was fined for contravening the new anti-money-laundering rules that the UK government passed. According to the FSA, between December 2001 and April 2003, Abbey systematically flouted the compliance rules that FSA imposed on banks to monitor money laundering and demonstrated a clear disregard of regulatory directives. When Abbey launched an internal review of its own compliance system, it found that a third of the branches failed to check their customers' identification properly and others did not regularly share accurate information with the bank's central compliance function. Abbey's failings also reflected that its overall compliance monitoring was disorganized and generally lacking over a prolonged period. Moreover, Abbey was slow, in some cases up to four months late, in reporting suspicious activities to the appropriate police agency.

7.3   Operational Loss Events

Operational loss events are commonly classified by the frequency with which they occur, as well as the severity of the potential loss. As shown in Figure 7.2, operational risk management practices focus on two general loss types: loss events that occur often, but with low impact or severity (high-frequency/low-impact event); and loss events that occur infrequently, but with high impact (low-frequency/high-impact event). Banks generally are not concerned with the other extremes: low-frequency/low-impact events would cost more to manage and monitor than the losses from these events would merit, and high-frequency/high-impact events, which would imply a very poorly managed bank that was destined to fail. As shown in Figure 7.2, operational risk management should strive to ensure that high-frequency operational risk events are very-low-severity events, and that high-severity events are very-low-frequency events.

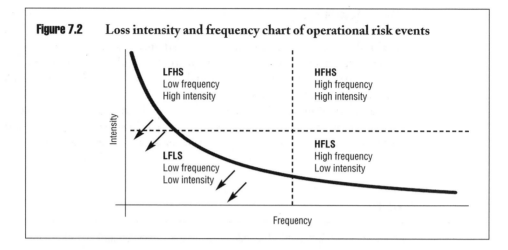

Figure 7.2   **Loss intensity and frequency chart of operational risk events**

7.3.1   High-Frequency/Low-Impact Risks (HFLI)

At an individual incident level, losses from **high-frequency/low-impact (HFLI) operational risks** may be minor, but collectively, HFLI events are considered important enough to include in the bank's business decision-making processes. Many financial service providers will factor in these kinds of losses within their product pricing structures. For example, petty fraud and process failures can occur relatively frequently (high frequency), but with relatively low cost, and so are viewed as a "cost of doing business." HFLI risk is generally managed by improving business efficiencies.

EXAMPLE

Credit card fraud in the form of unauthorized purchases is common. Identifying potentially unauthorized charges on credit cards is integral to any bank's operational risk management function. To identify and prevent unauthorized charges, complex computer programs analyze every single transaction for each credit card. Based on the location, the frequency, the type, and the amount of the transactions, these programs establish a spending pattern unique to each card.

When a credit card that is primarily used to pay for groceries in rural Germany is suddenly charged with the purchase of expensive jewelry in a different part of the world, the bank's software identifies the jewelry transaction as a pertinent deviation from the card's spending pattern. The risk management function usually suspends any further transactions for that particular card and immediately contacts the owner to inquire whether the transactions were in fact made or authorized by the owner.

If the credit card transactions were made without the consent of the credit card owner, the bank has successfully identified a compromised credit card and will invalidate or cancel the transactions. Then, the bank will replace the compromised card with a new credit card.

This process is costly. When banks adjust their credit card pricing structure, fees, annual interest rates, and membership fees, it is often to provide for the costs of fraud detection and deterrence. Credit card fraud is HFLI—high frequency, low-impact. Though costly, it would be of much higher impact if banks did not aggressively monitor cardholders' usage.

7.3.2   Low-Frequency/High-Impact Risks (LFHI)

Low-frequency/high-impact operational risks represent a challenging dimension for risk managers. Because losses from this category of operational risk rarely occur, these events are difficult to model and predict. But because losses from these events can be extremely large, LFHI risks must be considered and managed. Rogue traders, terrorist attacks, and fires are examples of LFHI risks. LFHI events can result in the collapse of a bank.

EXAMPLE

The brokerage and investment bank Cantor Fitzgerald lost its New York City headquarters in the World Trade Center terrorist attacks of September 11, 2001. The company lost all 658 employees who were in the office that day, about two-thirds of its work force. However, thanks to the dedication and commitment of its remaining employees, the cooperation of its clients, and the support of its backup resources (the result of business continuity planning), Cantor Fitzgerald was able to restart its business within a week, ensuring its clients' needs would be met and its remaining personnel would continue to be employed.

7.4   Operational Risk Management

The **operational risk management** process aims to reduce the bank's overall risk level to one that is acceptable to both the bank's senior management and its regulatory supervisor. The typical operational risk management process can be split into five fundamental steps illustrated in Figure 7.3:

Figure 7.3   Steps in the operational risk management process

- *Identification.* The first step is to consider all the bank's services, processes, and procedures and identify the potential risks and controls in place relating to each service, process, or procedure. Process mapping and self-assessment questionnaires are common methods used in identifying operational risks.
- *Assessment.* The next step is to consider each identified risk and assess the effectiveness of existing controls in mitigating the risk's potential impact. The risk assessment process provides a good indication of the bank's risk profile at both aggregate and individual business unit levels, and highlights those areas that require improved controls.
- *Measurement.* Operational risk measurement involves quantifying the potential losses from each identified risk. Operational risk can be approximated using simple measures based on the size of the organization or particular business units or modeled based on frequency and severity, as discussed in the previous section.
- *Mitigation and control.* Once operational risks have been identified, assessed, and measured, additional controls and process improvements can be developed and implemented to further mitigate identified risks to levels that are consistent with the risk level of the organization. Process design enhancement and segregation of duties are examples of methods for reducing operational risk.
- *Monitoring and reporting.* Operational risk management (and all risk management) requires ongoing monitoring of risks and concise, timely communication to bank managers, employees, and regulators. Regular risk reports on operational risk events allow bank management to better understand and assess the operational risk profile of the institution and to allocate required resources effectively to safeguard against unexpected increases in risk events.

7.4.1   Functional Structure of Operational Risk Management Activities

Banks can choose among several organizational structures to manage operational risk. These designs differ in implementation and location within the bank's internal organization. Usually, the bank's operational risk management function is a part of the following business structures:

- A *centralized risk function* is responsible for risk management across the entire bank.
- A *business line risk function* is responsible for evaluation of an individual business line.
- An *individual business unit risk function* is responsible for operational risk management for a business unit and supported by a central risk management group or function.

To achieve efficiencies, banks commonly adopt a mixed approach. Many banks locate the **risk analysis** function centrally at the headquarters, or main office, level. The **risk monitoring** functions are located as close to business units as possible. Defining clear roles and responsibilities for the operational risk management functions strengthens the operational risk management system. Independent of how a bank structures its risk analysis, monitoring, measuring, and management functions, there are two main approaches to building a companywide operational risk profile:

- The **top-down approach** first establishes a general assessment of risk from the highest or broadest levels within the organization; see Figure 7.4. It then refines this portfolio-level assessment by breaking the risks down into their individual components, carefully reviewing the individual processes and their attendant risks. This analysis always moves from a broad-based approach to an increasingly more specific approach—from a portfolio level, to a business line level, to the business unit level—to better gauge the risk's potential effects. The results of this analysis are then used to assess the gravity of both the individual risks and their financial effects, and to provide inputs for the firm's operational risk capital calculations.

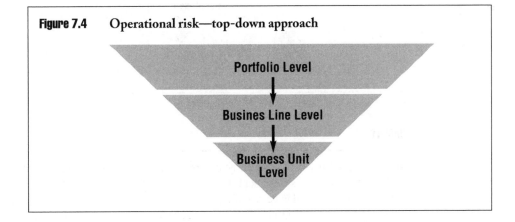

Figure 7.4　　Operational risk—top-down approach

EXAMPLE

In 1990, Bankers Trust, a New York-based bank, initiated a top-down approach to assess its operational risks. One of the first steps in this process was to ask the bank's key business line managers about potential loss scenarios within their business that "kept them awake at night." For each of these businesses each "desk" manager was then asked to assess the operational risks they encounter. Then, they quantified past losses for each business and assessed the likelihood that these risks could occur again. Managers were also asked about effective risk response approaches to mitigate the impact of these operational risks. This review led to the creation of an extensive inventory of risk classes. The inventory was then used to quantify the bank's overall exposure to each type of operational risk.

- In the **bottom-up approach**, first the risk management function assesses all processes within each business unit separately and benchmarks each unit's risk profile;

it then aggregates identified risks at a corporate level. The information is presented to a risk management committee or other oversight risk control function to generate a companywide risk profile. This risk profile is the aggregate of risk profiles of each individual business process; see Figure 7.5. Based on these results, the bank's operational risk capital is assessed.

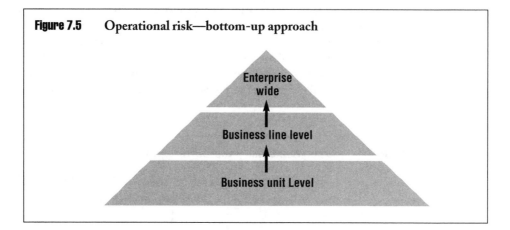

Figure 7.5   Operational risk—bottom-up approach

EXAMPLE

Bank of Tokyo-Mitsubishi UFJ created a complex risk self-assessment database in which each risk event was analyzed. The system contained 103 different types of risks. For each risk event, the appropriate risk types had to be identified, and managers had to assess what the potential losses could be, predict how frequently these events would likely occur each year, define factors that could predict the occurrence of the risk event, list procedures that could reduce these operational risks, and assess how effective the procedures could be.

Although the operational risk assessment approach of Bankers Trust and Bank of Tokyo-Mitsubishi UFJ seem similar, there is one fundamental difference between the two. Bankers Trust, based on its historical experience, created a companywide operational risk inventory, which then helped it to quantify its aggregate operational risk exposure. Bank of Tokyo-Mitsubishi UFJ looked at each of its business processes and, based on this self-assessment, developed operational risk management and measurement approaches. It then based its calculations of the bank's aggregate operational risk exposure on these results.

Whichever of these approaches—top-down or bottom-up—a bank adopts, it must be consistently maintained and appropriate to the overall risk profile of the bank. Factors that influence this decision include the size, sophistication, nature, and complexity of the bank's activities.

7.4.2   Operational Risk Identification, Assessment, and Measurement

Operational risk management begins with the identification and assessment of the risks inherent in the bank's services, policies, and procedures. The contemporary best practices used to study, assess, and analyze operational risks include:

- *Audit oversight.* The focus is on a review of individual business processes by external auditors, this practice is usually used to supplement the bottom-up approach.
- *Critical self-assessment.* Each business unit analyzes the nature of the operational risks it faces. This subjective method leads to an inventory of various risks, including an evaluation of the frequency and severity of past losses. Often this approach would include the development of risk control processes, such as checklists and questionnaires. This is a bottom-up approach.
- *Risk mapping.* This relates process flows, organizational units, and business units to various operational risk types to help management understand the location of operational weaknesses within the bank. This is considered a bottom-up approach.
- *Causal networks.* A map of the factors that directly or indirectly cause an operational risk event is created. Using complex models, these causal networks are used to measure the magnitude and distribution of operational risk losses and improve the understanding of them. This bottom-up approach is widely used because it captures the causes of risks.
- *Key risk indicators.* These measures the change in risks over time so it can be estimated how risky activity is using objective statistical methods. This approach builds on the assumption that as activities with key risk indicator of an activity increase, so will the likelihood and magnitude of an operational risk event from an activity. Using early warning signs—increased staff turnover, trade volumes, number of failed trades, the frequency and severity of errors within one business unit, etc.—potential losses can be estimated. This approach can be both top-down and bottom-up.
- *Actuarial models.* The focus is on the frequency and magnitude of operational risk losses and is based on internally collected or externally sourced information. This approach uses mathematical modeling methods from the insurance industry and can be used from both a bottom-up or a top-down modeling approach.
- *Earnings volatility.* The earnings of various operational units within the bank are analyzed and the historical changes in the earnings are calculated. This approach assumes that variations in earnings reflect operational risk events and not changes in the business environment. It relies heavily on historical data and thus is a back-ward-looking measure of risk. A shortcoming of using earnings volatility as a measure is that changes in operational risk management approaches within a business due to improved processes or better understandings of risk events are not quickly recognized in this top-down approach.

7.4.3   Example of Operational Risk Measurement and Management

To better understand the operational risk management process, consider the following simple example in which a bank reviews the process mapping of a check deposited in an account. The process of depositing a check at a bank usually consists of the steps shown in Figure 7.6.

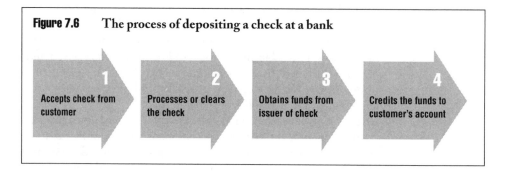

Figure 7.6   The process of depositing a check at a bank

1 Accepts check from customer

2 Processes or clears the check

3 Obtains funds from issuer of check

4 Credits the funds to customer's account

In identifying the potential operational risks, the bank considers employees' responsibilities at each step of the process and the possible operational risks that present themselves along the way. Suppose that during this process, the bank notices a number of problems that occurred, for example, with clearing international checks deposited in customer accounts from certain countries.

In assessing the problems with international check deposits, the bank finds that for the 50,000 transactions of a total value with EUR 6 billion it processed last year involving foreign checks from three countries, 950 experienced problems and processing errors, or about 2%, resulting in a loss to the bank of EUR 100,000. The bank concludes that international check processing for these three countries classifies as a high-frequency, low-impact event: correcting each of the 950 events costs the bank EUR 105 in personnel and other related expenses. The bank has now sufficient historical information to estimate both the distribution of frequency and severity of future losses from international check deposits.

To mitigate these losses, the bank decides to implement a control that causes checks from these three countries to be flagged for special attention to ensure they are properly cleared.

Finally, the bank monitors and reports the frequency and severity of losses from all international check deposits so that managers can identify patterns, trends, and clusters of errors, providing valuable objective and other analytical information that will assist in preventing problems and/or determining the root cause of an event (failure). Bank supervisors also have access to these reports through their oversight function, and will review them and make recommendations to bank management if they uncover issues of importance.

7.5 BASEL II AND OPERATIONAL RISK

The Basel II Capital Accord made operational risk management a new priority. Under Pillar 1 of the Accord, banks are required to quantify operational risk, measure it, and allocate capital as they do for credit risks and market risks. Basel II defines operational risk as the risk of loss resulting from inadequate or failed internal processes, people, and systems errors, or external events. Basel II outlines principles for developing and operating an operational risk framework that addresses the following:

- Development of an appropriate risk management environment internally
- Risk identification, assessment, monitoring, and mitigation/control
- The role of bank supervisors
- The role of disclosure

Basel II expects banks to manage operational risk to reduce the probability of adverse risk events. Properly managing operational risk should directly improve the bank's calculation of its operational risk capital.

Operational risk capital is capital allocated against possible operational losses. In drafting Basel II, the Basel Committee was aware that introducing an operational risk capital requirement could significantly impact the amount of regulatory capital that banks need to hold. The committee also recognized that requiring banks to value their operational risk and calculate risk capital (the first time for many banks) may present onerous challenges and expenses, particularly for smaller banks with simple risk profiles. For some banks, the cost of implementing highly complex methodologies for calculating operational risk capital could very well be greater than the benefits to be derived. So the Basel II Committee allowed flexibility, suggesting banks could use any one of three different approaches to calculate operational risk capital, or any combination of the three approaches:

1. Basic Indicator Approach
2. Standardized Approach
3. Advanced Measurement Approach

By allowing banks to choose from the three approaches, the Basel II framework encourages banks to become more precise in their approach to assessing the operational risks and calculating operational risk capital. Each approach is increasingly more sophisticated and more costly to implement than the previous one, but each is also believed to target a bank's operational risk capital requirement more accurately. The more accurate the analysis and assessment, the more certain a bank can be that it is not overestimating its actual operational risk capital needs, which would reduce its potential profitability.

7.5.1   Basic Indicator Approach

The **Basic Indicator Approach** uses the bank's total annual gross income as a risk indicator for the bank. This approach assumes that the more income the bank earns, the larger it is and the greater its operational risk. The bank's required level of operational risk capital is computed as a fixed percentage of the bank's annual gross income averaged over the previous three years (excluding negative and zero annual gross income years from both the numerator and denominator). The fixed percentage as set by the Basel Committee is currently 15%.

Given its simplicity, the Basic Indicator Approach is certainly the least costly in terms of internal systems and support. However, it is a generally inferior alternative for measuring the magnitude of operational risk—the bank may be setting aside more capital to cover operational risks than it needs to. Most banks engage in a wide variety of different types of businesses, each with an inherently distinctive risk profile, specific internal operational risk monitoring requirements, and earnings potential. That all business activities represent the same level of risk is a potentially hazardous oversimplification, and therefore, the fixed percentage set by the Basel Committee attempts to overestimate the risk potential, resulting in a higher operational risk capital requirement. In practice, the Basic Indicator Approach is limited because it is not a true indicator of risk and does not require a methodical review of the bank's services, policies, and procedures. However, it is simple and requires little in the way of direct expense.

EXAMPLE

AlphaBank makes loans only to corporate entities with assets in excess of EUR 200 million and high-net-worth individuals with assets in excess of EUR 10 million. It also focuses its business to deal with only a select number of these corporations and high-net-worth clients. BetaBank specializes in home mortgages and equity lines of credit to a wide, rapidly expanding, and predominantly retail, customer base. Both banks have the same positive gross annual income for each of the past three years. AlphaBank's business is likely to present less operational risk. Yet, under the Basic Indicator Approach, both banks would calculate their operational risk capital allocation as the same proportion of their gross income.

7.5.2   Standardized Approach

The **Standardized Approach** to calculating a bank's operational risk capital requirement attempts to address some of the concerns related to the lack of risk sensitivity in the Basic Indicator Approach. The Standardized Approach divides the activities of a bank into eight business lines and then applies a fixed percentage, or **beta factor**, against the average positive annual gross income (over three years) of each. The beta factor varies, depending on the business line, as seen in Figure 7.7. Once the capital requirement for each of the eight lines is calculated, the eight values are aggregated to arrive at the bank's operational risk capital minimum.

Figure 7.7   **Beta factors to calculate operational risk capital in the Standardized Approach**

Business Unit	Fixed Percentage (Beta Factor)
Corporate finance	18%
Payment and settlement	18%
Trading and sales	18%
Agency services	15%
Commercial banking	15%
Asset management	12%
Retail banking	12%
Retail brokerage	12%

The Standardized Approach refines the Basic Indicator Approach by recognizing that operational risk can vary by business unit. For example, a bank's trading and sales business unit is considered to carry a higher overall operational risk than its asset management business unit. The beta factor used in the calculation can be specified by the bank's regulator and can be adjusted to reflect the relative riskiness of diverse banking operations.

By splitting the bank into separate business lines and assigning a different risk calculation percentage to each, the Standardized Approach attempts to link a bank's operational risks more closely to its capital requirement. While this may be a better approach for many banks, the Standardized Approach is limited—it does not capture the bank's actual operational risk, as it does not involve detailed risk assessment.

EXAMPLE

GammaBank operates several different business lines and is evaluating the operational risk capital estimates that the Basic Indicator Approach and the Standardized Approach provide. The relevant annual gross income for the various business lines for the past three years is in Figure 7.8.

These two approaches offer two different minimum capital calculations; using the Standardized Approach, the operational risk capital estimate is CHF 0.90 million less (CHF 20.25 million − CHF 19.35 million = CHF 0.90 million).

Figure 7.8   Comparision of Risk Capital Charge under the Basic Indicator Approach and Standardized Approaches for GammaBank

	Annual Gross Income in CHF Millions			Basic Indicator Approach	Standardized Approach
	2006	**2007**	**2008**	**Beta Factor**	**Beta Factor**
Corporate finance	20	30	25	15%	18%
Retail banking	35	55	30	15%	12%
Commercial banking	55	60	20	15%	15%
Agency services	15	10	5	15%	15%
Retail brokerage	10	25	10	15%	12%
Total	**135**	**180**	**90**		

Basic Indicator Approach:
    Operational risk capital charge = (135 * 15% + 180 * 15% + 90 * 15%) / 3 = 20.25

Standardized Approach:
    2006 component = max(0, 20 * 18% + 35 * 12% + 55 * 15% + 15 * 15% + 10 * 12%) = 19.5
    2007 component = max(0, 30 * 18% + 55 * 12% + 60 * 15% + 10 * 15% + 25 * 12%) = 25.5
    2008 component = max(0, 25 * 18% + 30 * 12% + 20 * 15% + 5 * 15% + 10 * 12%) = 13.05
    Operational risk capital charge = (19.5 + 25.5 + 13.05) / 3 = 19.35

7.5.3   Advanced Measurement Approach

The **Advanced Measurement Approach (AMA)** is the most sophisticated approach to calculate operational risk capital and allows the bank to use internally generated models to calculate its operational risk capital requirements. Use of the AMA is subject to stringent regulatory requirements and rigorous bank supervisory oversight. The Basel Committee has not recommended any particular models for banks to use under the AMA, leaving it up to the bank to develop its own internal operational risk measurement systems.

In developing the bank's AMA, the bank may draw from its own risk experiences, including its loss history. The bank can complement this information with the pooled loss histories of other institutions. Moreover, the bank can consider, model, and measure its own business and internal control environment. Clearly, developing the methods and infrastructure to model and measure operational risk is significant and costly. The benefits are twofold. First, the Basel Committee presumes (and regularly monitors the validity) that the bank's AMA provides a more accurate assessment of a bank's operational risk, thereby allowing banks to move away from the simple, overly conservative weights used in the Basic Indicator and Standardized Approaches. Second, banks using the AMA benefit from the careful consideration of its business practices that must occur in assessing and measuring operational risk.

7.5.4   Criteria for Using Different Approaches

Banks must meet a "credibility" test in order to use the two more sophisticated approaches. Credibility is determined by the bank's regulatory supervisor, who compares the operational risk capital requirement the bank calculates against the requirements calculated by similar peer banks using the same approach. This comparison allows the bank supervisor to make an educated determination as to whether the bank's results are fairly stated and "credible" relative to those of its peers. If the results are not credible, the supervisor can direct that the bank use a simpler methodology to calculate its operational risk charge.

The Basic Indicator Approach, being the simplest, sets no criteria for adoption. Banks must meet certain stipulations in order to use the Standardized or Advanced Measurement approaches:

- **Standardized Approach**
  To use the Standardized Approach, the bank must have a dedicated operational risk function and systems in place to support it. Internationally active banks must also have systems and procedures to collect, store, maintain, and report internal operational risk data. The operational risk management function of an international bank must have clear lines of responsibility, and the bank must provide incentives for improving the management of operational risk throughout the firm. As a practical matter, the bank's supervisors can insist on a testing and monitoring period before allowing the Standardized Approach to be used for regulatory purposes.

- **Advanced Measurement Approach**
  Banks using the AMA are subject to strict qualitative and quantitative criteria. The bank must fulfill the Standardized Approach criteria regarding international banks and must augment its internal processes with external operational risk data. It must also develop and properly implement a dedicated and appropriate operational risk framework. The bank must also actively involve major business lines, control areas, audit areas, and the bank's board of directors and senior management in its operational risk oversight.
  - **Qualitative Criteria**
    The bank must adhere to a minimum set of quality standards, including those focusing on the independence and design of the operational risk measurement, management, and monitoring structure.
  - **Quantitative Criteria**
    To ensure that an internal model meets required standards, the Basel Accord specifies that the bank must be able to demonstrate that its approach captures potentially severe loss events and that the bank must maintain rigorous procedures for operational risk model development and independent model validation.

Lastly, as determined by its regulatory supervisor, a bank wanting to deploy the Advanced Measurement Approach is subject to a compulsory period of supervisory monitoring.

A bank does not have to start with the Basic Indicator Approach. Provided the bank meets the criteria outlined by Basel II and its regulators, it can implement either the Standardized Approach or the Advanced Measurement Approach. A bank can also migrate down from a more advanced methodology to a lesser one. Such a move requires the approval of the bank's regulatory supervisor, however. If the bank's regulator is not satisfied with the bank's advanced approach calculations, or if the bank subsequently fails to meet certain regulatory and/or Basel requirements, the regulator can require the bank to revert to a simpler approach.

The Basel II Accord will also allow a bank to use a mix of approaches for calculating operational risk capital. For example, if the bank meets preset criteria, its supervisor could allow it to use the Basic Indicator Approach or the Standardized Approach for some parts of its operations and the Advanced Measurement Approach for others.

7.5.5   Basel II and Operational Risk Management

As mentioned, Basel II requires, for the first time, that banks hold regulatory capital against their operational risks. It is expected that approximately 12% of a bank's capital will be held against these types of risk. The Basel Committee has adopted both a quantitative and a qualitative approach to determine comprehensively a bank's operational risk capital. Inherent in these requirements is the fact that banks need to understand their own operational risks, be able to collect operational risk loss data, and create functions that focus on managing, monitoring, and mitigating operational risks. Banks, regulators, and supervisors understand that the processes relating to and associated with operational risk analysis, operational risk event measurement and management, and risk capital calculations are dynamic and not just one-time or yearly reoccurring events.

CHAPTER 8

Regulatory Capital and Supervision under Basel II

T he Basel II Accord seeks to maintain stability in the international banking industry by defining a three-pillar framework for capital adequacy. Pillar 1 outlines
approaches to measuring a bank's credit, market, and operational risk and sets minimum
capital requirements based on the measured risk exposures. Pillar 2 describes how
supervisory review is to be used to oversee bank management and to encourage best
practices in risk management. Pillar 3 aims to use market discipline by defining disclosure requirements that allow market participants to readily assess a bank's capital
structure and adequacy. Beyond the mandates of regulatory capital, bank management
has a responsibility to address the long-term well-being of the organization. Economic
capital is the capital level a bank must maintain to withstand large but unlikely losses
so that it can survive over the long term.

Chapter Outline

- 8.1 Bank Regulatory Capital
- 8.2 Basel II Minimum Capital Requirement
- 8.3 Pillar 2—Supervisory Review
- 8.4 Pillar 3—Market Discipline
- 8.5 Beyond Regulatory Capital
- 8.6 Banks, Bank Risks, and Regulation

Key Learning Points
- The Basel II Accord provides a general framework for how a bank's overall
  capital should be structured, defines "tiers" of eligible capital, and provides specific
  rules on the relationships between different tiers.

- According to Basel II, the eligible capital for regulatory purposes must be greater than or equal to 8% of the risk-weighted asset value.
- Pillar 2, supervisory review, ensures compliance with minimum capital requirements and encourages banks to use the best risk management techniques and address risks beyond the scope of Pillar 1.
- Pillar 3 focuses on disclosure requirements to provide transparency with respect to a bank's capital structure, risk exposures, and capital adequacy.
- Economic capital establishes the capital level a bank must maintain to withstand large but unlikely losses so that it can survive over the long term.
- Banks use economic capital models to decide the level and structure of capital. The development and implementation of a well-designed economic capital model can help a bank identify, understand, mitigate, and manage its risks more effectively, leading ultimately to a more effective and stable bank.

Key Terms

• Basel II minimum capital requirement	• Regulatory capital
• Confidence level	• Risk-adjusted return on capital (RAROC)
• Credit risk disclosure	• Shareholders' equity
• Disclosure	• Subordinated term debt
• Economic capital	• Supervisory review
• Expected losses	• Tier 1 capital
• Innovative capital	• Tier 2 capital
• Market risk disclosures	• Tier 3 capital
• Probability distribution of credit losses	• Unexpected losses
	• Undisclosed reserves

Regulatory Capital and Supervision under Basel II

8.1 BANK REGULATORY CAPITAL

The Basel II Accord defines a three-pillar framework to achieve consistent capital adequacy requirements for active international banks.

- Pillar 1—Minimum Capital Requirements
- Pillar 2—Supervisory Review Process
- Pillar 3—Market Discipline

The goal of Pillar 1 is to set capital requirements as a function of the credit, market, and operational risk exposures of the bank. Much of Pillar 1 focuses on explaining the permissible approaches to measuring a bank's credit, market, and operational risk. As discussed in the previous three chapters, Basel II defines, for each risk type, several approaches to estimate the bank's riskiness, from basic to more sophisticated, as shown in Figure 8.1.

Figure 8.1 Methods for calculating capital according to Basel II

	Credit Risk	Market Risk	Operational Risk
Approaches (ordered from least to most sophisticated)	• Standardized Approach • Foundation Internal Ratings-Based (IRB) Approach • Advanced IRB Approach	• Standardized Approach • Internal Models Approach	• Basic Indicator Approach • Standardized Approach • Advanced Measurement Approach
Result	Risk-weighted asset value for credit risk	Market risk capital charge	Operational risk capital charge

By implementing and executing an approach for each risk type, the result will be a risk-weighted asset value that corresponds to that risk. As discussed in this chapter, Basel II also defines the eligible capital for regulatory purposes and, finally, sets a minimum capital requirement as a function of the risk-weighted asset values.

Pillar 2 of Basel II describes how bank supervisory review is to be used both to determine that banks meet the minimum capital requirements and to encourage best practices in risk management. Pillar 3 defines disclosure requirements that allow market participants to readily assess a bank's capital structure and adequacy, thereby allowing market discipline to further compel banks toward sound capital practices.

8.1.1   Bank Regulatory Capital

A bank's **regulatory capital** is the minimum capital that regulators require the bank to maintain. Equity capital is usually the primary asset that makes up the bank's regulatory capital. The Basel II Accord provides a general framework for how a bank's overall capital should be structured and defines guidelines for eligible capital. In particular, Basel II defines "tiers" of capital and provides specific rules on the relationships between different tiers that must be followed to meet mandated minimum capital requirements.

8.1.2   Tier 1 Capital

The amount of **Tier 1 capital** held by a bank is considered a core measure of its financial strength. The primary element of Tier 1 capital is **shareholders' equity** (the amount of capital left over after subtracting the bank's liabilities from its assets). To this core Tier 1 capital, a bank can add **innovative capital** such as complex financial instruments that have both equity and debt features. Bank supervisors place strict rules on this innovative Tier 1 capital. The complex financial instruments that can be considered for the Tier 1 capital are beyond the scope of this book.

8.1.3   Tier 2 Capital

Tier 2 capital is the second most important type of capital that can be used to meet a bank's regulatory minimum capital requirements. Tier 2 capital may consist of **undisclosed reserves** and certain **subordinated term debt**, debt issued by the bank that ranks lower on the repayment scale than depositors in the event of a bank default. For example, one type of undisclosed reserves is revaluation reserves, where a company's asset is revalued and the new higher value is recorded on the company's books.

EXAMPLE

AlphaBank owns government bonds that have increased in value by USD 20 million. The bank is considering selling the majority of these bonds in the near future. However, the bank cannot actually realize this profit until it sells the bonds. As such this price appreciation is considered "unrealized" profit. If these bonds can be revalued according to regulatory guidelines and with bank supervisory consent to reflect their "unrealized" profit, this "unrealized" profit of USD 20 million can be added to a reserve account and used for Tier 2 capital calculations.

The Basel Committee also defines rules governing the ratios that banks must maintain between different classes of capital. One primary restriction is that Tier 2 capital cannot be greater than Tier 1 capital.

8.1.4   Tier 3 Capital

Tier 3 capital includes a wider variety of subordinated debt than that allowed for Tier 2 capital and may include profits from the bank's trading activities. *Tier 3 capital can only be used to support the market risk the bank takes in its trading book.* Instruments that can be counted as Tier 3 capital are generally too risky to be used for material portions of a bank's capital calculation. For example, using trading profits in the capital calculation is obviously risky, as the trading profits could disappear at any time.

8.1.5   Deductions and Adjustments from Regulatory Capital

Certain capital items cannot be included in a bank's regulatory capital calculation. Typically these are:
*   Goodwill—this arises when the purchase price of a business is greater than the book value of the capital of the acquired company. Goodwill is a subjective assessment by the market and so is not included in the capital calculation.
*   Investments in subsidiaries engaged in banking and similar activities under certain conditions.
*   Shares held by the bank in another bank.

8.1.6   New Capital

Usually, growing banks retain some of their profits to add to their Tier 1 capital base. Retained capital allows the bank to support new business without raising new capital from activities such as issuing new shares, issuing debt, or seeking private investors. Raising new capital can be a time-consuming and expensive process.

The Basel Committee allows interim annual profits, adjusted for some items, to be added to Tier 1 capital as long as the bank's auditors also allow it. This is particularly useful for banks with rapidly growing balance sheets. If these banks were forced to wait until the end of their fiscal year before profits could be counted as regulatory capital, they might need interim injections of capital from shareholders to maintain their business growth.

8.2   BASEL II MINIMUM CAPITAL REQUIREMENT

As discussed in previous chapters, the Basel II Accord requires banks to measure the riskiness of their assets with respect to credit, market, and operational risk. Given the approved approaches to calculating the riskiness with respect to credit, market, and operational risk, banks will have derived the following values:

- Total risk-weighted assets for credit risk, denoted by RWA_c
- Market risk capital requirement, denoted by CR_m
- Operational risk capital requirement, denoted by CR_o

Then, the total risk-weighted assets (RWA_T) value for the bank is:

$$RWA_T = RWA_c + 12.5 * (CR_m + CR_o)$$

In addition, banks will have calculated their eligible regulatory capital (RC) roughly as follows:

$$RC = \text{Tier 1 Capital} + \text{Tier 2 Capital} - \text{Deductions}$$

The **Basel II minimum capital requirement** states that:

$$\frac{RC}{RWA_T} \geq 8\%$$

In words, the eligible capital for regulatory purposes must be greater than or equal to 8% of the risk-weighted asset value. Naturally, the Basel Committee retains the ability to adjust the 8% minimum parameter according to historical results over time.

There are additional capital calculations for credit and market risk.
- *For credit risk:* Eligible Tier 1 and Tier 2 capital for credit risk must be greater than $8\% * RWA_c$.
- *For market risk:* Eligible Tier 1, Tier 2, and Tier 3 capital for market risk must be greater than CR_m.

EXAMPLE

Bank JKL has used approved Basel II approaches to calculate its credit, market, and operational risk values as follows:
- Total risk-weighted assets for credit risk, RWA_c = USD 1,200 million
- Market risk capital requirement, CR_m = USD 40 million
- Operational risk capital requirement, CR_o = USD 60 million

In addition, Bank JKL has the following capital:
- Tier 1 capital: USD 150 million
- Tier 2 capital: USD 110 million
- Tier 3 capital: USD 0 million
- Deductions: USD 10 million

Then, using the formulas above,

$$RWA_T \;=\; RWA_c + 12.5 * (CR_m + CR_o)$$
$$=\; 1{,}200 + 12.5 * (40 + 60)$$
$$=\; USD\ 2{,}450\ million$$

$$RC \;=\; \text{Tier 1 capital} + \text{Tier 2 capital} + \text{Tier 3 capital} - \text{Deductions}$$
$$=\; 150 + 110 - 10$$
$$=\; USD\ 250\ million$$

$$\text{Capital ratio} \;=\; \frac{RC}{RWA_T} \;\geq\; 8\%$$

$$=\; 250 / 2{,}450$$
$$=\; 10.2\%$$
$$\geq\; 8.0\%$$

Regulatory capital ratio = USD 250/USD 2,450 million = 10.2%, which exceeds the minimum requirement 8%

Since the Bank JKL capital ratio exceeds 8%, Bank JKL meets the minimum regulatory capital requirement of the Basel II Accord. In fact, any eligible capital level in excess of USD 196 million (= 8% * USD 2,450 million) will satisfy the minimum regulatory capital requirement for Basel II.

Actual examples of regulatory capital can be seen by viewing the interim quarterly financial reports of several large international banks. Figure 8.2 shows the capital composition, risk-weighted asset breakdowns, and capital ratios from posted second quarter 2008 financial reports from UBS,[1] HSBC,[2] Barclays,[3] and BBVA.[4]

In all of the cases for the four banks:
- Tier 1 capital is greater than or equal to Tier 2 capital, as required under Basel II.
- Credit risk is the dominant contributor to risk-weighted assets, as credit risk is generally the biggest risk for banks.

---

1.   From "UBS Financial Reporting, Second Quarter 2008," available at http://www.ubs.com.
2.   From "2008 Interim Report, HSBC Holdings plc," available at http://www.hsbc.com.
3.   From "Barclays PLC, Interim Results, Figures 2008," available at http://www.investorrelations.barclays.co.uk.
4.   From "BBVA, Quarterly Report, January-June 2008," available at http://www.bbva.com.

- Capital ratios comfortably exceed 8%, the minimum requirement of Basel II. Basel II defines the minimum requirement, but bank management may set higher thresholds to maintain a target credit rating and/or to avoid potential increases to regulatory charges if the bank were to fall below the regulatory minimum.

Figure 8.2   **Sample regulatory capital reports**

	UBS[1] (million CHF)	HSBC[2] (million USD)	Barclays[3] (million EUR)	BBVA[4] (million EUR)
Shareholder equity and other Deductions	56,203 (18,703)	154,787 (46,936)	37,069 (9,369)	30,270 (9,556)
Tier 1 Capital	**37,500**	**107,851**	**27,700**	**20,714**
Subordinated debt and other Deductions	14,181 (1,012)	53,781 (14,682)	18,775 (1,306)	13,355 (490)
Tier 2 Capital	**13,170**	**39,099**	**17,469**	**12,865**
Other Deductions	0	0	(717)	0
Total Capital	**50,670**	**146,950**	**44,452**	**33,579**
Credit risk	260,578	1,071,482	283,746	Not provided
Market risk	19,195	52,533	40,462	Not provided
Operational risk	43,404	107,466	28,531	Not provided
Total Risk-Weighted Assets	**323,177**	**1,231,481**	**352,739**	**268,357**
Capital Ratio	**15.7%**	**11.9%**	**12.6%**	**12.5%**
Min. Capital Req. (8%)	**25,854**	**98,518**	**28,219**	**21,469**
Capital Surplus	**24,816**	**48,432**	**16,233**	**12,110**

8.3   Pillar 2—Supervisory Review

This review by bank supervisors ensures compliance with minimum capital requirements and encourages banks to develop and use the best risk management techniques. Pillar 1 defines the calculations to determine the minimum regulatory capital required with respect to market, credit, and operational risk. Pillar 2 sets out the principles of the supervisory review process that national authorities should use (in addition to the Pillar 1 capital calculations) to evaluate a bank's capital adequacy.

In particular, Pillar 2 addresses three main areas that are either not covered or fall outside the scope of Pillar 1.

1. Risks not fully considered by Pillar 1, such as credit concentration risk where a bank would have too much of its risk concentrated (e.g., in home loans in a certain part of a country)
2. Risks not considered at all by Pillar 1 (e.g., interest rate risk in the banking book)
3. Factors external to the bank (e.g., business cycle effects)

In addition, Pillar 2 defines the supervisory assessment of a bank's compliance with the minimum standards set for the use of the more advanced methods of capital calculation in Pillar 1.

Review by bank supervisors is not a substitute for good management. The board of directors and senior management of a bank have the responsibility to ensure that they maintain adequate capital to support the bank's business activities, including those beyond the scope of Pillar 1.

Bank management is responsible for developing an internal capital adequacy assessment process (ICAAP) that evaluates the risk and control environment across all the bank's operations. Capital assessment is an ongoing process that is an integral part of managing a bank's business activities. The process not only evaluates current capital requirements, but also estimates future capital requirements. Bank management uses the estimates for each of its businesses to set capital targets that are aggregated to determine the bank's overall capital requirement. Bank management then monitors the bank's actual capital requirement, as determined by the business it conducts against its previously estimated targets as part of its oversight of the bank's operations.

The quality of the internal capital assessment process is evaluated by the supervisory authorities. This evaluation, combined with other factors, determines the target capital ratio set for the bank. Any deficiencies in the process may result in an increased capital ratio requirement for the bank imposed by the supervisor. Higher capital requirements imply that less funds are available to lend or invest, which may result in lower profits. Banks therefore have a commercial, as well as a prudential, incentive to develop and maintain a high-quality capital assessment process.

Although bank supervisors can raise the capital ratio in response to deficiencies identified during a review, they may also use other measures to address perceived deficiencies, such as:

- Setting targets for improvements in the risk management structure
- Introducing tighter internal procedures, or improving the quality of staff through training or recruitment
- In extreme cases, curtailing the level of risk the bank can incur or business activity it can engage in until the problem is resolved or controlled

The Basel Committee sees the supervisory review process as an active dialogue between a bank and its supervisor. The two should be working together to identify and, if necessary, take rapid action to restore the bank's capital position to a satisfactory level.

8.3.1   Four Key Principles of Supervisory Review

Pillar 2 identifies four key principles of supervisory review, described in detail here.

Principle 1
Banks should have a process to assess their overall capital adequacy in relation to their risk profile as well as a strategy to maintain their capital levels.

Bank management bears primary responsibility for ensuring that the bank has adequate capital to meet its current and future requirements. Its capital targets must be set with integrity and be consistent with its risk profile and environment. The capital targets must be integral to the bank's strategic planning and should incorporate extensive stress testing.

In particular, Basel II describes five features of a rigorous capital assessment process:

- *Board and senior management oversight.* Bank management is responsible for understanding the nature and level of risk taken by the bank and monitoring the relationship between the level of risk and the bank's capital requirement. The board of directors or its equivalent must set the level of risk that the bank is willing to take (risk appetite) and establish an internal framework to assess risk, relate the level of risk to capital targets, and monitor compliance with internal limits and controls. The framework should also incorporate a capital planning process that is consistent with the bank's strategic business plan.
- *Sound capital assessment.* The target capital ratio should be related to the bank's strategic business plan, and there should be a transparent link between risk and capital.
- *Comprehensive assessment of risk.* All material risk exposures should be measured or estimated, including those risks identified by Pillar 1 and others, such as interest rate risk, liquidity risk, and credit concentration risk.
- *Monitoring and reporting.* The bank must establish a system for monitoring and reporting risk that allows management to assess how changes in risk affect its capital requirements. Bank management should receive regular reports that show the bank's capital level and its capital requirements. The reports should allow management to evaluate the level and trends of material risks, evaluate the sensitivity and reasonableness of current risk measures, and determine that the bank holds sufficient capital against the various risks and that it is in compliance with established capital adequacy goals.

- *Internal control review.* The bank's internal control framework is a key element in the capital assessment process. An effective review of this framework should include an internal or external audit.

Principle 2
Supervisors should review and evaluate banks' internal capital adequacy assessments and strategies, as well as their ability to monitor and ensure their compliance with regulatory capital ratios. Supervisors should take appropriate supervisory action if they are not satisfied with the result of this process.

The **supervisory review** process may involve on-site visits, off-site reviews, meetings with bank management, reviewing relevant work carried out by external auditors, and monitoring periodic reports. The regular review process should:
- Closely examine the calculation of risk exposures and the translation of risk into a capital requirement
- Focus on the quality of the process and on the quality of internal controls around the process
- Ensure that the composition of the capital held is appropriate for the scale of the business activity it supports
- Evaluate how the capital assessment process is monitored and reviewed by bank management
- Ensure that targets are appropriate for the current operating environment
- Ensure that the bank takes into account the effects of extreme or unexpected events when setting capital targets
- Identify any deficiencies in the capital assessment framework

On completion of the review, supervisors should take action if they are not satisfied with all or part of a bank's risk assessment process.

Principle 3
Supervisors should expect banks to operate above the minimum regulatory capital ratios, and they should be able to require banks to hold capital in excess of the minimum.

The minimum capital requirements set in Pillar 1 provide a baseline for banks and supervisors to gauge capital levels. In practice, banks will maintain a buffer above the minimum capital requirement, due to:
- Risks/business activities not properly covered by Pillar 1
- Bank-specific conditions that warrant additional capital
- Local market conditions
- Need/desire of the bank to maintain or achieve a high credit rating

- The need to ensure that the bank will not be required to raise capital quickly if market conditions change

From the supervisory review process, supervisors may also require banks to hold additional capital if they are not convinced that current capital is sufficient for the risks faced by the assets of the bank.

Principle 4
Supervisors should seek to intervene at an early stage to prevent capital from falling below the minimum levels required to support the risk characteristics of a particular bank and should require rapid remedial action if capital is not maintained or restored.

If a bank is failing to maintain its capital requirement, supervisors can use their discretion in taking action to correct the situation. Bank supervisors can require a bank to suspend dividend payments and/or raise extra capital to restore its capital ratio. If the problem is likely to take some time to resolve, supervisors could increase monitoring the bank and require the bank to submit a plan to restore the capital ratio to a level set by the supervisor.

Bank supervisors can increase a bank's capital requirement as a short-term measure while underlying problems are resolved. The increase in capital could be withdrawn when the supervisor is satisfied that the bank had overcome its operating difficulties.

8.3.2   Specific Issues to Address During Supervisory Review

The four principles in Pillar 2 describe a framework for supervisors to use in developing their own review procedures. The Basel Committee has also identified a number of other important issues that should be included in all supervisory reviews. These are issues that either form part of the standards set for the use of the advanced calculation methods or cover areas not directly addressed in Pillar 1—for example, stress testing and scenario analysis in liquidity testing.

Interest Rate Risk in the Banking Book
As discussed in Section 2.2, interest rate risk in the banking book refers to the potential loss in a bank's lending and deposit activities due to changes in interest rates. The Basel Committee considers interest rate risk in the banking book a significant risk that needs capital support. However, the Committee also accepts that the nature and management of this risk is very diverse across the international banking community and that this risk should be addressed under Pillar 2. Bank supervisors have discretion to implement a mandatory capital requirement if they feel it is appropriate for their own banking community. The committee recognizes that the reporting of this risk relies on the banks' own internal risk management systems. Supervisors also require reports based on a standard interest rate shift to allow for comparison across the banks under their jurisdiction.

If a bank is deemed to be holding insufficient capital to cover its interest rate risk, supervisors must require the bank to reduce its risk, hold more capital, or implement a combination of both.

Stress Tests under the Internal Ratings-Based (IRB) Approach in Pillar 1

Banks using the IRB Approach must ensure that they have sufficient capital to cover the IRB Approach's requirement. They must also have sufficient capital to cover any deficiencies identified in the credit risk stress tests carried out as part of the IRB Approach.

Definition of Default

The Basel Committee defines the event of default to have occurred when either or both of the two following events have taken place:

1. The bank considers that the obligor is unlikely to pay its credit obligations to the banking group in full, without recourse by the bank to actions such as taking formal possession of any collateral held.
2. The obligor is past due more than 90 days on any material credit obligation to the banking group. Overdrafts will be considered as being past due once the customer has breached an advised overdraft limit or been advised of a limit smaller than its current outstanding obligation to the bank.

Banks must use the Basel-referenced definition of default in their internal estimates for the probability of default (PD), loss given default (LGD), and exposure at default (EAD). However, bank supervisors will issue guidance on the interpretation of the default definition in their own jurisdiction. Supervisors should evaluate the impact of how a bank interprets the definition on the calculation of its capital requirement.

Residual Risk

Pillar 1 allows banks to mitigate their credit exposures by using collateral, guarantees, or credit derivatives. The capital offset allowed against an exposure assumes that the risk-mitigating method (sometimes referred to as a hedge) has been perfectly executed. However, there may be residual, legal, or documentation risks that could result in the bank having a greater exposure than it had originally recorded. Banks should develop policies and procedures to minimize their exposure to such residual risks. Banks must evaluate the quality of their policies and procedures to determine whether their credit exposures should or can be fully offset by their mitigation methods. Supervisors will review the bank's evaluation and will take action if they feel the process has deficiencies.

Credit Concentration Risk

A risk concentration is any single exposure or group of exposures that has the potential to generate losses that could jeopardize a bank's ability to carry on its business. Credit risk concentration is the most common concentration risk because lending is often a bank's primary activity.

EXAMPLE

In January 1998, Hong Kong-based Peregrine Investment Holdings, one of Asia's independent investment houses, went into liquidation with outstanding debts of some USD 400 million. Concentration risk was a principal cause of the collapse as Peregrine had lent approximately 20% of its capital base to Steady Safe, an Indonesian taxi and bus operator that went bankrupt.

Risk concentration is a major cause of banking problems. Credit risk concentration can take different forms and may include:

- Significant exposures to a single counterparty or financially related group of counterparties
- Exposures to counterparties in the same economic region or geographical location
- Exposures to counterparties that are dependent on the same business activity or commodity
- Indirect exposure to credit mitigation methods such as holding a single type of collateral

Banks must identify and manage credit risk concentrations as part of their risk management process. Credit risk concentrations should be defined in relation to the bank's operations and relevant risk limits and exposures set either in relation to regulatory capital requirements or in relation to total assets. Banks should ensure that their internal procedures are effective in identifying, measuring, monitoring, and controlling credit risk concentrations. Concentration risk is not covered by Pillar 1 requirements.

Operational Risk

The use of gross income as a proxy to reflect operational risk exposure under both the Basic Indicator Approach and the Standardized Approach may in some cases underestimate the risk. Supervisors should examine the nature of the bank's business and compare the risk calculations with similar banks in their jurisdiction.

Securitization

Through securitization, the bank removes (sells) and transfers its credit risk to the investors who are buying the securitized product. As a result, the bank needs less capital on its books—securitization brings capital relief. The bank supervisory review of the securitization process should examine how completely the securitization has transferred the bank's risks, determining whether the bank has retained any residual risk(s). If some risk remains, supervisors may decrease or remove the capital allowance calculated under Pillar 1. The aim is to determine a level of capital allowance that reflects the level of credit risk transferred by the securitization.

8.3.3   Accountability and International Cooperation

There is an element of discretion in the supervision of banks because banking activity is subject to different local regulations. Bank supervisors should ensure that their discretionary supervisory activities are carried out with transparency and accountability. Criteria for the review of capital adequacy for financial institutions should be publicly available. The criteria should include any policies that impose capital ratios above the minimum set in Basel II. Any decision to impose a higher capital requirement on an individual bank should be explained to the bank, specifying the reasons and the corrective action required.

International banks are likely to be active in a number of jurisdictions. As such, they will be subject to supervision by their home authority as well as each host authority in countries where they have banking operations. This situation is usually referred to in literature as home-host matters. The new Basel II Accord requires closer practical cooperation between home and host supervisors to help reduce the supervisory burden on such international banking groups.

The home supervisor should lead the coordination effort between itself and the host supervisors (those supervisors who would oversee the bank's branch operations in another country) responsible for a banking group's operations. The aim should be to reduce the implementation burden on banks and conserve supervisory resources by avoiding redundant or uncoordinated validation work.

8.4   PILLAR 3—MARKET DISCIPLINE

Disclosure is the dissemination of material information that allows a proper evaluation of a bank's business. This information guides investors and the market and gives bank customers a clearer view of the bank's operations and risk exposures. Disclosure requirements ensure that corporate entities share pertinent information about their financial performance with investors, with the information being presented according to generally accepted standards.

Both privately held and publicly traded companies are required to produce financial statements: profit and loss reports, balance sheets, and tax reports. These statements must be signed by the company's external auditors and reflect relevant, generally accepted accounting principles. To perform this task, auditors are required, among other things, to test and verify the quality of the company's internal controls as they relate to its financial reporting.

Publicly traded companies must also make additional disclosures required by the exchange on which their shares are traded, often known as "filings." The filings reflect the shareholders' information needs and contain very detailed financial information. In some countries, the management of publicly traded companies must also certify, subject to incurring legal liability for falsely doing so, that the company's financial statements correctly and fully reflect the actual financial position of the company. In the United States, this is required under the Sarbanes-Oxley Act.

EXAMPLE

In the mid-1990s, Parmalat, an Italian dairy and food corporation, aggressively bought other dairy and food companies all around the world through the use of debt instruments. By 2001, many of the newly bought companies were losing money. Irrespective of the poor performance of its portfolio of companies, the company continued its aggressive expansion, but instead of financing it with debt, Parmalat issued complex financial products, including derivatives. Derivatives enabled the company to hide its losses and the significant debt it had accumulated. By the end of 2003, the fraudulent accounting practices at Parmalat were exposed, including the selling of credit-linked notes to themselves. Parmalat's bank, Bank of America, released a document attesting that EUR 4 billion reported to be in Parmalat's bank account was not there. The actual extent of the accounting fraud has been estimated to be about EUR 14 billion. The firm was declared insolvent, and eventually the CEO, Calisto Tanzi, was sentenced to 10 years in prison for financial fraud. While Parmalat was not a bank, many banks are publicly held companies and are just as accountable to their shareholders as was Parmalat. A bank's failure to meet disclosure requirements of an exchange, regulator, or supervisor can have equally disastrous effects.

Pillar 3 focuses on disclosure requirements to complement the minimum capital requirements (Pillar 1) and supervisory review process (Pillar 2). Pillar 3 disclosure focuses on capital information, not financial performance, and addresses the company's:
- Capital structure
- Risk exposures
- Capital adequacy

Pillar 3 requires that the information considered for disclosure be material to the company's operations and investors' evaluation of the company's operations. The Basel II Accord considers information material if "its omission or misstatement could change or influence the assessment or decision of a user relying on that information for the purpose of making economic decisions." But under Pillar 3, banks are not required to disclose proprietary or confidential information, including confidential customer information.

Under Pillar 3, most banks make their disclosures every six months. There are three exceptions to this standard:
1. Small banks with stable risk profiles are permitted to make yearly disclosures.
2. Large, international banks must publish their Tier 1 and total capital adequacy ratios, as well as those ratios' components, quarterly.
3. Banks can make their qualitative disclosures of a general nature (meaning information about the bank's principles and procedures that it uses to assess its risks) yearly.

8.4.1 Accounting Disclosures

Basel II recognizes that risk disclosures and financial disclosures are dissimilar, and reconciling these two different types of disclosures can be expensive and time-consuming, if not unfair, for banks with stable risk levels.

Given the different purposes of financial accounts—investor information—and regulatory risk reports—relationship between risks and capital—any detailed reconciliation between risk disclosures and financial disclosures would be costly and difficult. For many banks, such reconciliation would involve significant systems expenditures. Basel II therefore suggests that banks publish their annual report and other financial statements separately from the required supervisory regulatory reports.

8.4.2 General Disclosure Requirements

The Basel II Accord requires banks to develop formal disclosure policies and processes to validate their disclosure and to reevaluate what information should, and should not be disclosed in the future. These policies and procedures should be approved by the bank's board of directors.

Pillar 3 requirements apply to both quantitative and qualitative disclosure with regard to the following:
*   *Bank, group, and subsidiary structure.* Disclosure requirements generally apply to the consolidated banking group—the entire bank, with all its banking and non-banking subsidiaries.
*   *Capital structure.* Banks must disclose details of their capital structure. The qualitative disclosure focuses on the different types of capital the bank has, while the quantitative disclosures include the following:
    -   Amount of Tier 1 capital, by capital source (shares, reserves, etc.), amount of Tier 2 capital, and amount of Tier 3 capital, if needed
    -   Deductions from capital, if needed
    -   Total regulatory capital
*   *Capital adequacy.* The bank must discuss how it assesses its capital adequacy, a qualitative disclosure; and the bank's capital requirements for credit risk, market risk, and operational risk, its total capital, and its Tier 1 capital ratio, all quantitative disclosures.

8.4.3 Disclosing Risk Exposure and Risk Assessment

Pillar 3's risk disclosure requirements depend on the approach the bank uses to calculate its required risk capital. The complexity of the approaches used by the bank will dictate what information needs to be disclosed.

General qualitative disclosure would include information on:
*   Risk management objectives and policies relating to each defined risk area

- The structure and organization of the relevant risk management function
- The use of hedging and risk-mitigating strategies

Quantitative disclosure requirements are complex, and any detailed listing would be lengthy. Generally, **credit risk disclosures** include information on:
- Gross and average credit exposure by major products
- Geographic, industry, and maturity distribution of exposures by major products
- Loans, provisions, and write-offs by industry, by counterparty, and by geographic area

Generally, **market risk disclosures** include information on:
- The capital requirements for the four main types of general market risk: interest rate risk, equity risk, foreign exchange risk, and commodity risk
- High, average, and low value-at-risk (VaR) values over the reporting period and an evaluation of the reliability of these calculations

There are no quantitative operational risk disclosure requirements other than those covered in the capital adequacy disclosures.

Finally, banks with interest rate risk in the banking book have to disclose information that allows a qualitative assessment of the models used to assess these risks. Model inputs include assumptions on prepayments and withdrawals of deposits. The quantitative disclosure concerning a bank's interest rate risk would reflect the effects interest rate changes have on the earnings or value of the bank.

8.5 BEYOND REGULATORY CAPITAL

Without question, meeting regulatory capital requirements does not relieve the board of directors and senior management of a bank of their responsibility to provide competent and prudent bank leadership and oversight, including the maintenance of adequate capital to support the bank's business activities beyond the scope of regulation. By design, regulatory capital defines the minimum capital requirement determined by a government agency whose primary concern is banking safety and stability for the general public.

EXAMPLE

In 2007, the global banking system started to experience capital adequacy issues related to the United States subprime mortgage market. In 2008, these issues became acute as losses were being incurred at unprecedented rates by banks as housing prices fell and borrowers defaulted on their loans. Banks were forced to raise capital from external sources. Refer to Figure 8.2. For example, if UBS experienced losses related to the subprime market and credit bubble that resulted in a reduction of its Tier 1 capital by 35% or CHF 19,671 million, its capital ratio would have dropped to 9.6%.

Although above the 8% minimum, it would be too close to provide confidence to the markets and its counterparties regarding its ability to withstand further losses in its portfolios. This example would also be the same for HSBC, Barclays, and BBVA.

In fact, real estate market values fell sharply in 2007 and 2008, affecting most of the banks around the globe. Although banks attempted to raise capital in any number of ways to shore up their balance sheet, ultimately every bank became concerned about the balance sheet of its banking counterparties and questioned whether all possible losses were being disclosed and positions were being valued properly.

This resulted in a freezing of credit in the financial system as banks became unwilling to lend funds to each other and to their customers. This catastrophic situation forced governments to establish programs aimed at restoring confidence in the banking system and recapitalizing their banks so that the banks would resume lending money.

Unfortunately, a solution to this problem has not yet been found despite the efforts of thousands of individuals and the injection of trillions of U.S. dollars and other global currencies into the financial system.

The topics previously discussed in this chapter relating to supervision and oversight are now the subject of much discussion and regulatory investigation. Numerous issues such as whether bank management exercised proper oversight, whether bank leadership was competent and prudent in its managerial activities, and whether banks were properly valuing their positions, among numerous other factors, are now being debated.

Regulatory capital mandates are designed to help ensure that in the event of distress or the failure for an individual bank, capital levels are adequate to prevent any individual bank's problem from becoming a system-wide problem. As such, the time horizon relating to regulatory capital calculations tends to be short term—10 days for market risk capital in Basel II, for example. Regulators want to ensure that the bank's capital would cover losses if its assets had to be liquidated quickly. Regulatory capital initiatives must be well defined, well tested, and broadly applicable. The methods for calculating regulatory capital are more rigid and focused on particular risks that all banks are likely to face, namely credit, market, and operational risk.

A key component of Pillar 2 is directed at supervisory evaluation of the quality of the bank's internal capital adequacy assessment process (ICAAP). Bank management must consider the long-term health and success of the bank, decide its risk tolerance, and set the capital level to be optimal with respect its acceptable trade-off between risk and reward. Higher capital levels imply that less funds are available to lend out or invest, lowering profits. But higher capital levels also imply greater ability to absorb losses, which improves a bank's credit rating and lowers borrowing costs. Given the immense impact of this decision, bank managers must maintain a high-quality capital assessment process that addresses all the particular risks faced by that bank, not just those identified by regulators.

Economic capital is a related concept to regulatory capital. Economic capital reflects the capital level a bank must maintain to withstand large but unlikely losses so that it can survive over the long term. It measures potential, though unexpected, losses that would have to be covered by capital. Economic capital as a risk measure evolved from the value-at-risk (VaR) methodology (see Chapter 5). Both bank supervisors and bank management find VaR an important tool because it considers the vital question:

> *"For a particular confidence level (e.g., 95% of the time), what is an upper bound on how much could the bank lose in the next time period (e.g., 24 hours, week, month, or year)?"*

Recall from our earlier discussion (chapter 5), VaR does not represent the absolute worst-case loss but the worst loss for some percentage of the time (e.g., 95%). Note that an alternative and equivalent question answered by VaR is:

> *"In the worst 5% of possible scenarios for the next time period, what is the least the bank could lose?"*

Economic capital considers the same question as VaR but is particularly concerned about the worst-case losses at a very high confidence level beyond what the bank considers normal losses that will be a part of running a business. Economic capital modeling involves estimating a probability distribution for the bank's potential losses, meaning deriving the likelihood of each possible loss value or ranges of loss values.

8.5.1 Calculating Economic Capital

Banks can calculate the economic capital needed for the whole bank or they can calculate it separately for various risks or types of losses such as loan losses or trading losses. In the AlphaBank example below, we calculate economic capital for loan losses. The process is represented graphically in Figure 8.3.

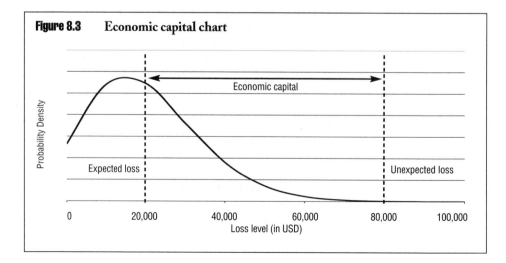

Figure 8.3   Economic capital chart

The first step is to estimate the **probability distribution of credit losses** for a particular period of time. We follow the common approach and consider a one-year time horizon. The horizontal axis in Figure 8.3 represents potential losses (plotted as positive numbers). The vertical axis represents probability. The curve plotted is a probability density function of losses. The area under the curve equals to the total probability of any loss, and each point on the curve represents the relative likelihood of that level of losses occurring in the next year. Note that the curve represents loan losses, and the minimum possible loss is zero, which would indicate that no loans defaulted during the period. The loss distribution shown is typical in that there is a high probability of relatively low losses and a lower probability of high losses.

In Figure 8.3, the dotted line labeled **expected loss** represents the average loss over the next year. Since this amount is expected, presumably the bank has included this into its cost estimates and used it to price its loans so no capital needs to be held against it.

The crucial next step in determining economic capital is the calculation of the **unexpected losses** and this requires the selection of a **confidence interval**, that is, the percentage of time actual losses will be less than or equal to the unexpected loss level. For the purposes of determining economic capital, the level is set very high: 99.97% would be a typical level. In Figure 8.3, the dotted line labeled "unexpected loss" represents the loss level such that there is a 99.97% probability that losses will be less than or equal to that amount. **Economic capital** is the difference between unexpected losses and expected losses; that is, economic capital is the amount of capital need to cover losses beyond the amount of losses that have been priced into the product. As discussed in Chapter 1, the more capital a bank keeps also means that it will earn lower returns as it cannot use that capital to generate returns elsewhere. Therefore, bank management can set the confidence level to meet its comfort level in the trade-off between risk and return.

EXAMPLE

AlphaBank extends a one-year loan to Charlie Customer for USD 10,000. Suppose that, based on information provided, AlphaBank determines that there is a 2% chance Mr. Customer will default on the loan and no money will be returned to the bank. The current one-year T-bill rate is 4%, which is considered risk free. The bank sets the interest rate on the loan to Mr. Customer to account for the risk it is taking by lending to him.

At the end of the year, there are two possible scenarios:

Scenario	Amount repaid to bank	Probability
Default	USD 0	2%
No default	USD 10,000 * (1 + r)	98%

If the bank is indifferent between receiving the risk-free rate and the rate on this loan, it can set the interest rate on the loan so that it receives compensation for the risk of default. To set the interest r so that the bank is compensated for the risk of default, the expected payoff of the loan must equal the expected payoff of investing the same amount of money in the one-year T-bill.

For the one-year T-bill, the payoff is straightforward—it is the amount invested times the T-bill interest rate.

Payoff of one-year T-bill = USD 10,000 * (1.04)
                           = USD 10,400

For the loan, the payoff has two components—the payoff if default does not happen (which is the amount invested times the loan interest rate) and the payoff if default does happen (which is USD 0 assuming no recovery).

Payoff of loan   = USD 10,000 * (1 + r) * 0.98 + USD 0 * 0.02
                        = USD 9800 * (1 + r)

Hence, the bank can set the interest rate r on the loan so that the expected payoffs are equal.

USD 10,400 = USD 9800 * (1 + r)
r = 6.12%

Hence, the "expected" loss of USD 200 is reflected in the price the bank places on the loan.

Now suppose that the bank makes the same USD 10,000 loan (one-year, 4% interest, 2% probability of default with no recovery) to 99 other customers: A2, A3, A4, ..., A100. For simplicity, suppose that the default of one customer has no impact on the default of any other customer. To get the loss distribution, we can consider each scenario of possible number of loan defaults and calculate the both the loss and the probability, as seen in Figure 8.4.

Figure 8.4   Loan defaults and probabilities

Number of Defaults, n	Probability that n Loans Default	Probability that n or Fewer Loans Default	Probability that n or More Loans Default
0	13.26%	13.26%	86.74%
1	27.07%	40.33%	59.67%
2	27.34%	67.67%	32.33%
3	18.23%	85.90%	14.10%
4	9.02%	94.92%	5.08%
5	3.53%	98.45%	1.55%
6	1.14%	99.59%	0.41%
7	0.31%	99.91%	0.09%
8	0.07%	99.98%	0.02%

By setting the interest rate to 6.12%, the bank has priced the **expected loss** into each loan. With 100 independent loans, the expected loss of the portfolio of loans is USD 20,000, since the expected loss of each loan is USD 200 and there are 100 loans. However, as shown in Figure 8.4, there is a 32.33% chance that there are more than two defaults. For a confidence level of 99.97%, we need the smallest number n such that the probability of n or fewer losses exceeds 99.97%. As shown in Figure 8.4, to ensure that the capital level exceeds the loss level 99.97% of the time, the capital level must cover the losses of eight defaults, or USD 80,000. Hence, the **unexpected loss** of the portfolio of loans is USD 80,000, and **economic capital** is USD 60,000, which is the difference between the expected loss of USD 20,000 and the unexpected loss of USD 80,000.

The USD 60,000 is the level of capital needed to withstand an unexpected, but reasonably probable (3 in 10,000) loss. This is the needed economic capital for credit losses. Similar calculations must then be done for other risks, such as market and operational risks, to obtain a level of economic capital for each risk. Ignoring possible diversification benefits, the sum of these economic capital levels is the amount of economic capital the bank needs. Alternatively, if the bank is calculating economic capital for the entire bank in one step, it combines different measures of risk. For example:

- *Trading losses* are measured daily with thousands of transactions a day.
- *Credit losses* are generally measured annually since transactions that can lead to credit losses are less frequent.
- *Operational losses* are also generally measured annually. Operational risk models require data on operational risks that often are difficult to quantify, and assembling sufficient relevant operational risk data poses some difficulty.

Clearly, there are similarities between the calculation of minimum regulatory capital discussed throughout Chapters 4 to 7 and the calculation of economic capital and the same practical difficulties both face. The data to create distributions of losses are difficult to assemble. Unlike regulatory capital, economic capital models can be internally developed models that try to capture specific characteristics of the individual bank and can be more flexible about capturing the effects of features such as diversification, liquidity risk, interest rate risk, and reputational risk. In addition, because economic capital is more concerned with the long-term survival of the bank, the typical time horizon is one year. Note that the time horizon defines the period over which losses are estimated, but does not imply how frequently a bank calculates economic or regulatory capital. That is, to calculate its economic capital, a bank may estimate its potential losses over the next year every day. Finally, note that economic capital is an internal bank metric; although bank supervisory agencies look at this and evaluate the bank's approach, economic capital is not the same as required regulatory capital.

Banks use economic capital models to decide on the level and structure of capital. The development and implementation of a well-designed economic capital model can help a bank identify, understand, mitigate, and manage its risks more effectively, leading ultimately to a more effective bank.

8.5.2   Risk-Adjusted Performance Measures

Since the formal development of economic capital as a bank management tool, banks have also used economic capital to support capital allocation and to evaluate profitability consistently across business lines. **Risk-adjusted return on capital (RAROC)** was developed by Bankers Trust in the late 1970s as a means of evaluating profitability from activities with very different risk profiles. Formally, RAROC is defined as follows:

$$\text{RAROC} = \frac{\text{Profit} - (\text{Economic capital}) * r}{\text{Economic capital}},$$

where r is the risk-free interest rate. Banks can use RAROC as a means of setting expected thresholds that must be met prior to initiating a new activity and as a means of evaluating the performance of different business units or activities.

EXAMPLE

Suppose that two business units (A and B) each return a profit of USD 5 million over the last year. However, suppose that business A is a much more risky business. In particular, for business A, the expected loss is USD 4 million and the unexpected loss at a 99.5% confidence level is USD 23 million. For business B, the expected loss is USD 5 million and the unexpected loss at a 99.5% confidence level is USD 18 million. Suppose the risk-free interest rate is 5%. Then, as shown in Figure 8.5 below, RAROC shows business B to have a higher return on a risk-adjusted basis than business A.

Figure 8.5   Expected loss, Economic capital, and RAROC

	Expected Loss	Unexpected Loss	Economic Capital	Profit	RAROC
Business A	4.00	23.00	19.00	5.00	21.32%
Business B	5.00	18.00	13.00	5.00	33.46%

8.6   BANKS, BANK RISKS, AND REGULATION

This book provides readers with an introduction to banks, bank risks, and bank regulation. Risk management is a complicated but extremely important and timely topic. Banks and their supervisors recognize, especially given the effects of the global financial upheaval of 2007 and 2008, that good risk management practices are vital to the safety and soundness of today's global and highly interconnected banking system. Risk management serves as the basis for international banking regulations—the Basel Accords set standards to mitigate risks inherent in the banking business.

Chapter 1 introduced banks and their business. Banks play a very important role in the economy through three core banking functions—collecting deposits, arranging payments, and making loans—and banks must manage the risks associated with each. Chapter 1 described different types of banks and the various risks banks face, such as credit, market, and operational risks.

The second chapter examined bank management and focused on corporate governance, financial statements, asset and liability management, and loan losses. Corporate governance sets operational guidelines to manage the often conflicting interests of bank stakeholders. Financial statements provide a comprehensive view of the bank's performance and include an accounting of the bank's assets and liabilities and outcomes of business transactions. Banks manage their assets and liabilities to reduce risk and maximize returns to shareholders. To mitigate the risk of loan losses (default, credit risk), banks build up reserves in their financial statements.

Chapter 3 focused on bank regulation. Regulation encourages banks to operate prudently, thereby reducing the risk that one bank's failure causes a series of failures. Regulation includes system-wide support mechanisms to provide industry stability. Regulatory tools include licensing and supervision. Supervision involves monitoring bank operations and activities to identify a liquidity crisis, take steps to avert a bank run, prevent contagion, and stop panic. Basel Accords I and II set international regulation protocols that acknowledge that risk is related to, and can be minimized by, a minimum regulatory capital standard. Deposit insurance, an increasingly important tool in supporting the stability of the financial system, guarantees deposits.

Chapter 4 introduced credit risk. This chapter defines and explains the source of credit risk, credit products, and the features of specific retail and commercial credit products. Banks distinguish between retail and commercial borrowers and tailor products by maturity, repayment method, loan use, types of security (collateral), or restrictions (covenants) to meet each borrower's unique financial needs.

Chapter 5 explored credit risk, the steps of the credit process, how banks treat credit risk, and the Basel II Accord's guidelines to measure and manage credit risk. The Basel II Accord provides three primary approaches to measure the capital a bank holds against its loan portfolio: Standardized, Foundation Internal Ratings-Based, and Advanced Internal Ratings-Based Approaches.

Chapter 6 explained market risk. Trading financial assets exposes banks to market risk. General market risk occurs when all financial instruments are affected by market movement. Specific risk is the risk an individual financial instrument moves more, or less, than the market does. To quantify this risk, the value-at-risk methodology is used. This approach estimates the potential losses over a certain time period at a specific confidence interval. The Basel II Accord provides two alternative processes for market risk measurement: the Standardized Approach and the Internal Models Approach.

Chapter 7 discussed operational risks. Operational risks are present in all bank transactions and activities. Failing to understand operational risk increases the likelihood that risks will go unrecognized and cause devastating losses. Basel II identifies five operational risk events: internal process risk, people risk, legal risk, external risk, and systems risk. All are often interrelated. The Accord characterizes operational risk events by frequency and impact. Banks focus on high-frequency/low-impact and low-frequency/high-impact risks. The Basel II Accord provides three approaches to calculate operational risk capital: Basic Indicator, Standardized, and Advanced Measurement.

Chapter 8 addressed the three pillars of the Basel II Accord. Pillar 1 outlines approaches to measure a bank's credit, market, and operational risk and sets minimum capital requirements based on measured risk exposures. Pillar 2 describes how supervisory review monitors bank management and encourages best risk management practices. Pillar 3 describes market discipline and the requirement to disclosure of a bank's capital structure and adequacy to market participants. Economic capital is the capital level banks must maintain to withstand large but unlikely losses. The Basel II Accord provides a framework to structure a bank's overall capital, defines "tiers" of eligible capital, and sets rules on the relationships between tiers. Banks use economic capital models to determine the level and structure of capital. Well-designed economic capital models help banks identify, understand, mitigate, and manage risks to perform more effectively.

Glossary

Advanced Measurement Approach   The Advanced Measurement Approach is a sophisticated approach to calculate operational risk capital and allows the bank to use internally generated models to calculate their operational risk capital requirements.

Asset and Liability Management (ALM)   Asset and liability management (ALM) function in a bank manages the risks that arise due to the mismatches between assets and liabilities in terms of maturity, liquidity, interest rates, etc., and typically focuses on the interest rate risk in the bank's banking book and the bank's liquidity risk.

Asset-Backed Security (ABS)   Asset-backed securities, backed by pools of mortgage loans or other types of securitizable cash flow generating assets, are sold to investors who then receive payments based on the cash flows generated by the assets in the underlying pool.

Asset-based loan   Asset based loans allow the borrower to pledge a specific asset or a combination of assets, such as inventory, machinery or equipment, as collateral to cover a loan.

Asset conversion loan   Asset conversion loans (self-liquidating loans) are loans that are repaid by converting the asset that is used to collateralize the loan into cash.

Asset transformation   Asset transformation is the process of creating a new asset (loan) from liabilities (deposits) with different characteristics by converting small denomination, immediately available, and relatively risk-free bank deposits into loans—new relatively risky, large denomination asset—that are repaid following a set schedule.

Assets   Assets are the various loans, investments, and anything of value that the bank owns.

Balance sheet   The balance sheet shows all the assets, liabilities, and equity the bank has at one particular point in time.

Balloon payments   Balloon payment is a large payment at maturity that includes the repayment of the principal and in certain cases all the accumulated interest.

Bank   A bank takes deposits, makes loans, arranges payments, holds a banking license, and is subject to regulatory supervision by a banking regulator.

Bank for International Settlements   The Bank for International Settlements, BIS, established in Basel, Switzerland, in 1930, is the principal center of international central bank cooperation.

Bank panic   A bank panic occurs when a large number of depositors at multiple different banks simultaneously demand the return of their deposits.

Bank run   A bank run occurs when a large number of depositors at one bank simultaneously demand the return of their deposits.

Banking book   The banking book of a bank is the portfolio of assets, primarily loans, a bank expects to hold until maturity when the loan is repaid fully; typically refers to the loans the bank underwrites.

Banking license   A banking license, issued by a banking regulator or supervisor, allows a bank to engage in banking activities under the condition that the bank agrees to be supervised by regulatory or supervisory authorities.

Basel Accords   The Basel Accords (Basel I Accord, the Market Risk Amendment, and the Basel II Accord) are the cornerstones of international risk-based banking regulation, the results of a collaborative attempt by banking regulators from major developed countries to create a globally valid and widely applicable framework for banks and bank risk management.

Basel Committee on Banking Supervision   The Basel Committee on Banking Supervision is a forum for regulatory cooperation between its member countries on banking supervision-related matters, was established by the central bank governors, and consists of senior representatives of bank supervisory authorities and central banks from major economies.

Basic indicator approach (BIA)   The Basic Indicator Approach uses the bank's total gross income as a risk indicator for the bank operational risk exposure and sets the required level of operational risk capital at 15% of the bank's annual positive gross income averaged over the previous three years.

Basis point   A basis point is one-hundredth of one percent, or 0.0001.

Beta factor (operational risk)   The beta factor is the fixed percentage of average positive annual gross income (over three years) of the eight different business lines bank may have and is used to calculate its operational risk capital.

Bid-ask-spread   The bid-ask spread is the difference between the buy price or rate (bid) and sell price or rate (ask) of a financial instrument.

Board of directors   The board of directors has the ultimate responsibility for the management and performance of a company, is responsible for the bank's governance, and is elected by the shareholders.

Bond   A bond is a legally binding contract through which the borrower (also referred to as the issuer of the bond) borrows the principal, an amount specified in the bond, from an investor and in exchange pays a specified amount of interest, usually at regular intervals, and repays the principal either at maturity or during the life of the bond.

Borrower   A borrower is one who receives money from a lender in exchange for a promise to repay the full amount borrowed (the principal) plus an additional amount (interest) at a future date(s).

Bottom-up approach   The bottom-up approach analyzes all processes within each business unit separately and benchmarks each unit's risk profile; it then aggregates identified risks first at the business line and eventually at a corporate level to generate a company-wide risk profile.

Business risk   Business risk is the potential loss due to a weakening in the competitive position.

Call option   A call option gives its holder the right, but not the obligation, to buy a specified asset at a specified price at some future date.

Capital adequacy   Capital adequacy is achieved when a bank's capital ratio meets or exceeds the minimum capital ratio, which under the Basel Accords is 8% of risk weighted assets and can be satisfied with Tier 1, Tier 2, and Tier 3 capital. Tier 1 capital has to account for at least 4% of risk-weighted assets; the remainder can be satisfied through Tier 2 and, in the case of market risk capital, Tier 3 capital. National banking regulators can deviate from these minimum capital adequacy ratios.

Capital ratio   Capital ratio is the relationship between Risk-Weighted Assets and regulatory capital.

Cash flow-based loan   A cash flow-based loan provides funds that are repaid from the cash flow generated from the borrower's operations.

Central bank   A central bank is the principal monetary authority of a country, or a group of countries, and may also exercise regulatory and supervisory responsibilities over other banks, arrange payment between banks, and when needed, provide stability to the financial and banking system.

Charged-off loan   A charged-off loan is a loan that has been removed from the bank's financial statements because the bank believes that it will collect nothing of the loan from the borrower.

Clearinghouse   A clearinghouse guarantees the financial performance of a trade on an exchange by becoming the buyer to each seller and the seller to each buyer and clears the trade between the parties by processing payments and the exchange of instruments.

Collateral   Collateral is an asset pledged by a borrower to secure a loan or other credit and is forfeited to the lender in the event of the borrower's default.

Commercial bank   A commercial bank offers a wide range of highly specialized loans to large businesses, acts as an intermediary in raising funds, and provides specialized financial services including payment, investment, and risk management services.

Commercial paper   A commercial paper is an unsecured, short-term debt security issued by a typically large, financially strong, organization that uses the proceeds to finance its operations with a maturity range of 30 to 50 days or less.

Committed facility   A committed facility is a type of loan whose terms and conditions—such as margins, fees, and duration—are clearly defined in a formal agreement by the bank and are imposed on the borrower, and the facility is funded.

Commodity   Commodities are generally physical items such as food, oil, metal, or other fixed substances that are relatively homogenous in nature.

Commodity risk   Commodity risk is the potential loss from an adverse change in commodity prices. This applies to all commodity positions and any derivative commodity positions such as futures contracts.

Compensating balances   Compensating balances are deposits the bank requires the borrower to deposit in the bank for the duration of the commitment in exchange for extending a committed or an uncommitted facility.

Confidence level   Confidence level expresses the degree of statistical confidence in an estimate.

Consortium   A consortium denotes a cooperative underwriting of loans by a select group of banks.

Contagion   Contagion is the transmission of an isolated financial or banking crisis across borders.

Core banking services   The core banking services are deposit collection, loan underwriting, and payment services.

Corporate borrower   Corporate borrowers range from small local companies to large global conglomerates.

Corporate governance　　Corporate governance is a set of relationships framed by corporate bylaws, articles of association, charters, and applicable statutory or other legal rules and principles, between the board of directors, shareholders, and other stakeholders of a organization that outlines the relationship among these groups, sets rules how the organization should be managed, and sets its operational framework.

Cost of funds　　The cost of funds is the interest rate, required return, or other compensation associated with securing and using capital.

Counterparty credit risk　　Counterparty credit risk is the risk that the other party to a contract or agreement will fail to perform under the terms of an agreement.

Coupon rate　　The coupon rate is a percentage of the principal borrowed, and determines the coupon payment, the promised and regularly paid interest payment to the buyer of a bond or other debt security.

Covenant　　A covenant is an agreement that requires one party to refrain from or engage in specified actions and is imposed on the borrower by a lender to prevent a potential deterioration in the borrower's financial and business condition.

Credit analysis　　Credit analysis or credit assessment is the process of assessing risk as measured by a borrower's ability to repay the loan.

Credit concentration risk　　Credit concentration risk is the risk stemming from a single large exposure or group of smaller exposures that are adversely impacted by similar variations in conditions, events, or circumstances.

Credit Rating Agency (CRA)　　A credit rating agency evaluates the creditworthiness of various borrowers, issuers, or credits.

Credit risk　　Credit risk is the risk of loss due to nonpayment of a loan, bond, or other credit.

Credit risk capital　　Credit risk capital is capital allocated against possible credit losses.

Credit risk mitigation technique　　A credit mitigation technique reduces credit risk through the use of such things as collateral, loan guarantees, securitization, or insurance.

Credit score　　A credit score is a number that relates the relative strength of each borrower to a larger group of borrowers and indicates the relative chance of default.

Currency　　A currency is a generally accepted form of money—coins and bills—used in a country or a group of countries issued by their governments, central banks, or monetary authorities.

Cyclical financing   Cyclical financing funds temporary and recurring increases in inventory, production, and sales due to changes in the business cycle.

Default   Default, the failure to pay interest or principal according to contractual terms, occurs when a debtor is unable to make a timely payment.

Default Risk   Default risk is the potential loss due to default.

Deposit   A deposit is money entrusted to a bank for safekeeping in a bank account that allows the depositor to withdraw these funds and any interest paid by the bank on the deposit.

Deposit insurance   Deposit insurance is a promise by a government or an insurance system that, in the event of a bank failure, bank depositors will receive their deposits with that bank either partly or fully.

Derivative   A (financial) derivative is an instrument whose value "derives" from the value of a related underlying financial asset or commodity , and includes swaps, options, forwards, and futures.

Disclosure   Disclosure is the dissemination of material information about the conditions of a business that allows for a proper and transparent evaluation of that business.

Dividend   A dividend is that part of the earnings of a corporation that are distributed to its owners. A dividend is a distribution to shareholders and typically entails the payment of cash or additional shares.

Economic capital   Economic capital is the amount of capital the bank needs in the case of loss events, covers all risks across a bank, and is essential for the bank to survive in the long term.

Equity   Equity is the capital raised from shareholders plus retained earnings and reflects the ownership interest in a corporation.

Equity risk   Equity risk is the potential loss due to an adverse change in the price of stock.

Exchange   A (financial) exchange is a formal, organized physical or electronic market-place where trades between investors follow standardized procedures.

Exchange rate   Exchange rates reflect the relative value of one currency in relation to another currency.

Expected loss, EL   An expected loss describes the mean annual aggregate of losses or, more practically, the size of losses that can be expected to occur.

Exposure at default (EAD)   Exposure at default is the maximum loss the lender may suffer in case of a default.

External risk   External risk is associated with a potential loss caused by external parties, is beyond the direct control of the corporation, and includes natural disasters, power shortage, or terrorism.

Fair market value   Fair market value is the price the asset would fetch if sold immediately on the market to a willing buyer.

Financial asset   A financial asset derives its value from a specific contractual claim and includes bonds, loans, stocks, money, currency, derivatives, deposits, etc.

Financial instrument   A financial instrument is a representation of an ownership interest claim or the contractual or contingent claim to receive or deliver cash, another financial instrument, or asset, and can either be a cash instrument (e.g., cash, securities, loans, bonds, notes, equity) or a derivative instrument (e.g., forward, future, option, and swap).

Financial intermediation   Financial intermediation is the process bringing together those who need financing, such as businesses and governments, with those who provide financing, such as lenders, banks, and private investors, and facilitating the flow of capital between them.

Financial stability   Financial stability indicates that shocks and disturbances impacting the financial markets and financial institutions do not restrict their ability to continue intermediating financing, carrying out payments, and redistributing risk satisfactorily.

Five Cs of Credit   The Five Cs of Credit is an abbreviation of a widely used credit analysis framework that focuses on the character of borrower, the capital provided by the borrower, the business, economic and other conditions faced by the borrower, the financial and legal capacity of the borrower, and the various types of collateral and other types of credit support mechanisms offered by the borrower.

Fixed interest rate loan   A fixed interest rate loan is a loan where the interest rate on the loan does not change during the life of the loan.

Floating interest rate loan   A floating interest rate loan is a loan where the interest rate on the loan is tied to an underlying index or base rate and, as a result, may change during the life of the loan.

Foreign currency cross rate   A foreign currency cross rate is the exchange rate between two currencies against a third.

Foreign exchange rate   A foreign exchange rate specifies the price one currency in terms of another currency.

Foreign exchange risk   Foreign exchange risk is the potential loss due to an adverse change in foreign exchange rates.

Forward   A forward (contract), a derivative, is a nontransferable contract that defines the delivery of specified asset (e.g., commodities, currencies, bonds or stocks), at a specified price, at a specified quantity, on a specified future date.

Fractional reserve banking   Fractional reserve banking is a banking system where only a small fraction of the total deposits must be held in reserve, with the balance available to be invested in loans and other securities.

Funding liquidity   Funding liquidity refers to a bank's ability to have funds available to repay depositors on demand and to fund loans when needed.

Funding liquidity risk   Funding liquidity risk refers to a bank's potential inability to have funds available to repay depositors on demand and to fund loans when needed.

Futures   A futures (contract), a derivative, is a standardized and transferable contract traded on an exchange that defines the delivery of specified asset (e.g., commodities, currencies, bonds, or stocks), at a specified price, at a specified quantity, on a specified future date.

General or systematic market risk   Systematic risk represents the effect of unexpected changes in macroeconomic and financial market conditions on the performance of a wide range of assets, and represents the risk of an adverse movement in market prices that are applied across a range of financial assets, including fixed income, loans, equity, and commodities.

Headline risk   Headline, or reputation, risk is the potential loss due to a decrease in a bank's standing in public opinion.

Hedging   Hedging attempts to reduce risk by matching a position with an opposite and offsetting position in a financial instrument that tracks or mirrors the value changes in the position.

High Frequency Low Impact, HFLI events   HFLI events occur frequently, but each event has a low impact on the operations of the bank.

Hybrid security   A hybrid security is a financial instrument that has both equity and debt features.

Idiosyncratic risk   Idiosyncratic risk represents risks that are particular to the conditions and circumstances of one or a defined group of individual borrowers, assets or securities.

Illiquidity   Illiquidity is the inability to make payments when they are due.

Income statement   The income statement records all the revenues (income) and costs (expenses) that the bank has encountered over a specific time period, such as one month, one quarter, or one year.

Inflation rate   Inflation rate, the price of money, is the change in the purchasing power of money expressed as an annual percentage change.

Innovative capital   Innovative capital includes complex financial instruments that have both equity and debt features.

Insolvency   Insolvency occurs when liabilities exceed assets; while not synonymous with bankruptcy or illiquidity, it typically leads to either or both.

Institutional borrower   An institutional borrower is a financially sophisticated organization such as a large publicly traded company, a hedge fund, a large bank, or a large insurer, who borrows substantial amounts of capital using debt securities or direct borrowing.

Insurance   Insurance provides financial compensation for loss; in exchange for periodic payments the insurer guarantees the insured a sum of money upon the occurrence of an adverse specific event.

Interbank loan   An interbank loan is a loan between banks.

Interest rate   Interest rate, the price of credit, is the rate charged for accessing and using borrowed funds.

Interest rate margin   The interest rate margin is the difference between the interest income the bank earns on its assets and the interest expense it pays on its liabilities.

Interest rate risk   Interest rate risk is the potential loss of value due to the variability of interest rates.

Interest rate risk in the banking book   The interest rate risk in the banking book reflects the fact that bank assets and liabilities have different maturities, are priced off different interest rates, and are repriced at different points in time.

Internal Models Approach   The Internal Models Approach relies on the bank's own internal risk management models and determines the regulatory minimum capital requirement for market risk based on the bank's VaR calculations.

Internal process risk   Internal process risk is the potential loss resulting from improper execution of processes and procedures in conducting a bank's day-to-day operations, internal processes.

Internal ratings-based (IRB) approach   The Internal Ratings Based approach to determine the regulatory minimum capital requirement for credit risk uses the bank's own information. IRB includes two different procedures that have methodological differences to forecast the different risk factors.

International bank   An international bank is a large commercial, investment, or merchant bank with operations in different countries.

Investment bank   An investment bank predominantly deals with corporate and institutional customers, issues financial securities in the financial and capital markets, provides advice on transactions such as mergers and acquisitions, manages investments, and trades on its own account.

Investment grade credit rating   An investment grade credit rating is one at the high end of the credit rating scale and is typically considered to imply a low probability of default.

Investment portfolio   An investment portfolio held by a bank or an individual contains various investments that typically include stocks (equity), bonds, loans, financial derivatives (options, futures, etc.), investible commodities such as gold or platinum, real estate, or similar assets of value.

Junior debt   Junior debt is subordinated to more senior debt but has priority over equity.

Legal risk   Legal risk includes, but is not limited to, the risk associated with the uncertainty of legal actions or the application or interpretation of contracts, laws, or regulations and can include potential exposure to fines, penalties, or punitive damages resulting from supervisory actions, as well as private settlements.

Lender of last resort   The lender of last resort, typically a central bank, assists banks facing unusually large and unexpected funding and other liquidity problems, or a systemic crisis by providing financing to the banks.

Lessee / lessor   A lessee contracts with a lessor to use an asset that lessor owns, and in exchange for the lessee's right to use the asset, it will make regular contractual payment(s) to the lessor.

Letter of credit   A letter of credit guarantees payment by a bank on behalf of its customer who pays a fee to the bank for providing the guarantee.

Level amortization   Level amortization repays the loan and interest on the loan with equal payments that include both interest and principal payments.

Leverage   Leverage, reflects the amount or proportion of debt used in the financing structure of an organization; the higher the leverage the more debt the company uses.

Liabilities   Liabilities consist of a bank's deposits and its borrowings.

LIBOR   LIBOR, London Interbank Offered Rate, is a daily reference rate based on the average interest rate banks in London charge other banks, on the offer side of the transaction, when borrowing and lending.

Licensing   Licensing provides license holders the right to operate a bank and the licensing process involves an evaluation of an entity's intent and ability to observe the regulatory guidelines that will govern the bank's operations, financial soundness, and managerial actions.

Line of credit   Line of credit is a typically short-term, uncommitted credit facility.

Liquidity   Liquidity refers to either market (transactional) or funding (payment) liquidity.

Liquidity crisis   Liquidity crisis is a situation when the bank is not able to make payments when they are due, secure needed funds, or trade on the markets.

Liquidity risk   Liquidity risk can be market (transactional) liquidity risk and funding (payment) liquidity risk.

Loan agreement   The loan agreement is a legal contract between the bank and the borrower and includes a description of undertakings and understandings, such as the principal, the stated interest rate and its calculation, the schedule of payments and repayments, the use of collateral, covenants, etc.

Loan loss reserve   A loan loss reserve, or "allowance for loan losses" or a "credit loss reserve," is the portion of loans set aside to absorb anticipated loan losses.

Loan-to-value, LTV, ratio   Loan-to-value ratio is the ratio of the loan and the collateral supporting the loan.

Long position   A long position, the opposite of short position, represents the ownership position of an asset; when the asset's value increases, the position increases in value and when the asset's value declines, the position decreases in value.

Long-term lending   Long-term lending has a maturity exceeding 15 years and finances major capital projects or expenditures.

Loss given default (LGD   Loss given default, the actual loss the lender suffers in the wake of a default, is the function of the recovery rate and the exposure at default.

Low Frequency, High Impact, LFHI events   LFHI events occur infrequently, but each event has a significant impact on the operations of the bank.

Margin   Margin (requirement) is the amount investors must post to their brokers and the brokers are obligated to post with the clearinghouse, and is determined by various considerations, including the different types of instruments the broker trades on the exchange, the risk of the instrument, and the overall trading volume.

Margin call   Margin call is the additional amount that needs to be deposited to fulfil the margin requirement imposed by the clearinghouse or the broker.

Marked-to-market   Marked-to-market (accounting) assigns a value to an asset that reflects the value it would fetch on the market.

Market discipline   Market discipline is the external monitoring and influencing another bank's risk-taking activities based on the disclosure of relevant financial, risk or other information that allows external assessment of risk-taking.

Market liquidity risk   Market liquidity risk refers to the ability to trade assets with negligible price concessions.

Market or trading liquidity   Market or trading liquidity refers to the ability to trade in and out of a position without significant price concessions.

Market risk   Market risk is defined as the risk of losses in on- and off-balance-sheet positions arising from movements in market prices and under the Basel II Accord encompass the risks pertaining to interest rate related instruments and equities in the trading book, and foreign exchange risk and commodities risk throughout the bank.

Market Risk Amendment   The Market Risk Amendment of 1996 required banks to maintain regulatory minimum capital against the bank's positions in various market-traded financial assets such as foreign exchange, fixed income, equity, commodities, and derivatives. It is now superseded by the Basel II Accord which incorporated significant proportions of the amendment.

Market risk capital   Market risk capital is capital allocated against possible market losses.

Maturity   Maturity is the time period until a loan, bond or other credit is repaid fully.

Medium-term lending   Medium-term lending has a maturity not exceeding three or five years and finances ongoing investments in machinery, equipment or facilities, or cyclical needs.

Monetary stability   Monetary stability reflect the extent the value of money can be maintained and, as a synonym of price stability, implies low and stable inflation.

Money   Money serves as a medium of exchange, legal tender, basis for trade, and acts as a unit of account and store of value.

Money creation   Money creation is the creation of additional money, within a fractional reserve banking system, through a bank's lending an initial deposit multiple times.

Money multiplier   The money multiplier, the inverse of the reserve requirement, indicates how much additional money each unit of money, deposited with a bank, creates.

Mortgage   A mortgage finances the purchase of real estate that serves as collateral.

Net income   Net income is the difference between total revenue and expenses.

Net interest income   Net interest income equals the difference between the interest income the bank earns on its loans and other financial assets, and the interest expense it pays to its depositors and other lenders.

Noninvestment grade credit rating   Noninvestment grade credit rating is a low credit rating and implies a relatively high probability of default.

Nonperforming loan   Nonperforming loan is a loan whose borrower fails to make, or makes delayed, payment.

Nonsystemic risk   Nonsystemic risk is risk that is restricted to a limited number of entities, typically one company, and does not affect others.

Off-balance-sheet activity   Off-balance-sheet activities are not recorded on the balance sheet, and include asset, debt, or financing-related activities such as derivatives or loan commitments and other contingent exposures that could pose a risk to the bank.

Operational loss event   Operational loss event is a loss that is the result of operational failure.

Operational risk   Operational risk is the risk of loss resulting from inadequate or failed internal processes, people, and systems, or from external events. This definition includes legal risk but excludes strategic and reputational risk.

Operational risk capital   Operational risk capital is capital allocated against possible operational losses.

Option   An option conveys certain rights to the buyer of an option; the two main types of options are a call option and a put option.

Over-the-counter (OTC) market   The over-the-counter market is a decentralized market without a physical marketplace, where both standardized and nonstandardized securities and other financial instruments are traded.

Paid-in-capital   Paid-in-capital is the (equity) capital that the owners have invested in the corporation.

Pastdue loan   A pastdue loan is where the repayment of principal and interest are in doubt because the borrower has missed several payments to the bank or the bank has a clear indication that the borrower may not repay the loan.

Payment system   A payment system is the infrastructure that settles financial and other transactions or transfers funds between financial institutions using established procedures and protocols.

People risk   People risk is associated with a potential loss resulting from intentional or unintentional employee actions, such as improper recordkeeping, misuse of information, or fraud.

Performing loan   A performing loan is a loan whose borrower is making payments as agreed.

Permanent financing   Permanent financing provides capital either through equity or long-term debt to purchase, develop, and operate long-term fixed assets, such as factories, equipment, and machinery.

Pillars 1, 2, and 3 of the Basel II Accord   The Basel II Accord consists of three pillars. Pillar 1 focuses on minimum capital requirements for the three major risks bank face: credit risk, operational risk, and market risk. Pillar 2 focuses on supervisory review and processes for capital adequacy. Pillar 3 focuses on market discipline and transparency.

Portfolio   A portfolio is a collection of investments, such as stocks, bonds, and cash equivalents, held by an institution or a private individual.

Portfolio management   Portfolio management involves determining the contents and the structure of the portfolio, monitoring its performance, making any changes, and deciding which assets to acquire and which assets to divest.

Prime lending rate   The prime lending rate is the rate the banks typically charge their best customers.

Principal   The principal is the amount borrowed on a credit and excludes interest or other charges.

Private offering   A private offering raises capital by selling new securities to a selected group of individuals that typically meet certain criteria, but not to the public.

Probability of default (PD)   The probability of default is the probability that a borrower defaults.

Project finance   Project finance provide funds for the completion of large scale industrial or infrastructure projects where the assets of the project are pledged as collateral for the loan and the realized income or cash flow once the project is completed is expected to repay the loan.

Provision for loan loss   Provision for loan losses is a cost recorded on the income statement that represents funds set aside to absorb anticipated loan losses.

Public borrower   A public borrower is typically a sovereign state, a provincial, or a local government including their sub-entities.

Public offering   A public offering raises capital by selling new securities to the public.

Put option   A put option gives its holder the right, but not the obligation, to sell a specified asset at a specified price at some future date.

Recovery rate (RR)   The recovery rate is that fraction of a defaulted obligation that can be recovered.

Regulatory capital requirement   Regulatory capital requirement specifies how much minimum capital a bank must hold to guard against the various—market, credit, and operational—risks it takes.

Repurchase agreement or repo   A repurchase agreement, repo, is a contract between two parties in which one party sells the other a security at a specified price with the obligation to buy the security back at a later date for another specified price; they are widely used by central banks to provide support to meet a bank's short-term liquidity.

Reputational or headline risk   Reputational, or headline, risk is the potential loss resulting from a decrease in a bank's standing in public opinion.

Reserve requirement   The reserve requirement, in the fractional reserve banking system, is the proportion of funds a bank must keep in reserve to meet regulatory requirements and limits how much money an initial deposit could potentially create.

Retail bank   Retail banks primarily service individuals, or consumers, and small and medium enterprises (SMEs).

Retail borrower   A retail borrower is an individual ("consumer") who borrows money to purchase homes, cars, and other goods or services.

Retained earnings   Retained earnings is that part of corporate earnings not returned to the owners as dividends.

Risk appetite   Risk appetite is the level of risk exposure an investor is willing to assume in exchange for the potential for a profit.

Risk management   Risk management is a structured approach to monitoring, measuring, and managing exposures to reduce the potential impact an uncertain event happening.

Risk-adjusted return on capital (RAROC)   RAROC, a risk-based profitability measurement, calculates the risk-adjusted financial performance of an operation or business unit.

Risk-weighted assets   Risk-weighted assets equal the sum of various financial assets multiplied by their respective risk-weights and off-balance-sheet items weighted for their credit risk according to the regulatory requirements outlined by banking regulators and supervisors.

Savings accounts   Savings accounts typically limit the number of withdrawals a depositor can make over a specified period of time.

Savings and loans (S&Ls)   S&Ls, or thrifts, primarily offer loans to individuals to finance residential housing, car, and other retail or consumer purchases.

Scenario analysis   Scenario analysis, or what-if analysis, assesses the potential outcome of various scenarios by setting up several possible situations and analyzing the potential outcomes of each situation.

Seasonal financing   A seasonal loan finances a temporary and predictable short-term demand, such as seasonal increases in inventory or farm-related financing.

Securitization   Securitization is a process where relatively illiquid cash flow producing assets (e.g., mortgages, credit cards, and loans) are pooled into a portfolio, and the purchase of these assets in the portfolio is financed by securities issued to investors, who then share the cash flows generated by the portfolio.

Securitizing assets   Securitization is a process where relatively illiquid assets—mortgages, credit cards, and loans—are pooled into a portfolio and the portfolio is then transformed into a security; as a result the credit risk of the individual assets is transferred to the investors who buy the securitized product.

Security   A (financial) security is a fungible financial instrument that may be required to be registered with a regulatory authority.

Senior debt   Senior debt has priority in default over all other more junior and subordinated debt.

Settlement risk   Settlement, or Herstatt, risk is the risk that a counterparty fails to perform as agreed and does not deliver a security, or its value after the other counterparty has already delivered on the same transaction.

Shareholder   A shareholder, stockholder, or equity holder, is one of the owners of a corporation, typically has the right to elect the board of directors, may decide in corporate matters, and may receive dividends.

Shareholders' equity   Shareholders' equity, the difference between assets and liabilities, is the shareholders' investment in the company, which typically equals the amount the shareholders have invested in the company and retained earnings.

Short position   A short position, the opposite of long position, represents either the selling of a borrowed asset, the writing of an option, or selling a futures position; when the asset's value increases, the position declines in value and when the asset's value declines, the position increases in value.

Short-term lending   Short-term lending has a maturity less than one year and finances temporary requirements, or seasonal needs.

Sinking-fund amortization   Sinking fund amortization repays the loan and interest on the loan with payments, where the principal repayment is a constant, but the interest payments change as the outstanding balance is reduced.

Small and medium enterprise (SME)   A small and medium enterprise is usually a partnership, a proprietorship, an owner-operator, or other types of small business and corporation whose sales, assets, and headcount falls below a certain limit.

Solvency   Solvency is when assets exceed the liabilities, and typically implies the ability to repay debts and other obligations when they come due.

Sovereign borrower   A sovereign borrower is a government of an independent state or a country that issues bonds or borrows to finance large capital or infrastructure investments, such as roads or railways, or to fund government spending.

Specific, nonsystematic, unique risk   Specific, nonsystematic, unique risk is the risk of an adverse movement in the price of one individual security or financial asset due to factors specific to that particular security or issuer.

Speculation   Speculation involves the buying (long position), holding, selling, and short-selling (short position) of financial assets, commodities, foreign exchange, or derivatives, in the expectation that price fluctuations will generate a profit; a position that is not hedged or when simply buying or selling the asset with the hope of earning a profit.

Spillover effect   Spillover effect is a spreading of concern.

Stakeholder   A stakeholder is someone with an interest in the future of a business, enterprise or organization, and usually includes individual customers, borrowers, depositors, investors, employees, shareholders, regulators, and public.

Standardized approach   The Standardized Approach to calculate the bank's credit and market risk capital is the simplest approach outlined in the Basel II Accord for these risks. For operational risk, this is an intermediate level approach.

Strategic risk   Strategic risk is the potential loss due to poor business decisions or their incorrect execution.

Stress testing   Stress testing assesses the potential outcome of specific changes that are fundamental, material, and adverse.

Supervisory review   Supervisory review is a process that national bank regulatory or supervisory authorities use to evaluate a bank's capital adequacy in relation to the risks and capital the bank has.

Swap   A swap, a derivative, allows two counterparties to exchange streams of future cash flows with each other.

Systemic risk   Systemic risk is the risk of a systemwide breakdown in the banking or financial system.

Systems risk   Systems risk is the loss resulting from the insufficient protection of information technology against disruption, damage, or loss caused by hazards such as systems failure, security breaches, or data theft.

Temporary financing   Temporary financing provides capital through short- or medium-term debt; includes seasonal and cyclical loans.

Tier 1 capital   Tier 1 Capital in the Basel Accords is the core capital of the bank and refers to equity capital and to certain types of disclosed reserves, as well as particular debt/equity hybrid securities.

Tier 2 capital   Tier 2 Capital in the Basel Accords is supplementary capital and refers to undisclosed and certain disclosed reserves, general provisions, general loan loss reserves, hybrid capital instruments, and subordinated debt.

Tier 3 capital   Tier 3 Capital in the Basel Accords is a specific type of supplementary capital and refers to certain type of short-term debt that can partially satisfy regulatory minimum capital requirements for market risk only.

Top-down approach   The top-down approach provides initially an overview of the bank's overall risk exposure and then analyzes identifiable risks at first the business line and then at the business unit level; as the analysis moves to business line and business unit level, the analysis is conducted in increasingly greater detail.

Trade receivables   Trade receivables result from credit sales, where the company extends credit to its customers to purchase its products or services in anticipation of payment.

Trading   Trading is the exchange between traders.

Trading book   The trading book of a bank is the portfolio of various positions in financial assets, instruments, and commodities that a bank holds with the intention to invest, to trade, or to hedge other positions in the trading book.

Transaction accounts   Transaction accounts are accounts where the depositor can withdraw the deposits on demand using checks, debit cards, or similar payment instructions.

Uncommitted facility   An uncommitted facility is a loan with loosely specified terms and conditions but with an understanding that the funds will be made available by the lender when the borrower demands.

Underwriting   Underwriting assesses the borrower's eligibility to receive a credit, a loan or a bond, by analyzing financial and other information furnished by the potential borrower or obtained elsewhere.

Unexpected loss   An unexpected loss describes the loss in excess of the expected loss and is expressed with a certain confidence level.

Universal bank   Universal banks complement their offering of core banking services with a wide range of other financial services, particularly insurance.

Value-at-risk (VaR)   Value-at-risk measure risk by calculating the potential loss exceeding a specified confidence level using statistical analysis.

Wholesale bank   A wholesale bank serves, as an investment or merchant bank, corporations with banking and advisory services that are specific to the need of large businesses.

Written-down loan   A written-down loan is a loan that is past due, and the bank has made a determination that it will not be able to recover fully the amount it has lent to the borrower.

Yield curve   A yield curve illustrates the relationship between bond yields and their maturity.

Index

AUTHORS

Richard Apostolik is President and CEO of the Global Association of Risk Professionals, Inc. (GARP). Prior to joining GARP Rich worked with Bankers Trust's (Deutsche Bank) Strategic Ventures group where he focused on developing financial risk management initiatives designed to provide credit risk mitigation and management services to financial service companies. There he was the co-developer of CoVar, a dynamic counterparty credit risk mitigation system while also specializing in advising clients about the broader strategic applications of the use of derivative risk management systems and financial structuring arrangements.

Prior to Bankers Trust, Rich was J.P. Morgan & Co.'s global head of energy brokerage activities and COO of its global listed product businesses. Before joining J.P. Morgan, he ran his own consulting firm, providing advice on start up operations and management issues to such major financial institutions as Deutsche Bank, Fuji Bank, Discount Corporation of New York and J.P. Morgan. He was also responsible for the start up of S.G. Warburg & Co.'s North American futures and options business. Rich possesses a BSBA degree with a major in Marketing, an MBA and Juris Doctor from the University of Dayton. He was an attorney with the US Securities and Exchange Commission, practiced law with a private law firm in Chicago and was the Chicago Mercantile Exchange's House Counsel.

Dr. Christopher Donohue heads the GARP Research Center and the GARP Digital Library and is a member of the FRM® committee. He is responsible for managing the development of GARP risk management programs, and conducting and supporting research in financial risk management topics.

Previously, Chris was a Partner at a hedge fund where he was responsible for the development of asset allocation tools for pension funds and automated trading systems. Prior to that, Chris was a Director in the Global Research Center at Deutsche Asset Management where he led product research and development in the areas of asset liability management, asset allocation and consumption optimization for endowments and optimal portfolio management with transaction costs. He also previously worked as the Director of Optimization Technology at Alphatech, a leading-edge technology and research defense contractor, where he led algorithm development for intelligence aircraft path planning and sensor scheduling systems. Dr. Donohue has published several articles on portfolio management and optimization. He has a BA from Hamilton College in Mathematics and a Ph.D. from the University of Michigan in Operations Research.

Dr. Peter Went is a Senior Researcher at the GARP Research Center where he develops risk management programs and conducts research on financial risk management topics.

Peter is a member of the board of directors of both a publicly traded bank and a privately held technology company. He has been a professor of finance at Bucknell University in Lewisburg, PA, and taught at the University of Nebraska and at the Central European University in Budapest, Hungary. He has also worked as an investment analyst for a Nordic boutique investment firm in Stockholm, Sweden. Peter has published several articles in finance journals. He has a Ph.D. in Finance from the University of Nebraska, and degrees from the Stockholm School of Economics and the Stockholm University School of Law as well as the Chartered Financial Analyst (CFA®) designation.